# TALES FROM THE TENT

# JESS SMITH

was raised in a large family of Scottish travellers. This is the second book in her bestselling autobiographical trilogy. Her story begins with *Jessie's Journey: Autobiography of a Traveller Girl* and concludes with *Tears for a Tinker: Jessie's Journey Concludes*. She has also written a novel, *Bruar's Rest*. As a traditional storyteller, she is in great demand for live performances throughout Scotland.

# TALES FROM THE TENT

## JESSIE'S JOURNEY CONTINUES

### JESS SMITH

BIRLINN

First published in 2003 by Mercat Press Ltd
Reprinted in 2003 and 2005
New edition published 2008 and reprinted 2012 by
Birlinn Limited
West Newington House
10 Newington Road
Edinburgh
EH9 1QS

*www.birlinn.co.uk*

ISBN-13: 978 1 84158 719 6

British Library Cataloguing-in-Publication Data
A catalogue record for this book is available from the British
Library


Set in Bembo and Adobe Jenson at Birlinn

Printed and bound by Clays Ltd, St Ives plc

# Contents

# ILLUSTRATIONS

# Acknowledgements

There is a countless army who inspired, prodded, encouraged, laughed and cried with me whilst I was writing this book—many thanks for staying the course.

Dave the rock; Daddy and Mammy—never far away; Bonnie, Rosie, Rebecca, Meghan, Nicole, Jason; The Golden Girls; wee pal—cousin Anna; Janet Keet Black; Mamie for Keith's poem; David Cowan; Glen neighbours; David Campbell the book man; Portsoy Peter (deceased).

A special thanks to Robert Dawson (my radgy gadgie); John Beaton; Catherine; Tom and Seán.

And a great big thanks to Michael G Kidd who wrote *Where do I Belong?* especially for me.

I am eternally grateful to the Scottish Arts Council, who through a fine grant allowed me the freedom to research further than I could otherwise have done.

*I dedicate this book to Mac,*
*of the old tattered journal*

# INTRODUCTION

Those of you who came with me on 'Jessie's Journey,' when I told you about my life in our blue Bedford bus with Mammy, Daddy, seven sisters and Tiny, the wee fox terrier that could run rings round rats, will have an idea where we are going. To those who did not, then let me take you through the Scottish travellers' life, a life of folklore, murder and mystery. Humour jumps on board too, folks!

Will you believe my tales? Perhaps aye, or maybe not. For what is fact and fiction in life when a falling snowflake can lead a young mother to trek upon a treacherous mountain in a blizzard perilously putting her two little boys in danger?

Would you like to hear of the threesome who dared to bury a Royal Duke in the wee coastal graveyard filled to capacity with tramps, vagabonds and tinkers? More to the point—was there room for him?

Those hounds of Harry's, were they really dead? Did he survive because it wasn't his time?

Deep beneath gorse bush and thistle, were those the fingers of a dead man? Or something even more sinister?

She killed her daughter! Didn't she?

Well now, are you with me? Are you coming, reader, into my world, the travellers' world, where children learn about Bonnie Princess Charlotte, and her evil quest to unite the clans? Think you can handle that? More to the point, will historians of Jacobitism accept it?

What a strange night old lovelorn Peter had when the mistletoe seller came a-calling...

Do you know there are creatures of the night that come within a moor wind? I hope you never have the misfortune to meet one! Perhaps a wee early warning never to unlawfully enter a place of the dead might help.

In *Jessie's Journey* I told you of life in the bus. What I failed to divulge was, as death claimed night, that there sometimes came the 'Tall Man'. Why?

I bet you'd love to hear Mac's story. I can say with hand on heart you'll never hear of another such start to a new life.

Why was Wullie Two so called? Laugh with me on this one, folks.

I have many, many tales and stories to share with you. Get the cup, boil a kettle, comfort the bones—oh, and don't forget to lock the doors, because you never know, now, do you?

So, reader, are you coming with me on the road?

You are!

Great!

Who needs sanity anyway?

# 1

## BACK ON THE GREEN

My bus home of ten previous summers was gone and everyone told me to stop greeting about its demise and get on with life. Sister Shirley reminded me daily that I was fifteen years old, with a whole life spread out before me. A world of wonder waiting to be explored, so get on with it.

But how could I? The neat bedroom she prepared for me with girlie curtains and bedspread to match stank of scaldy (settled) life and made me puke. I wished I was a road tramp with skin as brown as toads, eating out of deerskin lunzies and laying my filthy body down to sleep behind bumpy-stoned dykes, with a star-encrusted heaven as my roof. But a fifteen-year-old female wouldn't last long. On the other hand I knew survival wasn't impossible, not with the knowledge I'd accumulated on the road. We travellers are born survivors.

Shirley was kindness itself and tried her best to make me feel at home. So I bit my lip and said nothing about my true feelings.

The women at Fettykil Paper Mill in neighbouring Leslie, where Carl—Shirley's then husband—found me a job, mothered the life from me. They recognised how unhappy I was. One of them called Stella was from travelling stock and she said she knew how I felt. At break there would be a fairy cake or half a Mars Bar and sometimes a wee drink of ginger (lemonade) propped against the paper-bag-holer machine I used. I knew it was Stella who left those treats because once I had told her how my Mammy did things like that in the bus. Whenever the old tonsillitis left me with a vile taste in my mouth she'd put sweets and tit-bits under my pillow or in my sock, anywhere I'd perk up on finding them.

Still, all the kindness in the wide world failed to remove my misery, and one day round about three on a Friday afternoon I collapsed at the paper-bag-holer machine. Not before plunging its giant needle straight through the index finger of my right hand, may I add. The factory doctor asked me if a period was the reason. Embarrassment turned me pure red in the face and silent. So he diagnosed period pains, even though it wasn't anything to do with that. The nurse was a wee bit more concerned and asked if there was a problem. I don't know if it was her gentle voice or the way she tilted her head as she bandaged that throbbing bleeding finger, but it opened the flood gates and I told her of my yearning to be home on the road with my own folks. 'Lassie,' she whispered, 'away you go, pack your bits and pieces, and whatever you do don't come back here on Monday.' If I'd been offered a free dip at the contents of Fort Knox I'd not have been happier than when I left the high-walled paper mill as soon as I did.

I hugged Stella with tears of unbridled joy. She laughed and said, 'My God, girl, you'd think ye were gittin oot o' the stardy.'

'I feel like I've been in one,' I told her.

Shirley wasn't too pleased when she heard I'd had it with the scaldy life. In fact she was mortified, but what else could I do? What choice did I have? None.

Within three days Daddy and Mammy came over to Glenrothes and removed me, wee brown leather suitcase and all. I can't say I wasn't sorry to leave Shirley, because all through my young life she was the heart of the bus, she was a fire when there was no coal in Wee Reekie, and I knew we'd miss each other. She was now a scaldy; her days of travelling had ended, Scotland's roads were a wee bit quieter from then on.

Shirley may have left the road but the road never left her, and for starters here is a wee poem by her to give the coming chapters a bitty atmosphere.

# The Berries

*We a' went tae the berry picking,*
*Aye, when we were young,*
*Wi' oor luggies, hooks, strings and pails,*
*Boy, did we have fun.*

*We went in the summer, when the berries were ripe*
*And the sun was high in the sky,*
*Wi' oor sloppy joes, jeans and boppers sae white,*
*A bottle o' juice an a pie.*

*We met lots o' new friends and shook lots o' hands*
*And greeted the auld weel kent set.*
*Sticky juice o' the berries wis stuck roond oor mooths,*
*It's a sight I'll never forget.*

*We sookit the big yins, then made oorselves sick,*
*And mother wis fair black-affronted.*
*We turned a shade green, were in bed for a week,*
*A doctor wis a' that we wanted.*

*We grafted an blethered, rested and sang:*
*While filling oor pails it wis fun.*
*We a' went tae the berry picking,*
*Aye, when we were young.*

Charlotte Munro

Oh my, what a delight for the eyes of a traveller lassie who'd been locked off the road for a full two months! The berry campsite was brimming with trailers, hawker's lorries, vans and lurcher dogs. The women, with heads of thick hair wrapped in multi-coloured head squares, were all cracking and gossiping. Younger lassies showed off slender figures, flashing smiles and gold-ringed ears. Men were spitting on their hands and doing deals over horses or motors or whatever they fancied. I felt the giant butterflies bursting into life inside my young breast—I was home, back on the green. If you're not a traveller then you'll be thinking I went mad. If you are, well, need I say more?

Mary, Renie and Babsy circled round and hugged me until I worried if I'd have a chest to breathe again. That was a grand welcome, but nothing like the one wee Tiny gave me. I swear if yon dog could talk he'd have poured the love of every day he'd missed me through a tottie wet tongue right into my ear.

Without the bus, things would never be the same again, I knew that much, but I'd settle for the Eccles caravan and large Ford van Daddy had replaced it with. I named that motor Big Fordy. (Remember Wee Fordy? Makes sense, doesn't it?)

My parents realised they'd made a mistake by taking me off the road. I later heard Daddy tell Mammy that 'Yon lassie o' oors is like me when I was a youngster, Jeannie—a thoroughbred gan-aboot.'

Mammy nodded and said, 'Aye, Charlie, I'm thinking she's a throwback from the old yins.'

Something completely different had become a fixture in our circle—*a male*! Mammy's sister Annie's boy Nicky had joined us, and was to prove invaluable as Daddy's right-hand man with the spray-painting. He had his own caravan, and was the reason frying steak was on our menu from then on.

Someone else had joined our crew whilst I was trying out the scaldy life—Portsoy Peter. He was a pal of Daddy's, who went back as many years as my parents did. He hailed from Morayshire. I can say this, with hand on heart, that more folks than I care to remember came through our lives, but no one sticks so vividly in my mind as this expert of the gab art, Portsoy, King of the Con! He was a con-artist second to none. Soon I'll share some of his expertise with you, but first I'd like to tell you about 'Wullie Two'.

## 2

### A CONVERSATION WITH WULLIE

For as long as I could go back in my mind, Wullie Two was part of the 'berries'. Nobody knew much about him but the minute a fire was lit, there was Wullie. 'A wee bit simple,' some would say. Others would just say he never grew up. He wasn't violent or anything like that, in fact the opposite was the case. He would go to the pictures with us young ones, sit on the back of the seats and shout out at John Wayne, 'Git yer heed doon, man, the Indians are coming!' He believed that the film being projected in front of his eyes was really taking place. Then we would all shout at him, 'Git yer heed doon, Wullie, the picture-house man wi the torch is comin.' This of course was double the entertainment for us, laughing ourselves silly at the antics of Wullie as he dived below our feet, thinking he'd be turfed out before the film had ended.

This is a conversation I had on a quiet Sunday with the guid lad.

'Why are you called "Wullie Two", Wullie?'

'Weel, ma Mammy had four laddies, an as she wisnae very good wi names she cried us all the same. Wullie One, Wullie Two and so on.'

'But how come she called you all Wullie?'

'The scaldy hantel call a man's private johnny, a wullie, and as ma faither used his tae give us a "jump start", then that's why we're all cried that.'

'Have you any sisters?'

5

'Aye.'

'How many?'

'Only the one.'

'What's her name?'

'I dinna ken, but she wis a beautiful lassie.'

'Have you forgotten her name?'

A silent pause made me wonder if I'd upset him somewhat, so I asked if he didn't wish to answer. His response turned me silent.

'Ma sister nivver had a name, neither had she a man tae herself.'

'Was she fussy with lads?'

'No, she fell in love with a greyhound, and when she had a litter o' pups ma Dad sent her packing.'

I tried to stifle the surge of laughter welling in my throat, but I don't believe anyone could hold back after such a comment, so I let rip. When I'd composed myself Wullie's next words sent me back into overdrive.

'Ye may well laugh, but she's rich noo, yon sister o' mine, because ivery yin o' yon dugs went on tae tak first place on Scotland's racetracks, ivery yin!'

'Oh, Wullie, what a man you are. Where were you born, anyroad?'

'Ma Mither found me sleeping in a pot o' pea an ham soup, huddlin' in ahent a puckle boilt bones.'

Just when I thought my sides would split his finishing comment left me in stitches.

'It was rare an' warm in yon pot!'

So there you have it, folks, my memory of a born comic. No script, no rehearsal, just a pure untapped rarity of golden delight. However, the more I think about Wullie, the more a certain Rattray man's words keep turning over in my head. His nickname was Shakims, and as he said, 'Who's the more foolish—him who tells the tale or him who believes it?'

## 3

### A KINDRED SPIRIT

Here is the story of Mac.

The July sun was never as hot as it was that day, so once I'd reached the grand sum of one pound and ten shillings worth of berries picked, I dropped the wee metal luggie tied round my waist and headed home. The berry farmer wasn't too pleased with my early withdrawal from his heavily-laden fruit field and called after me, 'Where are you going, young un?'

I had hoped he wouldn't miss me, but as the rain had poured solid the two previous weeks, this cratur was desperate to see all hands on deck to transfer his yield of fruit, which was hanging heavy, from bush to baskets. I had no wish to lie, so as the pinky of my right hand had earlier suffered the fierce sting of a big orange and yellow bumblebee, I used this as my excuse. He tutted and warned me to 'mind and make sure you work double hard the morra.' Poor man, little did he know cousin Nicky had removed the bee's painful spike over two hours earlier, and although the pain was still there it certainly didn't warrant a 'sicky'. But after I'd soaked my head under the waterspout behind the farmhouse I was more than glad that the day's berry picking had come to a close. Betsy Whyte was outside her trailer boiling a kettle of tea water on an iron chittie and waved over to me. 'Aye, Jess, it'll be a sunbathe you'll be up tae, lassie.'

I laughed and asked her not to tell Mammy. Betsy was one of the nicest travelling women I'd ever met. Little did I know that some day in the near future she would be the greatest traveller writer of her time. (Both her books—*Yellow on the Broom* and *Red Rowans and Wild Honey*—would be renowned as classics.)

But you know something, if I hadn't left the drills that day then my meeting with Mac might not have taken place and a great deal of tales would have passed me by.

I went into the trailer where Mammy had, before going to join her brood on the field, a massive pile of drop scones cooling under a flannel dishtowel. Putting one in my mouth and another in my pocket for later I lay down to sunbathe under the hotter-than-ever sky. Just as my eyes felt heavy and Father Nod crept serenely over my body I was brought to life by a large being shading out the sun.

'Hello, lassie, I'm looking for my mate, Portsoy Peter. I was told he was hitching his yoke with Charlie Riley.'

I sat up to say he'd found the right place, but Portsoy wasn't in. 'I think he's at Perth and will be back about tea-time,' I told the stranger, then continued: 'I know that because he asked Mammy what was for tea, and when she telt him tattie soup and stovies he said there was no way he'd miss out on such a cracking meal.'

The big man asked politely if he could wait at our fire. 'I've come a fair distance tae see my old mate, it would be daft tae go away without a blether.'

It was nearing three in the afternoon so I enquired if this visitor fancied a cuppy?

'Only if I can have a share o' yer scone,' he mused.

'I'll get you another one, Mammy's made a wayn o' them. What's yer name by the way?'

'Mac, I'm simply called Mac.'

'What else, surely there's more to your self than three letters?'

'Well, you can put a lot into those three wee letters, lassie.' He smiled as he settled himself down onto the warm grass and lay beside me. Shielding his eyes from the sun's glare with his bunnet, then inserting a blade of grass between a fine mouth of shiny white teeth he told me how he came to be.

It was 1918 and old Widow Macgregor had just made safe her tent fire for the night. All of a sudden the flap door was wrenched back and a young lassie, still with the freckles on her face and the red on her cheeks, thrust a new born baby boy into the hands of the startled elderly woman. 'I canna keep it,' she cried, 'I dinna ken

8

how tae.' Those words were the youngster's parting call before she planted a soft kiss on the infant's brow and was gone into the dark night. The old woman had seen many bairns into the world, so she knew how to twine-tie the cord and wash its tiny frame. What worried her more was her awareness that it had not long left the womb, because it takes no longer for a new human to die than it does for a featherless chick deserted in the nest. Without a minute wasted, she wrapped the bairn in a shawl and huddled off into the night toward the tent of Marion Macdonald. She had a few wee ones. The widow had heard them playing in the birch woods and knew they lived less than a mile away up toward Tulimet. The tents were in darkness as she arrived by the moonlight's guidance.

Without waiting for permission, she forced her old frame in through the door of the Macdonalds' tent. 'A stupid wee lassie has had herself a baby, Mrs Macdonald—have ye the breast milk for it? Look, the poor wee thing hasn't even tasted a drop yet, I fear death is in the waiting for it if it doesn't see any sustenance.'

'Oh dear, I'm fair sorry for the mite, but my youngest is over the year and doesn't need milk. Mine dried up last month. But the lassie Macpherson might be able to help, did she not bury a stiff-born infant just the other day?'

The old woman, saddled with her precious burden, said she'd heard of the sad case, but were the Macphersons not over seven miles away? 'The baby would never survive that distance,' she said, biting into her knuckles in desperation.

'Not if my Jamie runs with him', answered Marion. Her Jamie was thirteen and 'could run with the Monarch', she proudly told the old woman. Marion speedily ripped out sheep's wool she'd sown into her children's mattress and began covering the wee boy's head and vulnerable back. Then she tied pieces of muslin all round his tiny frame, leaving a small hole for air at his mouth. As if packing a very valuable piece of china she placed the baby into a hessian sack and tied it to Jamie's back. To emphasise the importance of his task she placed two strong hands onto his young shoulders and said, 'for God's sake, laddie, go like the wind, for this wee bundle hasn't an hour of life left in him.'

Jamie took off into the night as sure-footed as the deer, and in no time was holding out the tiny parcel to the young mother in the throes of bereavement.

Soon the wee baby boy was suckling like mad, a life saved by the expertise of the travelling people. Sad to say, though, his adopted mother fell ill with fever, and in his eleventh month her life was cut short. Her sad husband, unable to cope, begged a farmer and his wife to take the bonny healthy boy. Which they did and brought him up as their own.

'And here I am, lassie, lying here on the grass beside you this very afternoon.' Mac finished his tale, turned onto his stomach and went to sleep.

I was intrigued, what a marvellous story. I had to hear more about my new friend.

'You still haven't told me why you're called Mac.' I awakened him with a prod into his ribs.

'Then you haven't been listening, lassie,' he said, rolling onto his side.

'I heard every word you said, it was fascinating.'

He then reminded me: the first old woman's name was Macgregor, the second was Macdonald, the third... Macpherson.

'Oh, I can see it now, their names all began with "Mac".'

'You've got it!'

'But why didn't you take the farm-folks' name—surely they gave you theirs?'

'I did! They were called—Macmillan!'

I laughed, so did he, then we shared another cup of tea and scone.

I liked this man, I felt a kindred spirit, and wanted to know more about his fascinating life. But soon the family would be home from the berries. I had a fire to kindle, tatties to peel and a kettle to boil.

The night settled itself around the campfire, which began to be crowded with lads and lassies whirling up a ceilidh. Some sang the old ballads, while others played an instrument. We were graced with a blaw from Mammy on her mouthie before she gave everyone a toe-tapper on her Jew's harp. She could fair make that wee piece of metal curl and twang between her lips, could my Mam! I told a ghost story or two, which saw old biddies pull collars tighter round their necks. Such were the horrors that fell wordily from my mouth, even I found it hard to believe they were 'made up tales' out of my head of many characters. At last Mammy scolded me for frightening the bairns, who'd scurried away to their beds. A tall lad from up north sang several Jacobite songs, which went down very well with his captive audience. But, strange to say, this particular choice of song didn't stir a single clap from my pal Mac. Later, when everyone had bedded down for the night, I asked him if he had had a 'whine' with the singer.

'Not at all, lass, it was those Bonnie Prince Charlie stories that I canna feel much for,' he answered.

'I love to hear them', I told him. 'It makes me feel all fuzzy inside to think he might have been our last king.' I then proudly added, 'what about our ancestors who gave their lives and their lands for freedom's sword?'

'Huh, what rubbish, that word freedom is as Scottish as haggis!'

I looked on in bewilderment while he ranted on about how, after Culloden, all our hardy beef was scoured out of the land and we were forced to live off mutton because that was all there was. If our English neighbours hadn't felt pity on our starving bairns and showed us how to survive the winters by eating sheep offal in its stomach, then a hell of a lot of us would have perished. 'Why do you think Robert Burns wrote a poem to the haggis? Because it fed the poor, that's why!'

Those words left my imagination in overdrive, but I hadn't enough insight to understand what they meant, so I prodded Mac to say some more. But he would go no further and told me to find out for myself.

He fell silent for a while before going into Portsoy's caravan (who, by the way, hadn't arrived back from Perth). When inside he called to me through the open door, 'Jessie, do you want to hear another side to that historical episode of yon Stuart?'

Now, anyone who knows me would swear to walk forever backwards if I didn't want to hear stories about my Scotland, fictitious or otherwise. So in no time I was sitting with knees under my chin, watching and waiting as Mac opened an old tattered suitcase he'd earlier slipped under Portsoy's bed, and carefully removed a single jacket, a pair of trousers and three or four odd socks, and put them on the caravan floor. Concealed at the bottom of the case he lifted out an old bulky journal that had seen better days, and laid it gently down. 'This, lassie, is tales told to me over the years by many, many traveller folks. You see, because of my beginnings I always felt drawn to the tent folks. You could say I was magnetically pulled into their midst by an invisible force outwith my control. The ancient stories fascinated me, and thanks to my adopted parents I was schooled in reading and writing. Now, I dare say many of the tellers were reluctant to see the spoken word go on paper, but it's amazing what a wee dram and a few fags could do. However there were a damn sight more that would not be bought for love nor money. I had a fierce arm chuck me into a grimy puddle many a time by those who believed in staying loyal and forbidding the writing down of the sacred tales. So a lot of the time I had to rely on memory. This story, though, I did have the blessing of the teller to put through the pen. Do you want to hear it?'

'Without a doubt.'

'Then, Jess, listen and do it well, for there's many who would spit in your eye for its hearing. I do hope you don't suffer the same fate as those first poor souls who dared tell the story of—

# 4

## THE SEVERED LINE

Who among us in Scotland has not heard of 'The Young Pretender', son of James Edward the 'Old Pretender', the rightful Stuart King of Scotland? No doubt very few. It brings the musician out in all of us, doesn't it, to hear the stirring battle call of 'Bonnie Prince Charlie' himself, and the Jacobite rising of the '45. How bold and daring were the exploits of his followers; lengthy novels depict his brave attempt to bring the Stuarts back their kingdom of Scotland, their birthright throne.

But! What if I told you a different tale, with twists and turns, and evil lies, hmm?

Come with me now to Rome where a lady lies, writhing and screaming in the last throes of her pain-wracked labour. Nursemaids, sweating and scurrying to and fro with hot water and swathings of cooled cloths, await the arrival of the King's new heir.

Outside, a fierce thunderstorm adds its tension to a nerve-stretched night. It is four a.m., the darkest hour; the lady pushes for the last time and a new-born scream cuts through the waiting ears of a small army of servants and doctors. The heir apparent has arrived. The clan chiefs, far off in tiny Scotland, will breathe hope again.

The new mother opens her exhausted eyes, and for a moment she sees on the face of her doctor a frightened look. He hands the baby over to a trembling nurse, who swiftly wipes its tiny frame before laying it down beside its mother, who pretends to be asleep. While her nurses make the place ready for his Majesty's arrival the lady pulls back the shawl to see she has… a beautiful daughter! The last thing she remembers before exhaustion sweeps over her is an enormous crack of lighting that lights up the entire room, but strangely leaves her infant clouded by a dark shadow.

When at last her eyes opened again it was her dear husband holding both her hand and the tiny fingers of their new–SON. The lady said nothing because she knew the chiefs would not accept a female child. She kept silent and went along with the lie that she had given birth to a healthy son, but she had to know if her natural child was alive or not. When her health returned she forced her handmaiden to tell the truth.

'It was not to be disclosed to another living soul, Ma'am, but in the same hour your child was born a scullery maid brought forth an illegitimate son. It was his Majesty's orders that the babies be switched.'

'Where is the kitchen lass, and does she still have my daughter?' asked the lady, shaking with emotion.

'Ma'am, she has been given a small dowry and, oh, please Ma'am, forgive me for telling you this, but she's been sent to Scotland!' The maid fell at the knees of her mistress and sobbed.

The Lady gently lifted her servant's head and said, 'Please tell me she has the child.'

'Yes, Ma'am, the baby is with her.'

Those were blessed words to her ears. She knew that her baby was lost to her forever, but at least a royal Stuart would grow, and, pray God, survive, within her rightful home on Scottish soil.

The scullery maid called her forced child Charlotte, and swore with every God-given breath to disclose to the lass, when the time was right, who she really was.

Within no time of their arrival in Scotland, in a part of Edinburgh, the scullery maid found a house of employment. Strangely, the wealthy family with whom she had settled took her child as well. Perhaps it was the distinctive blue of her eyes or maybe it was the bright red hair, one cannot say, but before long she was accepted as one of the family.

Within this family were three children who were privately tutored in the highest of education, music and the arts. When old enough, Charlotte joined them in their classroom and soon stood out as a bright and highly intelligent student.

Soon it was time! One night the woman whom she thought of as Mother sat young Charlotte, now eighteen, down and revealed the awful truth.

It was hard for her to understand the revelations pouring forth, and she at first refused to believe such apparent untruths.

'It is the God's truth, my lady. You are Scotland's rightful heir.'

'Then why do I not sit on the throne?'

'Because the chiefs would have you silenced. They have word from the Vatican that a young prince, my rightful son, is as we speak being groomed to bring Scotland freedom.'

'Then, mother, for that is who you will always be to me, time for planning.'

From that night onwards Charlotte lived only to be Queen!

Three more years passed, and having reached a certain status under the roof of her mother's employers she spread, not the wings of a fair dove, but the sharpened claws of a fierce bird of prey. Soon she found a position nursing in a home for recovering soldiers. In no time she caught the tired eye of a captain home from fighting in some far-off land. He was of blue-blooded stock with property, just what she was looking for. Her claws gently dug in to the heart of this man twenty years her senior. Before fewer than ten months had passed she was the honourable Lady Lister, seated in her new home three miles north of Inverness, with her so-called mother installed as housekeeper, and keeper of the secret. More important than anything else she was pregnant. 'If the clans do not accept my blood, then they will accept my son.' She swore her womb carried a male child. If it did not, then she would continue producing children until it did! For this was Charlotte's plan.

But oh, how the best-laid plans fall prey to fate.

Much to her horror her husband fell, fatally wounded, during a skirmish in France, and never lived to see his twin sons being born. More's the blessing on him, because the babies were so badly deformed that Charlotte dared not let any eye fall on them. How could she now approach the chiefs? This was not foreseen. But so deep had her intent become that she refused to be daunted. She would find a way, right or wrong.

There had still been no sign of the 'impostor'. Perhaps he would refuse an invitation from the now restless clans. After all, having lived a charmed existence under the cloak of rich indulgence in the fine palaces of Rome and France, he was hardly likely to put his life in danger for such a futile cause.

Seventeen years passed, her sons never having set an eye upon an open door or window. She herself found it difficult to spend any more time than necessary in that stinking room in the attic of Lister House, set in the thickest of Caledonian forests. Only her once mother, the now old and bent housekeeper, fed and cared for those sad cripples who had once held all her hopes of bringing the crown home from those greedy southern jailers.

Charlotte's plan to put Scotland into the Royal Stuarts' hands was indeed honourable, but she was becoming desperate, and desperate people do dishonourable things. In the days ahead, not only did she stoop to unmentionable depths, but the Devil himself would have been proud of her, to say the least.

I now take a moment, reader, to tell you that my host, narrator of this historic tale, closed his journal and reminded me of the time, which was entering a summer midnight hour. 'I think our friend Portsoy is for staying the night in Perth, lassie. Do you think he'll mind me kipping down on his bed?'

Mac certainly looked the worst for whatever journey he'd taken that day, and after all the poor soul was over sixty. I, however, was only fifteen, and this story would not keep in my head. I needed desperately to know its end.

Just then, before either of us could say a thing, the door opened and there was my Daddy with the man himself, old Portsoy Peter.

'This daft Morayshire man broke doon upon the Perth road,' laughed Daddy, 'I found him hitching a mile north o' Scone.'

I found it hard not to laugh at the poor soul's predicament, because he had been blowing a hardy trumpet that very morning about how his new-bought Bentley 'was the maist reliant motor vehicle in all the countryside.'

But when he saw his dear friend Mac lying sprawled upon his bed, storybook opened, he put the car aside for another day's conversation. Daddy asked me to fetch a pot of tea while the threesome had a wee crack. He'd been away himself most of the day at Stirling selling a vanload of brock wool.

Although pleased, as I always was, to see my father safely home, I was also annoyed that the pair had interrupted Charlotte's tale. 'Are we going to find the end of our story?' I prodded Mac on the arm.

Now, I know this seems a bit uncommon to say the least, given the ungodly hour, but Daddy said he'd haggled all day with the rag merchant and would take a tale before bedding himself. Portsoy, who'd heard Mac's tales before, was also in the mood for hearing it again. So, after going hurriedly back to the beginning of the story for our added listeners, Mac continued with 'The Severed Line.'

§

One day, while out walking in the thick forest with her old house-keeper, Charlotte was stunned to silence by the appearance of a small band of passing tinkers. It was not their lowly existence nor tiny abodes secured to bent backs that took her eye, but the fine fiery red hair cascading down a slender spine. The girl, Iona by name, was a mere fifteen, if that, with flashing green eyes and oh! that so thick red hair—the hair of the Royal Stuarts.

Charlotte was already sealing the fate of this impoverished band, and before that fateful day slowed to its end she had paid two hench-men to slit all their throats. All but the wench. She was gagged, bound hand and foot, and brought into the stately home. There she was forced up the winding metal stairway and thrown into the den of Charlotte's twin sons. 'I shall surely have my heir to this country now,' she cried, as she shook her fist at the heavens above and swore that this was a God-given day.

The two sons had grown up as twisted in mind as they were in their maimed bodies. The innocent tinker girl was subjected that night to the most horrific attack upon her small frame. Had the housekeeper not entered later to remove her shattered and torn body, no one knows what they would have ended up doing to Iona that night. Next day Charlotte insisted her sons taste more, and in she threw an exhausted and half-dead girl. This she did daily for a week, allowing both her sons to abuse her at will.

After that she imprisoned Iona in a tiny basement and waited. Within two months her housekeeper brought the news—Iona was pregnant. On the old housekeeper's advice a warmer, more comfort-able apartment was prepared to imprison the mother-to-be. After all, it would be a royal Stuart who was coming once again to the

Scottish nation, one whom the clans had been awaiting for a long time. They would listen and believe Charlotte when the truth was shown to them. She would be the Queen Mother and instruct the new heir. Oh, how she schemed and plotted!

Now, while all was being prepared, the old housekeeper began to think remorsefully on the road her life had taken. She could feel that her life was slowly dwindling and felt it wasn't Charlotte's fault but hers for disclosing the truth in the first place. She thought on the husband who had died far from his estate. She thought about the sadly malformed twins who had never been kissed or cuddled by a loving mother, and now poor Iona, whose family had been murdered for sake of this woman whom she had nurtured.

Any day now Iona would give birth and then what? What if it was a girl? Would she be thrown into the den of the twins once again? What if it was indeed a son? Of course, with her task complete, the young mother would never see another day. When would all this evil end? The old woman was the only one who could change things. Next day she set out to do just that.

While Charlotte slept, she went into the girl's room, and just as expected the baby was moving into position for birth. Dressing Iona, the old housekeeper silently led her out of the large house of Lister. On the way she told the lassie what Charlotte was planning to do. The pair walked on until, exhausted, they came to the shore. Iona was led into a small cave to hide and have her child without help. You see, the old housekeeper had her own safety to consider.

Charlotte was seething with the red anger when she found that Iona and the housekeeper had gone, and she rode out to procure once again the assistance of her two henchmen who were living in a dark hovel nearby. Riding madly through the thick forest the three came upon the old woman, who lied and said that when she rose that morning she too had found Iona's bed empty and set out to find her 'before you, my mistress, awakened.' Before walking off she called back to the death-minded threesome that she would take care of the boys, then she was gone into the forest.

As the day's sun was settling into the night sky, they were searching every inch of shoreline until a child's cry brought Charlotte and her hired killers to the cave. As they dismounted they saw a small figure silhouetted against the horizon; it was Iona standing above them on a ledge.

'Have you a son for the throne of Scotland, lassie?' Charlotte cried up to the visibly shaken girl.

'Aye, mistress, see for yourself. I've done ye doubly proud.'

Charlotte could hardly believe her eyes, for there, lying wrapped in a torn shawl, were not one but two sons, each already showing a fine red hairline.

'When I have my babies you know what to do with the tinker,' she whispered.

The henchmen nodded in unison.

Iona was more than aware of her impending doom, but she was not going to go without seeing Charlotte's face when the truth was revealed.

For as the lady of evil stooped to bundle up her heirs, two tiny heads rolled from their bodies at her feet!

'See, wicked Charlotte, see your severed line!' Those were Iona's last earthly words as she leapt to a watery grave.

Charlotte screamed towards the heavens, blaming everybody but herself.

'I will repeat this, others will be found,' she screamed over and over again.

Those men of depravity had come even to their limit when witnessing this dreadful scene, and without payment they rode off into the dark forest, hoping never to set eyes upon Lady Charlotte again.

However, when she at last arrived home yet another horror was to meet her eyes that day, because the old housekeeper had torched Lister House with Charlotte's twin sons locked within its walls. Charlotte and Lister House were never heard of or seen again. There are those who said she cursed Scotland from that day, and swore that the impostor would fail in any attempt he made to unite the clans. And that he did. Strange!

'Great story,' whispered Daddy, not wishing to wake Portsoy who had fallen asleep earlier. He turned and whispered to me, 'Mammy will want to know why you and me hadn't bedded until the second hour of the night, better no tell her we were tale telling.' I smiled and promised, but hey, who could fool Mammy?

He then went off to his bed. But not I, no, I was still standing on that ledge with Iona watching the babies' wee heads rolling at

Charlotte's feet. How could I sleep? I just had to ask Mac if there was any truth at all in this tale. He never answered. I couldn't help but smile to myself, though, as I watched him take those flashing white teeth of his that I'd admired all day, and pop them into a glass half-filled with water.

Next day the berries saw us swelling the purse. Mammy was rare pleased and thanked God for filling the drills with juicy fruit and the heavens with the sun. I wanted to hear more of Mac's tales, but he had lots of cracking to do with old Portsoy. I stood upon a wee stool and peeped through the window, to see the same glass Mac's teeth had snuggled into the night before filled to the brim with 'the cratur'. 'Oh well,' I thought, 'thon's a wild bit o' cracking taking place in that wee trailer this night, best I forget the tales for now.'

I wandered off and soon found a dozen or so girls of my age hanging about the farmer's giant hay barn. 'Let's monkey swing,' said one of the lassies. This game was to swing from the rafters and then drop down onto the hay, great fun it was too. The usual practice was to aim to go from one end of the barn to the other without falling. Whoever slipped first stood out, and so on until only one was left. Well, I can't say exactly how or why, but you-know-who fell and landed, not on the soft spongy hay, but on a great rusty pitchfork concealing itself under a layer of straw. Up it went into an inch of my foot. Two strong lassies dragged me squealing like a porkie all the way from the barn to our spot at the far end of the campsite. Every traveller in the place was up and over to see why my foot was dragging a pitchfork behind it. 'Take that lassie tae the doctor,' was one concerned voice. 'God, wid ye look at thon fit, it'll need tae be cut aff!' was another. My mammy knew exactly what to do, and soon my foot with the hole was steeped in an almost boiling basinful of water and Dettol. Half an hour later I was sat, my foot washed and swathed in miles of torn cotton sheet strips, with a cup of tea and a scone. All well wishers and nosy parkers gone, I hopped to bed with a foot as sore as the wildest toothache, and Mr Nod definitely did not come within a mile of me that night.

Next morning I was still immersed in the Charlotte story and failed to hear Mammy shout out to me to 'watch the fire, ye daft lassie!' Too late—I stumbled and fell over half a tree Nicky had positioned on the early morning blaze. 'Ouch!' I watched a great swelling instantly spread itself across my shinbone to add to my other injury. Everybody laughed and I said something stupid like, 'so glad to kick-start yer day's humour.' Mammy came immediately to my assistance with a damp cloth—then, when she saw my baggy eyes, she didn't half turn on the fury. 'Have you been filling your empty head with stories, how oftimes dae I say, there's a time an a place.' Before I could answer, Daddy came to my aid by saying, 'the tale she heard was a cracker, Jeannie, and if you mind oor Jess when its cold winter howling, then she'll tell it on a dark night.'

Mammy tutted, then ordered everyone to eat breakfast and get to work. I looked at Daddy who winked at me, then at Portsoy who in turn winked his eye at Mac. But it wasn't the story of Charlotte I'd heard two nights past that had caused my baggy eyes, it was the throbbing pain in my sore foot.

However Mac's tale of Charlotte did give me food for thought, and I just had to hear another tale. By teatime, me with my shiny shin, holey foot and baggy eyes were once again propped in old Portsoy's caravan, listening to another of Mac's tales.

This story was given to Mac by a young woman he met camping in a moor, and that was all he would tell me. He tells it through the woman's tongue. I do the same.

# 5

## THE TOMMY STEALERS

It was a beautiful place, with warmth and security. The moon shone on the hanging branches of several laburnum trees lining the pure green grass, and as my father unyoked the horse a flash of silver-white wings rose in brief splendour from an old oak. Mother imitated the too-wooing of the owl, then apologised to it for the disturbance.

My brother Tommy and I helped Father unload the cart while Mother filled a kettle from a clear flowing stream marking its territory round the outskirts of the forest. In no time the horse was munching on a casket of hay, the bowed tent was nestled snugly against an ancient stone wall, the fire was lit with a brag o' heart and we were enjoying a hot mug of tea.

'This is a good place,' said Dad, 'I think we'll make a day or two's lowie here'.

Mam gulped a mouthful of tea before replying that any place would be better than the last place, then added, 'God help us all if they ever find us.'

'They'll never find us, lass, and if they do then it's a fight to the death.'

Dad's words sent a cold shiver up my back and the hair rose on my neck as a shy rabbit scurried through the thick undergrowth over by some trees. My brother Tommy felt my fear and moved closer, entwining his arm through mine.

Dad smiled and said, 'now let's not be shanning ourselves like this, it's time for bed,' then added, 'look at the old moon, it's heavy on the western side of the heavens and we all know that means it's past two in the morning, so off to bed with the lot of us.'

I pulled the rug up under my chin as sleep was finding no place in me and thought back to the last place—and them! 'Will I ever sleep again?' I thought.

Sleep did come that night, but not in a restful slumber that a child of ten should enjoy. No, it came within a dark cloud of nightmarish memories, ones that would plague me for the rest of my life.

It was the day before that we had camped briefly with some travellers of Irish stock, who kept my father busy dealing his horse for theirs. After swapping mares they hitched up to move further up country. Nice folks they were.

The three strangers who wandered on to the green seemed pleasant enough as they shared some twist with Dad. Mother even gave them tea and a buttered scone. I remember hearing one ask Dad if we were the only travellers there. Yes, he told them innocently, there had been four or five Irish families but they'd moved on.

This seemed to please them and they settled back at our fire, spending what was left of the day with us.

Come teatime, Mother didn't have enough food and told them so, apologising.

'Oh, that's fine, because we're not here to eat your meat,' said one of the strangers, a tall man.

'No,' laughed another, 'we're here for him.' The older man had no sooner answered my mother than he stretched out a hairy arm and grabbed our Tommy. Father fumbled with a burning stick from the fire, then, brandishing it in the air, shouted, 'leave my son alone!'

The third man, a dirty creature, unshaven and raggedy-clothed, came up behind father and knocked him to the ground. Then a sickening thud from his navvy-booted foot rendered father unconscious.

I screamed at the man who was running off with Tommy to let him go, while Mother scooped a bucketful of burning ashes from the fire and in vain threw them over the second man. Within seconds the three fiends were out of sight, running off with our Tommy. Mother and I dropped to our knees beside father's lifeless body, sobbing uncontrollably. We'd heard the tales of body-dealers, men who targeted vulnerable people. Unscrupulous men with wicked intentions of selling them to doctors for the practice of dissecting. But until then we had never believed the scattered tales. There we were, then, victims of such demons. But some folks swear that God protects us! It certainly was true on that day, because who should discover that the horse father had changed with them was lame? Yes, the Irish lads. And while they were bringing the mare back they came across the body snatchers. When they saw and recognised Tommy it didn't take them long to sort out those evil men and bring him home.

Father was none the worse for his ordeal. It wasn't the first hammering he'd had. After thanking the Irish we packed instantly and set off. Mother told me to hold Tommy's little hand. I held it so tight it went pale.

Yes, my sleep was sorely troubled that night. But that was a long time ago.

The Great War of 1914 came with its millions of casualties. Father followed the call and was among them. Mother, being of delicate stature, found life without her man unlivable, so within a year took her place in the ground at his side. I had to be strong for Tommy. You see my young brother developed a stutter, and became the butt of endless jibes and jokes. One day before his tenth birthday his teacher asked me not to take him back to the school.

As he grew he became more and more withdrawn. No matter how hard I tried to love and protect him, Tommy found life unbearably hard. One dark winter night while a blizzard covered the country, my young brother walked out, barefooted and nothing on except pants and a thin simmit. I found him clutching a piece of paper. He was frozen dead. Scribbled on the paper was: *'I love you sister, but every night when I fall asleep those three strangers come back, I have to find peace. Forgive me, Tommy.'*

My brother died before reaching the age of seventeen.

'Oh Mac, you might have picked a story to cheer me up, that is so, so sad,' I told him.

'Funny is it ye want—well, here's a wee laugh for you.'

Mac closed his bulky journal and lit up a fag. Full-strength Capstan he smoked. Why did folks feel the need to kill themselves and call it enjoyment? This always made me think that we adults are stupid. But back to things in hand (and not Mac's fag by the way). No, this next wee tale was perhaps his way of cheering me up. All the more because the folks involved are relatives of mine.

# 6

## SANDY'S KILT

Sandy the piper was more than pleased with his day's takings. Well, that's understandable, because was oor lad no' just the country's best piper. He'd spent the better part of that July day on his favourite spot at the Pass o' Killiecrankie, piping tune after tune for Scotland's culture-keen tourists. Weary but happy, he'd wandered home, which was a snug wee wood-end on the outskirts of Pitlochry, to share his hard earned shillings with the dearest love of his life—bonnie Jeannie. When our hardy piper arrived, a grand plate of thick vegetable broth was waiting, followed by a heel-end of the best bread spread over with streaky bacon, to be swallowed down with Jeannie's milky tea.

'Ye ken this, my love, if ever a man had an angel for a wife, then he stands here in front o' ye.'

'And I'm the maist fortunate woman tae have Scotland's finest piper lay at ma side every night.'

Yes, an air of fine contentment spread itself over the little bended tent that teatime, and the bairns, all seven of them, played in amongst a forest floor of soft moss and grass fern.

Jeannie told Sandy that while in the town earlier she had met a dozen or so lads here for the games. She said his cousins and brothers were there, and why not go meet up with them for a dram. Sandy was grateful to his lass, but thought it might not be wise to drink the night before his *crème de la crème* piping event of the year. But Jeannie said she trusted him enough not to overdo the swallowing.

Now, perhaps this is the best time to tell you about Sandy's other love—his late father's Black Watch kilt. This said garment had been passed down to Sandy by old Sandy, and his intention was to do likewise for his own eldest son, wee Sandy, who was becoming a grand piper in his own right. The family were totally convinced that this garment of pitch-black and forest green held the power of all their good fortune.

'Take off the kilt, ma man, and wear troosers. I've a pair I hawked from an old gamekeeper. They're a wee bit coorse, them being rough tweed, but they'll do for a meeting wi' the lads,' advised Jeannie.

'Na, lassie, this is games weekend, everybody will be in the kilt. I'd look right oot o' place in troosers, folk would think me an Englishman.'

'Very well, but mind an' take good care o' yer faither's kilt.'

Sandy walked off briskly, near a whole jar of Brylcreem splattering his sideburns. To meet up for a couple of drams with his kin was all he intended, but oh, dearie me, we all know—when the drink's in, the maths are oot! Intentions or nae. And soon the couple of drinks became a wayn o' the cratur.

Jeannie put the bairns to bed before adding half a tree stump to the fire for her man to 'get a wee heat when he came hame.'

However, she didn't hear his homecoming, because sleep over-came the good lady, and at four in the morning what else should she be doing? Not wishing to wake the family, Sandy curled up at the fire like a shepherd's old collie dog and fell into a deep drunken sleep. But Ochone! Ochone! were matters not about to take a right serious turn?

'Rouse yourself, wee Sandy, and fetch the water can!' Jeannie screamed as loud as she could at the sight of her sleeping beloved laid on the ground with half his kilt flaming away. Great spirals of orange and yellow fire twisted and danced with the green and black of the travelling family's heirloom Sleeping Sandy's hindquarters were on fire! His oldest lad threw every ounce of water from the can over him. This brought our bold lad leaping from his bed of flattened and singed grass, and he began hooting and howling. 'A'm weel fumit, help me, bairns!'

Every one of them threw dirt and rags and whatever they could lay their hands on, and even the wee-est bairn whipped its dad with a broom branch.

However Jeannie was the one who was fuming. 'Look at the kilt, ye stupid fool o' a tinker's curse! Ye heap o' cow's dung, yer an excuse for a man!' She'd certainly changed her tune from the previous day. Her tongue was in unison with the fires of hell, and who could blame her?

'Mammy,' said one of the sleepy-headed bairns, 'what's that smell?' the wee yin was pointing at her father's smouldering rear-end.

Now if ever anything was sent to sober a body, then that was it—his bum was on fire! Like a wild dog that had just swallowed the gorse, he dived into the narrow burn, splashing madly at his burning flesh.

'See where the drink gets you! I said a couple o' drams, no half the f...... pub.'

Poor Jeannie, all she could think was how in the name of God was her breadwinner to perform today? The money made at Pitlochry Games was supposed to see them through a long winter ahead. They were doomed. And not to mention the 'luck' of granddad Sandy's kilt. Yes, life as she knew it was over.

Poor Jeannie threw herself in through the door of her wee tent and screamed until every roosting wood pigeon was a mile up in terror. Amazing how the gentle lady-love of Sandy's day before had changed. But she wasn't one for long grudges, was Jeannie, and soon had the half-burnt kilt spread out across her knee, stitching like a possessed demon at every damaged pleat, seven anxious children round her and a sobering Sandy slapping calamine lotion over his wee burnt bum in the background.

For over an hour she laboured, but as handy a seamstress as Jeannie was, this job was well and truly beyond her. Putting the kilt on the ground at her feet she apologised to old Sandy as if he himself was hovering in the spirit world wondering if his precious garment would soon be joining him. Still, Sandy wasn't a giver-upper, oh no, not him. Half a kilt or not, he'd wear it and be a piper. A plan formed in his head.

'Ye'll never do that, Sandy. Mark my words, that's a rubbish plan.' Jeannie and the kids shook their heads as Sandy the piper marched off to work that fateful day. His parting words were echoing in all their ears—'My faither's kilt is a lucky yin, and if it's as powerful as we ken, then the luck will be a power tae be reckoned with. Cheerio.'

As Sandy marched away down the road, he never heard the hysterical laughter coming from his brood. They had good reason. Even a blind man would have been in stitches, thinking on thon two wee red hips of Sandy's rubbing together with the sorest sway a body wearing the kilt can swagger.

Soon, though, our hero had himself secured in place hard up against a dry stane dyke. As the first few early morning tourists settled themselves into the Coronation Park where the games were to take place, Sandy gave his first tune on the pipes. One stirring tune followed another, and if ever a man had to prove himself then here he was. He was going to make amends to Jeannie (and his father's kilt) if it was the last thing he would do.

Half the day passed, along with caber-tossers, cyclists, relay-runners, pipe-bands, bonnie stewarty tartan lassies louping high in the air with every turn of their delicate toes. But still Sandy's collection bunnet lay at his weary feet, seeing a mere handful of pennies. He'd played every tune he knew twice, and still they walked by. It was beginning to dawn on him: his father's kilt had lost its luck, 'all burnt away,' he thought sadly.

'I'll play a lament for my auld Da, then its hame to face the real music; oor Jeannie's tongue.'

Sandy played his heart out through that last lament, and at long last a group of tourists began to circle round him. He played it again, louder this time. This brought a penny from one, sixpence from another, two halfpennies from a lady's wee laddie, then they left, all but one couple, who were Americans. 'That was damned fine playing, my man,' said the gent before adding, 'I remember a piper who played his regiment into battle. He was a damned fine piper as well. My wife here will tell you how often I speak of that Scotsman, although I ain't got a clue what his name was.'

Sandy couldn't have cared a toss, because his Jeannie was going to tar and feather him for taking home the measly pittance huddling at the bottom of his bunnet. No, it mattered nothing if the yank tourist reminisced or not.

'I wonder if you might do my dear lady a favour, piper?' said the gent, pushing his hand into his pocket and retrieving two beautiful five-pound notes.

Sandy's heart began thumping in his chest at the sight of the money. 'Whatever you like, sir, and, er, madam, you only have to ask.' With the man's next words, whatever heartfelt joy our piper had felt vaporised.

'Could you be so kind as to march up and down while playing your pipes?'

'March, ye say, lad. Well sir, if I could then it would be my dearest pleasure.' Sandy was desperate: he had to get his hands on that tenner. His marriage depended on it, but how, in heaven's starry heights, was he to walk with two reddened hips for the entire world to see? What Scotsman worth his salt would insult his national garb in such a way?

Sandy thought quickly. 'Ye see, sir, I was a fighting man myself, an while the wildest battle was raging I found myself along with two young soldiers. They were like yerself, sir, dear Americans, pals of mine. It happened like this. Hitler's bullets, sniping and whizzing like a whirlpool, were taking us out like flies. Man after man fell in that dark hole over enemy lines. One of my companions took it in the back, the other in the thigh. I had no option but to carry one on my back, the other laddie I dragged. On and on I went, and not the devil himself could separate me from my pals. I had to get them back to our own lines, but a hundred yards from there did I not take a blasted bullet in my right knee and then one in the left. Wounded and without the power of my legs, I still pulled and dragged those seriously injured boys to safety. Later they came to see me when they healed, but me, well sir, the power I lost that fateful day never returned to these legs of mine.

'Do you mean to tell us you gave up your own safety for my fellow countrymen?'

'I would have done it again, sir. They were fine boys, and I know what pain a mother suffers if her lad disnae make it hame. I can stand, but no much walking dae these legs of mine dae. My oldest boy pushes me here on a wee cart, and when the Games close he comes back for me.'

'Then a mere two fivers ain't enough for a hero like yourself.' The gent pulled out his wallet and handed Sandy a bunch of notes without even counting them. His wife, who up till then said nothing, removed another wad of notes from her handbag and stuffed them into Sandy's fist. He was completely dumbstruck. He'd never in all his life seen so much money. Luck, this half-burnt kilt had never been so lucky!

The couple, with the wool pulled over their eyes, walked away shaking heads at the wonderful bravery of this lowly piper. If they only knew. Sandy had spent the war as a storeman at Inveraray Barracks, and the nearest he came to a bullet was when one rolled from its box and hit his bunion.

'There are times when desperation leads a man to sink beneath his usual high moral standing, and this has been one,' thought Sandy as he marched off down the road with a healthier swagger than before, loaded! And, of course, with a mighty blister forming on his buttocks. Still, was his Jeannie not a dab hand with the needle?

But hey, talk about paying the piper!

### Black Watch

*1st Battalion (42nd) was raised in 1730 from six independent companies of Highlanders, for the protection of Edinburgh as a regiment of the watch. In 1751 it was numbered the 42nd. When it became amalgamated, the bright colours in the tartan were taken out, leaving only the dark green background as a tartan, and from this circumstance rose the title 'THE BLACK WATCH'.*

*In 1794, for gallant conduct at the battle of Guildermalsen in Holland, it won the 'Red Hackle' (on plume) which is worn in the men's bonnets. They are also known as the 'FORTY-TWAS'.*

Although my foot was beginning to throb like billy-oh, I was laughing. Who wouldn't laugh with the devil on that hilarious tale, I ask ye?

Next day Daddy and Nicky set off to spray-paint a farmer's outbuildings round about Kirriemuir way. Portsoy, who had been on the whisky with some ancient, well-to-do wife, was sunk into his bed with the drink-doldrums. His companion had the fortune to live in a stately home two miles north of Blairgowrie, and the misfortune to have acquired a fondness for 'the wee cratur'. I promise later on to share the character of oor lad with you, and how he seemed to be drawn to toffs and their ilk.

Mammy left me comfortably seated on piles of cushions, with true romance comics and a plate of sandwiches. Mister Sun had dominance over the early morning sky. So there I was, semi-invalid with a horribly pained foot. It hadn't been that bad until Mammy gave it another dip into a basin half-filled with almost unbearably hot water and Dettol, before she went berry-picking with my three siblings.

Our wee Tiny was panting at a lurcher bitch coming on heat owned by travelling folks from Cromarty. I called across to a good-looking fella that if my wee jugal got a slip at his bitch, then don't blame me. The laddie eyed up Tiny, no bigger than a size ten shoe, then at his bitch standing the height o' a wee pony, and split his sides laughing. I blushed scarlet and sank my head down into a comic. The laddie called over, did I need anything?

I shook my head, and kept reading, aware my cheeks were redder than before. Horrors, he came over and sat on the grass opposite. I cringed, because, since falling insanely in love with Betsy Whyte's son Wullie last year, I hadn't even looked at boys. Incidentally, the previous summer Wullie had tried to avoid my infatuated advances because he'd already had a girlfriend. No, men and me didn't work well at all. Anyway, when I'd sufficiently stopped blushing I raised my head to see a smothering of freckles cover the friendliest face I'd seen in a long while. With flashing blue eyes and thick curly blond hair, he didn't look half-bad, I can tell you.

'I heard the wild screams oot o' ye when thon graip found its way into this foot o' yours. I thought a terrible thing had happened, like ye were half dead or something, instead of a wee teeny hole intae the sole o' yer fit.' He went on, to my annoyance, 'you wimmin canna handle pain.'

'I am half-dead, you cheeky bisom. If poison gets hold, this leg of mine will be in deep dung, I can tell you. And as for pain I'd like to see a maternity ward full of gadjies!'

As I thought on what I'd just said about 'dung' and pregnant men the red returned, and not only covered my cheeks but most of my neck as well. All of a sudden this young man made me feel strange, my head was fuzzy, what was happening?

He apologised for making fun of my injury, saying he was just trying to cheer me up. Then, obviously embarrassed, he got up and walked his three lurchers. Tiny by now was nosed deep into the heaty bitch, and although what he wanted was a complete imposs-ibility, he wasn't taking no for an answer. The bitch rolled her eyes, and with a swish of her wiry tail let him know she was not remotely interested. The bite she gave was enough to say that her rear-end was a no-go area.

George (for this was the lad's name) asked if, when he returned, he could come over for a blether? I said 'okay' and my very first romance began. The look, the smile, the red face, yep—it must be love. From that moment my painful foot became more tolerable as I floated away on pink clouds with my man, George. Honest, folks, that's how fast it happened. A fifteen-year-old's first love. Is there anything more blissful?

We found through our blethers that we had much in common: high mountains, peaty burns, migrating swallows and much more. But above anything else was our love of the travelling history. I always believed our people were descended from ancient Egypt and were brought here as Roman slaves. Handpicked for our skills. Our masters had only one skill: the art of war. It's no secret Rome produced a mighty army. Hence their ability to conquer a great chunk of the Earth. But the craftsmen, builders and scholars were all slaves of the highest esteem. Of course when the Romans had to flee back home they had no place for slaves and left them behind. Now, if you were a native and had seen the tyranny of conquerors run rampant through your land for many years, then it's highly unlikely you'd have much time for the people brought with them. No, you'd want rid of them as well. Hence our wondering nomadic existence and fight for survival through a hostile world.

George had another theory, that we originated from Northern India and spread through the world, arriving in Scotland seven or eight hundred years ago.

I didn't accept this (and still don't). 'Where,' I asked him, 'do you get the title of gypsy from?' I went on, 'there are folks who call us gypsies and them who call us Romanies. Doesn't that speak for itself, Geordie my lad, we were Rome's Egyptian slaves.' After the clearances, Highlanders forced from hill and glen shared our nomadic lifestyle and were grateful for it.

George had his own ideas and wouldn't be swayed, but one thing we did agree on was our puzzlement as to why Scotland accepted and gave respect to descendants of those other conquerors, like the Vikings and the English, given the terrors they brought?

'Aye, an undivided world right enough,' we laughed, saying if big hairy three-headed spacemen come and help themselves to

Scotland it will make little odds who we think we are. We're all 'Jock Tamson's bairns', as the old folks would say.

In passing, it is worth a mention that Egyptian mummies have been discovered with the bagpipes amongst other treasures buried in their sarcophagi.

One thing our relatives had handed down in stone, however, was that a hell of a chunk of us were scattered and displaced Highlanders who had joined with gypsies for survival.

The farmer, bless him, had made me, from two pitchfork handles, of all things a pair of crutches, and by the end of the week my foot had healed perfectly.

Geordie's father, who by now was a permanent feature at our fire, gave me the next tale I am about to share with you. One of his lurchers had been splinter-speared while rabbiting. A gaping wound on the poor beast's side had rendered it near dead. A handful of spider moss was wetted, rolled into a ball and inserted into the wound. This pale green moss, which grows on the bark of the silver-birch tree, has powerful healing qualities. Old folks swear it is Nature's penicillin.

When I enquired of Geordie's father if he knew any stories, it was no surprise that the only tales he knew were to do with dogs. So, reader, if you've walked your old mongrel, and got the cuppy close by, then here is the tale of—

# 7

## HARRY'S DOGS

'So, old boy, I can only say sorry to you, but that's the way of it. Please close the door as you leave.'

Slower than he'd opened the heavy oak door of the factor's office, Harry closed it behind him. Not even a glance backwards at the big house did he take as, flanked by his lassies, his gun dogs, the old gamekeeper, with head hung, hobbled down the driveway towards the wee cottage in the glen. Mrs Brown, the shepherd's wife, came to meet him. 'Och man, me an' Wull are fair vexed at thon factor's decision. He'll no find a better gamey onywhere in the hale o' the country, and I'll tell him when he bothers tae bring his fine self in among us. Come you in fur a drappy tea, I'm thinkin ye'll be needin yin.'

Harry, usually reluctant to visit the kind lady's kitchen on account of her blethering tongue, felt in need of a bit company, so ushering his girls under her table he sank onto her husband Wull's chair by the fire. Something he'd never usually do, but today his mind wasn't on the niceties of good manners.

Mrs Brown talked incessantly while preparing girdle scones, stooping every so often to pet the dogs lying under her table and to pop a bit of cold cooked rabbit into their mouths.

'I mind when you an the old Laird were like brithers. Dae ye mind yon time, Harry, whin he fell an broke his ankle an you cerried him frae the quarry a' the way doon tae the big hoose, dae ye mind?'

Harry took a swallow of hot tea and nodded. The shepherd's wife could see his furrowed brow, and how hard he was trying to conceal a tear forming at the corner of his eye.

'He needs to be by himself,' she thought, and made some excuse that Wull had asked her to mind a sick ewe in the byre.

Alone now with his dogs, Harry thought back on his life as gamekeeper on his friend Sir Gregor McEwan's estate. They met during the war, he as a mere Private, Greg a Captain. After the war their friendship continued when Harry followed in his father's steps and became a keeper. Greg took over the running of his own father's estate and became laird.

During a blether while on a shoot, Harry discovered that a certain estate was looking for a good keeper. Imagine his surprise on discovering that the laird of this place was none other than his old buddy, Greg. 'Good God, Harry, what a great day this is, of all the keepers in the country there's none I'd rather have than you! How in the name are things doing with you?'

'Och, I'm the better for meeting up with your good self again,' was his answer.

Drams were downed by the bottleful as the friends cracked on into early light.

First off, Harry became under-keeper, then head-keeper, running the shooting on the estate with a free hand. Greg trusted his every decision and he never let him down.

A few years down the line, Sir Greg married a city girl, a pretty debutante who tolerated country living for a while. She was never happy away from the bright lights, and when their first and only child came along, a boy, she was determined he would be reared in the city. This unhappy union soon ended in divorce and so Greg threw himself into the running of the estate, spending any free time he had wandering through its vast expanse of moorland with Harry and his faithful gun dogs. Harry always believed those dogs were the only companionship a man needed, and so never found nor looked for the comfort the fairer sex offered.

And that's how it was from that day until three months ago, when suddenly his friend of over forty years lost his life. No one knew what had really happened, reports in the papers stated that the lorry driver had fallen asleep. It was just another fatal accident on a winding moorland road. The fierce gale and driving rain may have contributed to it.

It didn't matter to Harry how or what had happened, his best friend was lost to him forever. Never again to discuss the grouse, the deer and the high-flying flocks of wild geese over a 'guid auld malt'.

Greg's son had no intention of running the estate. Money and what it could acquire were all that motivated him! Those precious acres of land that his Father tended so lovingly were sold to whatever land developer offered the highest price.

However, exceptions were made for some of the land to accommodate the employed. Greg's will saw to it that they were given lifelong tenancy of their homes. But whenever the old laird had mentioned the details of this plan to Harry the old gamey used to say, 'well now, man, I'll be long dead before yourself, you being a well-heeled gent an all,' So the old friends never got round to arranging such things. When Greg brought up the subject, Harry refused to discuss it.

So here he was in that dreadful position of being homeless, but what troubled him more than anything were his ten-year-old gun dogs. Those faithful companions who had never lived a day without being in eyesight of their master. More heart wrenching was the fact that they were a gift to him after age took his last pair—a token of friendship from Greg. 'For yourself lad, to take you through the next ten years,' Harry remembered him saying when he handed over the six-month-old spaniels, one black and white, the other brown and dirty white.

He quickly thanked Mrs Brown for her kindness then excused himself and was gone; two dogs at his heels. 'Only one thing to do,' he thought, 'my lassies would pine without me. I have no choice, every keeper worth a spit of knowledge knows dogs without their master would be useless, better dead.' A shiver ran from bunnet to boot as he walked back to his wee cottage with the heaviest heart. In minutes, pack slung over his shoulder holding a few morsels of food, gun clenched in a tight fist, he set off for a mist-shrouded moor, dogs running in excited circles.

Within the hour a quiet stretch of heather-covered peat ground spread before him. 'Let's see the best o' ye, lassies,' he said, pointing his gun towards the heavens. Darting excitedly back and forth, with yelps and barks, the spaniels routed a fine specimen of a grouse. Up, up it flew. Harry hadn't lost his sharp eye to age. It fell like a stone, then another one fell, feathers falling like gentle snowflakes upon the purpled ground. The girls soon stood before him, proudly depositing the fallen prey at his feet.

'Well done, my beauties, now you shall feast at the rich man's table.'

The bewildered animals lay resting as Harry, instead of tying the fowl, plucked and gutted the newly-killed birds. He then built a fire and proceeded to cook the grouse, saying all the time, 'A feast for my ladies, my lovely ladies!'

It may have been a dog's instinct, who can tell, but after feasting on the prepared meal Harry's lassies become subdued, quiet as if they knew what fate waited them at their master's hand. High upon the windswept moor he walked them; hour upon hour passed before he sat each one down and said, 'you know I must do this my dear, dear friends, the choice has been taken from me,'

A strange eeriness crept upon the moor in the coming dusk. Silence followed the last whine as each of Harry's companions fell dead at the command of his shotgun. With tear-filled eyes he threw the offending weapon as far from his hand as he could possibly manage. High above crows circled and chased a single buzzard waiting to feast on the dead carcasses of Harry's spaniels. He would leave them to Nature: it was her place to dispose of them. His head hung from bowed shoulders. Tears fell freely from his old weatherbeaten face as he turned, not knowing or caring in what direction his tired legs were taking him.

Perhaps it was a sudden onset of mist, or maybe night fell faster than usual, but he didn't see the familiar lip of the quarry. All he remembered was tumbling and falling down, down, into the murky, thick, peat water. How long he hung on to a broken tree branch he had no knowledge, but one thing soon became apparent, he was losing the battle with that cold, watery grave. And indeed he was on the point of slipping under when suddenly two strong arms pulled him from almost certain death. It was old Wull and his youngest lad.

An early morning light pushed a welcome ray of sunshine through the small window of the shepherd's cottage bedroom. 'Hello lad, my, you gave us such a fright you did.' It was Mrs Brown. 'I have some brose, here, sit up and fill yourself, Harry. It's near death you've been for sure.'

Harry lifted a weak hand across his eyes, wiping away five days' unconscious sleep.

'Wull, come in here,' she called out, 'Harry's back with us.'

The shepherd rushed into the small bedroom, followed by his son.

'Oh, my maun, you didn't half put the frighteners on us right enough, how are you feeling?'

Harry lifted his frame from the bed, only to fall back flat, unable to say anything.

He lay stretched and sore and listened as his neighbours went on and on. It was a relief to hear them, but before he slipped back into a comfortable sleep he asked in a whisper, 'how did you know where I was?'

'How indeed! Your lassies, of course, did they not bark us out of our beds! But we don't know where they are. The lad here has searched high and low and can't find them anywhere. Ah well, no doubt they'll soon come at your whistle. Eh, Harry?'

As word spread that me and Geordie were paired, the lassies giggled and gossiped as to when we might be wed or what colour our weans' hair would be, seeing as mine was jet black and his a honey blonde. Soon Daddy was picking up wee bits of this information and, unbeknown to myself, he was not at all pleased—in fact, my father was downright angry.

I was growing up and Daddy was losing his wee lassie. His attitude puzzled me though, because already my four older sisters were wed and had his blessing because of it.

It was a Friday morning I will never forget. Daddy called me into the trailer and asked me to sit down. 'Jessie,' he said, in the quietest voice, 'in every family, especially one like ours with lots of lassies, there has to be the one who stays single.'

'Why, Daddy?' I asked, puzzled and bewildered by such a comment.

'That's the one who'll look after Mam and me when we're too old to see to ourselves. Can you understand me, lassie?'

I bowed my head. 'Yes, Daddy, I'm the one who will never know a man's love or the joy of my own bairns. Oh yes, I understand you perfectly well.'

'Promise me, lassie.'

'I promise.'

I knew very well that this is an unbreakable rule amongst travelling people. It was and is still to this day an unwritten law that elderly parents have to see respect and care from their family until the last breath. No matter what old age brings, whether the losing of the mind or bodily functions, family devotion must go all the way to the grave. Aye, and beyond, in many cases. Still, I always thought my strong parents would see to themselves. It never entered my head they would need tending to. I don't know if it was the thought that the two dearest people in the world to me would one day be incapacitated, or because I was the one chosen never to know a man's love or not, but my heart was pushing waves of tears into my throat. I needed solitude!

I had no wish to share my agony with Daddy or anyone else, so I ran and ran until I had left the campsite far behind me. For a while I wished that I were one of Harry's dogs. At least then there would be meaning and purpose to my life. All of a sudden a realisation spread through my young growing body; I wanted to be wee Jessie again. Never ever feeling the need to be grown-up, not ever. How long I lay in my nest of summer clover and wild daisies I do not know, but a spiral of troubled thoughts threw me into an afternoon of deep sleep. It was Geordie's voice that wakened me.

'Jess, my bonny lassie, what brings you up here to lie amongst the bluebottles and corn lice?'

I hadn't realised, but within my heaven of clover a herd of Friesian cows was munching away, happily depositing the contents of their bowels in circles of pancakes all around me. A light wind was blowing the tiny black lice from off a nearby cornfield and this heaven of mine was becoming less like a sanctuary and more like a farmyard on a hot sticky July day.

George lay down beside me and without a single warning kissed me hard on the lips. I was startled and perhaps embarrassed. I did not kiss him back, but rather pushed him away. He then became quite forceful. Those gentle hands that had previously helped me when my foot was pained became powered by something I had never encountered before. This once-tender boy who embraced me gently in dreams was foaming at the mouth and tearing madly at my clothes. Was he in for a shock! I jumped up, drew back my foot as far as possible and gave him the biggest kick between his legs. The scream he let forth sent cows, bluebottles and corn lice into the next glen.

'You ever try that again, and mark my words, laddie, I'll take those swelt walnuts between your legs and stuff them into the biggest toad I can find. Then with the greatest pleasure I'll ram yon stuffed puddock as far up your arse as it'll go, alright, bastard?' I gripped his tartan shirt collar and warned him in no uncertain terms to watch his sleep, because a regiment of rats and vampire bats were marching from hell's depths to eat that offending weapon from between his legs. Yes, Geordie lad, with hands clasping a painful swelt area of bruised manhood, would think twice before applying that kind of courtship to a lassie again. Served him right.

My days of courtship were well and truly over. If that was what men had to offer, then my parents would have no problems. Their old days would be taken care of by yours truly, and from then on I'd be a maiden aunt. The term 'auld spinster' didn't seem so bad, considering. I had hardly started with men and already I was finished. End of story.

From then on I reverted back to being a fifteen-year-old tomboy. Climbing the rear end out of my jeans. Shortest haircut and unwashed face looked good on me, and apart from the cursed once a monthers, I was as happy as a pig in smelly stuff.

Daddy, obviously annoyed with his part in my giving up ever man-hunting again felt obliged to make amends by unsuccessfully trying to buy Mac's journal. But nothing doing, my fellow storyteller would take his tales to the grave. And if rumour is half right, then my friend lost his life one fateful night after a wild night drinking in the Macduff Hotel. It seems he fell into the harbour and was drowned. It's said he went over with a battered brown suitcase clasped in his hand. Did it contain those magical tales from the tents, or did they give heart to some lonely man's fire?

Mac parted with a few more stories before he ended his visit. Later, as we wander through this book, reader, I'll pop them in.

Soon we had said our goodbye to the 'berries' and headed along the way to where Daddy was spray-painting over by Kirriemuir. This is a part of Scotland that shall live forever in my mind as the place of couthie folk. Farm people, workers of the soil and, much to my delight, traditional music lovers and storytellers.

Like us who also were agricultural workers, they had little time for idle hands. Everybody I met had a job of sorts. Woman baked and cooked from nature's larder, made their own cheese and butter and ate only the food that swam, flew and browsed within the Angus Glens. And the men, well, they worked the land from sun-up to sundown. I heard many a traveller wife say to her children 'to mind and eat yer grub an be big and strong like the ploughmen'—or, in cant, 'like the plughs.'

## 8

### THE GHOSTS OF KIRRIEMUIR

Why, I hear you ask, has she given a wee town that sits snuggled at the feet of the Angus Glens a whole section of the book? After all, we only stayed a week. Well, it could be because the famed author of 'Peter Pan' was born there, but it isn't. Or the fact that a great royal castle by the name of Glamis has its seat a few miles down the way, and it being the birthplace of Her Majesty Queen Elizabeth, the late mother of the present queen, but that's not the reason either. If, however, I swear to you that our entire campsite became a place of an immense haunting, would you believe me? Of course you wouldn't.

Give me a hearing, that's all I ask, then see what you think.

We found a wood a few miles outside the town in an area back-dropped by vast heather moorlands. Up a rough track on the way to our campsite we passed a mausoleum, the burial site of landed gentry.

Before I frighten the life out of you with the haunting of our campsite, I would be pleased to ease you gently in with this tale. Not all ghosts are terror-filled.

§

'It'll snow before nightfall, Peter, the blackbirds have eaten every scrap of crumbs I put out this morning and the goats have been butting the barn door to get inside!'

It wasn't usual for the old man to agree with his neighbour's wife, Mrs Beckett, but he'd felt the coming snow as far back as yesterday's dawn. The groaning pain in his joints told him it was time for it.

Mrs Beckett came as she did every year, basket filled with home-made mince pies, a little mulled wine, a slice of thick Christmas cake and one of her finest pork pies. In the Angus glens the womenfolk were famed for their 'porkies'.

She was a good woman who meant well, but her visit brought it all back, and he didn't need to be reminded.

On the eve of Christmas she came, her basket filled with festive fare. Helen and the dear lady would sit till after ten in the morning, chatting about this and that.

He remembered it so well, like it was yesterday, could see their smiling faces in his mind, the way his pretty wife covered her mouth when her friend mentioned so-and-so was having an affair with a certain person. 'You're an awfy lass, Mrs Beckett, you mustn't listen tae rumours,' she would say, before adding, 'who did ye say it was?'

Peter seldom listened to the women folk's banter, but although he didn't admit it, he enjoyed the whispering tones of their endless chit-chat.

But since *that* day, the silence was all he heard, and it was deafening.

'Mr Beckett sends his regards tae ye, he asks if you might like to spend Christmas wi' us. The goose, well, goodness me, it's far too big, I telt him the smaller one would do just fine. "Husband," I said, "that bird will feed our pigs for a month, it's a monster."' Peter lifted his stiffened body from the rocking chair, slowly straightened his back and thanked the dear woman for her neighbourly kindness. 'I will, as always, find your gifts maist tasty, Mrs Beckett, but am thinking it would be wise if ye were to leave now, as the sky grows thicker by the minute, and the three miles home will hinder ye greatly if it snows. Thank your man for his kind offer, but I'll stay here at hame, if it's a' the same with ye baith.'

'Och aye, of course I feel it, the biting wind already chills my face, but you know we would like nothing better, especially at this time!' Mrs Beckett wished she hadn't mentioned that! She saw old Peter flinch as if her words had opened a deep wound, spreading a look of pain across his old, craggy face.

She quickly sat the basket down and muttered she'd come back for it another time. 'I'm right sorry, Peter, this tongue o' mine, it must be the years pilin' on, I'm a mite forgetful. The man an' I wish ye a guid Christmas. We'll visit in the New Year, share a dram, weather permitting that is. Cheerio now!'

She had said enough. Angered at herself for her looseness of tongue, she bade him goodbye, pulled a thick woollen shawl from her shoulders, covered her head and was soon gone down the way she had come an hour before.

Peter shuffled inside, closed the heavy oak door, put a few more logs on the fire and sank down in his worn armchair.

'Helen, my lovely Helen, oh how I miss you. No living body could begin tae ken the depth o' pain in my heart for you. Why, my bonny dearie? Oh why did you leave our home all those years ago?'

Peter closed his eyes. The passing of thirty years hardly eased the pain which was more unbearable with each passing year.

It was like yesterday, the memory so clear in his head that he could almost see her! She sang a gentle carol while tidying up the small house, looking forward to the coming new year. 'Just think,' she called to him, 'it will soon be 1900, a brand new century!'—then continued with her singing.

She put his porridge on the hot stove and quietly went into the tiny bedroom, kissed his cheek as he was half waking, and reminded him in a whisper that young Maggie Brown's first baby was overdue and she'd promised to help at the birth.

'Goodbye, my love, I'll be back in a whiley. I think we're in for a white Christmas, the sky's grey, and the frost's liftin'.'

He'd had a bout of fever the week before and was more than relieved that Helen left him to a long lie. He heard the door close behind her, pulled the bedcovers over his head and couried down for a cosy sleep.

There was no need to concern himself about Helen's safe return, for countless times she had walked the half mile to visit the pregnant woman. She knew the way like the back of her hand, though, mind you, he would rather his wife had stayed at home on Christmas Day.

But not having children of her own, she just had to be there, she wouldn't have missed the birth for the world.

The young mother did indeed deliver a beautiful baby, a big healthy boy it was. Helen couldn't wait to get back home and give Peter every detail of the birth.

The new parents advised her to wait until morning; the wind and snow were swirling up such a fearsome storm! But she had no fear of a wee bit snow, and besides, was her heavy tweed coat not warm enough to keep out the worst of Scotland's blizzards?

Peter never knew what story his wife would have told of the infant's coming into the world.

Helen never came home.

Somewhere in the depth of wind and freezing snow his precious wife lost her way. Now only the glens carried the secret of her resting-place, for her body was never found. This was the reason for old Peter's intense heartache—no remains to grieve over, no body to bury, no graveside to visit!

His only consolation was that 'time doesn't stand still', and thankfully time for him was running out. That year heralded his own eighty-first, and in those days a ploughman seldom saw sixty, never mind twenty years more. Not a bone in his body failed to ache with a sore stiffness, and every so often a searing pain centred in his chest, then journeyed up his shoulder and down his arm, taking the breath from his body.

When Helen shared his life they had a fine wee croft, four sheep, two cows, quackies and pullets that laid many a tasty egg. A grand yield of corn kept bread and porridge on their table. Now the only thing left alive in the dilapidated croft were a few scrawny hens, long past laying. If it weren't for the old screeching cockerel, a passing stranger would think nothing existed there at all. This, however, was the way Peter preferred it. Like him, all around was dying!

The knock at the door jolted him from a troubled slumber. He ignored it, hoping whoever it was would think him out and go away. Not so! This person sounded desperate, the knocking became louder and more urgent. Peter, sufficiently angered, lifted his stiffened frame from the chair and shuffled toward the door.

A flurry of thick snow instantly covered his face, adding to his annoyance. 'Who's botherin an auld man on such a dreich day? Have yer say an be aff wi' ye!'

'Mistletoe, sir, would you buy my mistletoe?'

Peter looked down at a slightly-built lassie, no more than sixteen if she was a day, black curly hair blowing with the wind, cheeks blue with the cold, little button nose glowing red.

Her lips quivered and eyes filled with cold tears as she repeated her words; 'for tae kiss yer fair lady, sir, aneath the white berries, two pennies worth?'

'Look at the state o' the weather. Where are yer folks? Be gone now or it's a stick I'll tak tae yer hide if ye dinna git away from ma door!'

For some strange reason Peter's raised voice and angry words did not put fear into this youngster. Perhaps she had been shunned once too often that day and was past the point of caring, or maybe it was so cold, so very cold.

'Do buy a wee bit then, sir, before I go, or could you see yer way tae gie me a heat at yon warm fire, then I'll bother you nae mair!'

Peter could see the lassie edging her frame nearer, trying desperately to catch a little warmth radiating from his fire.

'Och, come in for five minutes then, the house will soon freeze if I keep this door open any longer, and no, I dinna want yer stupid branches, I ken whaur there's a tree full o' the stuff, that wad fill my house!'

She unloaded her pack and jammed the mistletoe between stacked logs near the house wall, before scurrying past her host to sit as close to the fire as she could, hands fanned out to the warm flames. The old man sat back down into his chair and watched her thin frame slowly stop shivering.

For a few minutes both said not a word, before she broke the silence by saying, 'This is a warm hoose with a cold heart! When did she die?'

He almost fell from the seat as her words cut into his very soul. 'Get yersel out now!' he shouted pointing at the old door. 'I've no place for a dirty tinker at my fireside!' She, a stranger to speak of his precious Helen! How dare she, the little bitch?

'Forgive me, auld man, it's just that I have the gift. Your hoose tells me a great love lived here, but didn't die here. If she had, then her heart would still be in this place, keeping you warm. You see, the warmth comes from the sticks in the fire, the cold from you.'

Peter's privacy had been invaded, not by a dropped word like Mrs Beckett's but an intrusion he never wished for while breath came from him. No! She had to go, snow or otherwise.

Outside the wind had increased to such an extent the little windows rattled loudly in their rotted wooden frames. The young girl rose swiftly, closed the torn curtains and latched the oak door.

'We're in for a wild night, auld man! It's my promise tae ye I'll say nae mair if ye gi'e me shelter here the nicht!' She sat down on the hard floor before adding, 'I'll sleep here on your floor and not ask for a morsel o' food if that is alright with your kind self?'

Peter, still shocked by her intrusion into what he regarded as something 'sacred', would not hear of such a person spending a night in his house. He pointed for a second time to the door, saying, 'you lot have nae soul, and folk like your kind are no deserving o' a decent body's menses. Be awa wi' ye!'

She hung her head, removed a tartan neck-scarf and cried silently into the crumpled cloth. Keeping her head down she begged, 'It's Death himself who will get me if I'm forced out in such a foul night. Please let me stay. Look! Like a dog I'll bide on yer floor in front o' the fire.' At those words she lay down, bringing small thin knees up under an elf-like chin.

Peter's heart had hardened through the years. He could not share his house with this tinker, even although the gales screamed round the little house and night had crept in. No, she had to go! He got to his feet, reached for his stick, then with a sudden jolt slumped back down as the chest-pain returned with a vengeance.

Clutching his neck as if all breath had been wrenched from his body, he tried to speak but only short gasps came from his throat.

'Oh my God! Old man, whatever ails ye?' The young girl was at his side, pulling his shirt neck open as if such a futile attempt might release his breath. She took the neckscarf, soaked it in a basin of water, and mopped his sweating brow.

He slumped forward in his chair, gave one long gasp and fell clumsily onto the hard floor. She pulled a small tattered cushion from his chair, propping up his head, and began shaking him by the shoulders. This seemed to help. Bit by bit the breath returned.

Although sweat oozed from every pore he began to shiver. 'Gi'e me my overcoat, lass, it hangs behind the door.'

She leapt to her feet, grabbed the grey relic from some long-past war and covered the shaking man.

He lay in that position for ages while she stacked the fire and gave him small sips of welcome water.

Perhaps an hour passed, before old Peter at last felt his body warm deep inside, the shivering slowly subsided and his breathing became less erratic.

'I think it would be a wise act for you to go to bed, auld man,' she said, as she gently lifted his hand, brushing it against her small face.

Peter, weakened and frail, nodded. 'I'm sorry, lassie, for bringing fear into your heart earlier. Ye see, my dear wife's memory—well, it's aye been sae precious.' Before he said another word she smiled an understanding smile, then put a finger to her lips, whispering, 'shh—I ken, I ken, don't tire yourself.'

Soon the small youngster had her host tucked warmly in bed, while she lay under his great coat on the cold, hard floor.

Outside, the storm was becoming as fierce as he'd ever known. It had a ferocious heart, just as it was the day it took Helen.

As if to remind him of that nightmare, the wind forced a crack in the window to lengthen, causing a nasty cold draught round his head. He pulled, with weakened fingers, a torn wool blanket over his ears as if in some way to deafen him to the awful sound, and he prayed never to see the morning.

In the pitch-dark of the long night Peter heard his bedroom door creak open.

'Auld man! Are you asleep? Has the pain gone?' He raised his head from a flattened feather pillow to see the small frame silhouetted against the opened door.

'In and out of baith, lass, sleep and pain. What is it you want?'

She moved to his bedside. 'The fire is clean out and my bones freeze on the hard floor. I know you must be cold as well, for it feels like ice in here. Can I sleep wi' you?'

'Oh lassie, that's impossible! Unheard of! Unholy!'

'What would the guid Lord say if we kept each other warm till morn? As it is, the storm isnae letting up, and if I stay on the floor I'll be dead in the morning. Aye, an your good self intae the bargain! Please, auld man, I'm freezin' already!'

His heart softened. He knew that without the lassie's help, the cold kitchen floor would have been his rest that night. What harm could be done?

Peter pulled back the blanket and within seconds the unlikely pair were huddled together. He felt instant warmth from the girl's body and moved closer, slipping an arm round her small waist.

Something strange began to happen! The young girl's frame had a familiar feel to it, and for some reason he knew this feeling. She did not move as he ran his hand over her head and shoulders. In the dark he could not see her hair but there was no curl to it, in fact the opposite. Long and silky hair cascaded through his quivering fingers. Helen had such hair!

At his touch she turned round to face him, the smell of her body filling his nostrils. He had never forgotten the smell of rose water. Helen dabbed a little on her breastbone each night. He took great pleasure from the fragrance when she gently laid his head on her body after a long hard day at the plough.

He held the girl close, running his hands over her small frame.

'My love! My love!' he whispered as time took him back to days long buried. They were running together, young, hand in hand, a warm summer breeze gently blowing her hair against his face. He closed his eyes and felt the silky smoothness. They'd stop every so often, embrace lovingly, and then kiss with all the passion in their youthful being.

'Helen, why did you leave me alone, my love? Oh, how I've missed you!'

He whispered in the young girl's ear over again, 'My love, why?'

Peter had been dreaming. Realising what he'd said and done, he sat up, feelings of guilt and shame rushing through his mind.

Utterly ashamed he cried out in the cold, darkened room. 'I'm sorry at what I have done. Oh Lord, what manner o' man am I? What has become of me? Lassie, please forgive this auld man, I'm not myself. You stay here, I'll go into the kitchen and light the fire…'

In the darkness the girl said nothing. It was silent, for the storm had subsided. A bright moonlight filled the sky, slivers of light shone through the cracked window and lit up her face, but it wasn't her he saw lying there, with arms stretched out to him, not the little tinker lass—it was his very own Helen, his beautiful wife had come home.

All pain left his body as he fell into a deep sleep.

He returned to his dream, holding tightly the hand of his lost love. As they walked off into the red sunset, he glanced over his shoulder and waved to a young mistletoe-seller, with curly black hair and a little button nose, skipping off down a heather-lined path, who waved back before disappearing over the brow of the hill.

§

Mrs Beckett, concerned for her neighbour, went back to visit early in the New Year. There was no sign of the old man and the house lay cold and empty, as if no one had lived there for years.

The few old hens had laid claim to the bedroom. Melting snow soaked floors and furniture. Where had old Peter gone? 'Did he,' she wondered, heartbroken, 'set off in the storm and, like Helen, become a mystery known only to the glens?' She would never know.

The good woman stood in silence, clasped hands and said a little prayer.

One last look round the house, then she would leave and take the sad news home to her husband.

Something, though, caught her eye. A notebook, covered in dust, lay half-open on the kitchen table. It was a small diary, Helen's, dated thirty years ago, the day she disappeared. Mrs Beckett picked it up, and carefully blew off the dust. It read:

*'Today my Peter sleeps long, the fever leaves him weak. Mrs Brown will deliver today. I hope it's a boy, they need a fine boy to start their family.*
*I feel snow in the air.*
*There was as strange early morning visitor, still, I felt it best to buy a little, even though Peter knows the whereabouts of a tree laden with berries. Still, she was such a small tinker to carry a heavy load.*
*She said one day that she'd come back and repay my kindness.*
*Sweet child. Bonny curly black hair.'*

Now if the couthy neighbour had dallied just a wee bit longer, and taken herself into the bedroom, then shooed away the hens from the tousled bed, she may have seen on the pillow an impression, clearly showing the mark not of one, but of two heads!

# 9

## THE BANASHEN

That is one of my all-time favourite stories. So where were we? Oh aye, this creepy place. I'm still sure you won't believe me and I'll lose you on this one, folks, but if you can stay with me then its grateful I'll be, because if you haven't experienced the supernatural then why be a judge?

I was the first to notice it. Mammy said there was nothing like it for spiralling through a damp washing and giving it a proper airing. Daddy said it put a grand heart into the fire. It sent wee Tiny curling into a tight ball behind the trailer wheel for shelter, but to me it meant only one thing—the voice of a 'Banashen.' That cold, sharp breeze blowing along the Earth's floor, rising no higher than knee level, told me a spirit was angry. An elderly woman once informed me that if a grave were disturbed then many would come. I didn't know what she meant at the time, but before our stay's end I found out all right, no doubting that!

Apart from the cold breeze blowing round our ankles that Monday morning it was quite pleasant for September. The heather heads were deep purple and cornfields ripe for cutting. Daddy and Nicky went off to spray-paint a farmer's sheds, while Mammy and I went hawking. Since my confinement with Shirley in Glenrothes and that horrible paper mill, Mammy and I didn't have many cracks, so this day's hawking would allow us time together. Anyhow, who could forget a day tramping amongst the kind country hantel of the Angus glens?

Nicky's wee brother Alan, their mother and her new man, big Wullie Young, who had arrived the night before, said they'd keep a heart in the fire and have soup ready for our return. My Auntie Annie was previously married to Jock Macdonald. His family was known amongst travellers as powerful street fighters. They were as proud a clan as any that lived and breathed in Scotland, and not only were they an extremely handsome folk, but their history tells of ancestors who held a circle of human shields around Charlie on the field at Culloden. All perished. They were thought to be descended from Glen Coe. My mother's younger sister, Mary, had married Charlie, brother of Jock.

During mid-morning, big Wullie and the lassies went for a rout amongst the silver birch wood. Soon they came upon the circular granite structure of a mausoleum. This giant building, standing about forty feet high, seemed an impregnable fortress. Undergrowth of thick ivy and gorse bush dominated its lower part. Sisters Mary and Babsy were desperate to see inside, but Renie wasn't so keen. She was our seventh sister, and although she never accepted it there was in her the power of the eye. Not, may I earnestly add, 'the evil eye', but rather that of the sixth sense. 'Come on, big Wullie,' she begged, 'don't you go looking for a way in there. It's a sacred place, and gives me the jitters.'

Big Wullie found Renie's fear quite disturbing and ushered the lassies away. Our Mary, however, was as curious a thirteen-year-old as you'd find anywhere and laughed off Renie's warnings. She spied a broken branch hanging from the high bank over onto the wall. 'Come on, Babsy, that's our way in,' she called. She hoisted Babsy up by the arm, and in no time the duo were out of sight and half way up the branch before big Wullie could stop them.

'You two bisoms get down here this instant, before the polis or a laird o' some kind spots ye breakin' an' enterin'.' He needed to raise his voice and shout my sisters down, but if you'd ever heard the roar from him then you'd know the whole of Kirrie would hear. He was aware of this, so told Renie to go back home, and that he'd fetch the girls down himself. She didn't need telling twice, and was soon gone out of the wood and up the road.

The big man rather sheepishly rolled over from the broken branch and landed inside the mausoleum. Mary and Babsy were already protesting their innocence, saying the padlock on the gate leading to the inner chamber had already been interfered with. It didn't take long to see they weren't the first intruders. The padlock was indeed wrenched off and lay in segments upon the stone floor. Very quietly they pushed inside and began whispering. Mary laughed at this and said she hardly thought the inhabitants were likely to hear them. Inside the dome, as far as the eye could see, were inscribed stone squares circling round the floor and going round and round all the way up to the ceiling. These were obviously containers for the ashes of departed family members. Some were little children who'd died of illnesses, some were soldiers lost in battles dating back hundreds of years, some were young women and old men, there were dozens of them. Big Wullie began to feel a strange panic in his chest and shouted at my sisters to 'get the hell out of this icy place!' Soon the threesome were heading back up the old track road to tell Auntie Annie about the creepy mausoleum of the landed gentry.

She was livid and told him so. 'Better the man you'll be if you took no part in the disturbance of the dead! See if I find out you had an evil hand in that kind o' thing then you'll feel the other side o' ma haun.' Auntie Annie was brandishing the soup ladle as near her man's face as she could, and if big Wullie hadn't said what he said next then he wouldn't have felt its soupy wallop.

'I only had a wee peep inside, wife, and by the way, what's wrong with the other side o' your haun?' Silly big fool of a man. Everybody who knew Auntie Annie knew her arm-reach was longer than that of any living man, you see she never misses.

Without seeking another word from the lassies or her man, she went back to stirring the soup. When we all gathered for supper she told us about the mausoleum. My Mammy, although she'd had a grand day at the hawking with me, was furious and didn't half lay into Mary and Babsy. She left Renie alone, knowing she'd have no stomach for such desecration. For the next hour the crack made no mention of the building that housed 'gone over the other side folk'.

Usually when we had eaten, we took our last long walk of the day—you know, the one that needs a lot of privacy. Men went in one direction, women the other. Somehow or other, though, in that particular gloaming we found that our paths met down on the old track road, standing outside the place of dead folks. Strange that we were all of the same curious mind, would you not say, reader?

Daddy hoisted Alan up, then said he'd go in last, let all us healthy youngsters go first. Mammy and Auntie Annie stood at the bottom, point-blank refusing to go any further. Portsoy was confident enough that there was still spunk in his bandy legs to tackle the climb.

Inside (and I can verify this because I was the first in) was an altar with a tiny casket in the middle, but, sad to say, its contents were long since scattered over the stone floor. 'This must have been a very important baby to be placed in this position,' I thought, 'and all these names—wow!' My eyes circled up and round the dome.

'Would you look at those words,' whispered cousin Nicky in my ear.

'What words?' I asked. Nicky took my chin and directed my gaze upward towards a long narrow stone cemented between the memorials to two Earls. It read:

> No eye shall gaze upon our rest,
> Unless it is in Heaven.
> No hand shall lay upon our rest,
> Unless it is forgiven.

I didn't quite understand those chiselled words, nor did I understand why there were spirals of icy-cold winds breathing sharply against my ankles. Still, all the while the voice of yon old woman echoed loudly in my head: 'Angry is the Banashen when graves have been disturbed.'

Mammy's whistle had all of us abandoning our curiosity and clambering over the wall back onto terra firma. Soon we saw the reason for her whistle, a handful of locals were heading towards our campsite. Whenever travellers were in the vicinity it was usual for local folks to join them for a ceilidh. Well, it was in those days, especially in the Angus glens. The hardy craturs had brought some home-brewed ale and soon the pipes were reeling, followed by lassies dancing and singing the old ballads. Mammy played her mouthy dry, and as the day wasted away a grand time was had by all.

Before we uttered our farewells to them, however, Daddy asked what significance the mausoleum held. For instance, did any superstitions linger around it? The dead, did they hold any position of high degree? Now, reader, do you know this, that not one of those folks, and I can say from memory there was a dozen, said a single word.

They just thanked us for a braw evening as they slowly walked out of sight and round a tree-lined bend.

Auntie Annie reminded us not to leave any belongings lying outside, just in case someone had an eye on something. Mammy told her our visitors were as honest as the day was long and not to be so mistrusting. Auntie said she trusted no one, and reminded us she once had a pair of pink knickers stolen from off a fence—and did the bugger not steal a shoe as well! Big Wullie laughed, and said there must be a right funny thief going about. 'Did you search for a one legged bloke who wore pink knickers, wife?' he joked. Stupid big man, you'd think he'd learn. Yes, this time he took the full force of both Annie's fists.

Well, the ale had worn off, and by midnight we were all sound to the world in our beds. Then it began. The haunting!

Now, for no apparent reason, I awakened and sat upright in my bed. Mammy did the same. In the hazy dark she asked what had wakened me? Suddenly, Daddy and my young sisters were also sitting up in bed, bewildered as to why they were awake. We peeped out from within the trailer curtains, out into the grey dark night, and, God in heaven, what we saw still sends eerie shivers travelling from my hair to my heel.

Sticks, still alight, were suspended in mid air. Washed clothes that Mammy had draped over a nearby fence were floating around in circles intermingled with basins, boots and tattie bags. In fact all that lay outside was going round and around in mid-air. We stared in utter terror to see if anyone else was witnessing this phenomenon, and, yes, Auntie Annie and big Wullie were both wide-eyed at their window. Nicky and Portsoy were a wee bit braver than the rest of us and opened their trailer door. Immediately they stepped outside the wind stopped, and everything fell with a clatter on the ground.

'This is a witch's doings,' called Portsoy, 'someone has put the evil eye on us.' He went on, 'Come on Charlie, you too, big Wullie, best we take what we can and move away this night.'

Before anyone could find the breath to answer Portsoy, the spirit wind came with such ferocity the feet were taken from beneath him and threw him hard upon the cold grass. I never knew the old yin could move so quickly. The moment he and Nicky were back inside their trailer again, every movable object began circling the campsite. This went on for at least an hour. Then, as quickly as it began, it subsided. Unable even to contemplate sleep we sat as if transfixed in our beds. Then it started, a noise unlike any we'd heard before. Metal striking metal. Then, the most horrific of all—the voices! Shouting, screaming, whispering voices! Inside our heads and outside there was no escaping those dispossessed souls, for that was the only explanation we could find—the dead were amongst us. It is almost impossible to put those moments into words. Whatever was in our midst that night, its sole purpose was to frighten the life from us. Renie was the first to stiffen and shriek hysterically, and in no time we joined in. Daddy stood up and shouted as loud as he had ever done at us to shut up. Soon we exchanged our hysterics for low whimpers, and this, along with the voices, lasted until a sleepy sun pushed its first rays beyond the heathery grouse-moor horizon.

So, friends, as I said previously, you may find that hard to believe, but as I also said, if you have never experienced the supernatural then perhaps it is best for you not to judge.

Without sleep and like brain-dead zombies we shuffled our bodies through the motions. By mid-morning Daddy answered Mammy by saying he definitely wasn't moving until the weekend, because of the farmer's sheds he still had to paint. Mammy practically ate him alive at this news, but she soon realised the spraying of the sheds would help provide for our winter's table. So, demons or not, we had to face more nights in that frightening campsite beyond the shadowy mausoleum.

Auntie Annie and big Wullie, well, they had no reason to bide another night, and by twelve they had packed up and gone. Old Portsoy said there was a bit of business needed seeing to at Aberdeen, and he'd be back on the Thursday. So, with those three gone, our fewer numbers looked forward with heightened fear to what might come that night when the blind bats took flight. We wondered if the Banashen wind would ever subside, because it was still blowing eerily through our lower limbs.

Nicky, Daddy and the rest of us gathered as many fallen tree branches as we could carry from the wood for a roaring fire. If anything came upon us that night then we'd sure as hell see it.

Darkness seemed to be waiting impatiently, and thank the gods the folks who visited the previous night came a-calling after tea. They were doubled in numbers and brought biscuits, cakes, ale again and numerous musical instruments.

The bothy ballads sung so traditionally would, had the night before not happened, been without doubt a joy, but none of us were ready to be serenaded. No, we were too afraid.

It was touching midnight before they upped sticks and headed off down the road. Mary mentioned, in a rather sheepish voice, our previous night's strange apparitions. She was perhaps hoping our glen folks might be able to throw some light on the matter, but once again no one said a dickey-bird. None of us took our eyes from the visitors until the last head bobbed round the bend and left us alone. Alone, and at the mercy of the Banashen wind.

Two hours in the dark passed, then three, and, so far so good, the metal clankers and voices left us in peace. Was it to be only one night of haunting? No, was it hell! Four a.m. ticked loudly from Daddy's alarm clock and the whole sequence of events began again. This time, however, it had more of a heart. The wind lifted and not only circled our belongings around, but intermittently threw things forcefully against our trailer walls. The metal striking metal was louder this time, as if nearing us. Nicky dived into our trailer and shouted he'd had it with this place, and that come the morning he'd be gone. Mammy, perhaps not wanting to lose her laddie (as she called him) ordered Daddy to get up and pack. The ghosts had won, we were leaving. The Banashen wind calmed when Daddy and Nicky gathered our bits and pieces from outside. Not one of us lassies, or Tiny either, ventured so much as a toe into the dark, and as we huddled together on the trailer floor, Daddy hitched big Fordy onto the trailer, and hurried off that haunted green. Nicky pulled his and old Portsoy's trailer behind us.

Whatever happened to us in that secluded spot remains a mystery. I later discovered that a great battle was fought in and around the area of the mausoleum. Did our disturbance of those sacred remains have anything to do with what happened? Perhaps it did.

# The Enemy Without

*When earth's adorned in winter's frock,*
*When sunshine all but falls asleep,*
*When life is cold and drab and lost,*
*I, the spiteful wind, will reap.*

*I hide then seek in hawthorn glens,*
*Pruning wings of invisible light,*
*Then choose at will, stout hunting grounds,*
*Dante's inferno, or Paris by night.*

*If pass me by a tall ship sailing,*
*So gentle trumpet tilt her deck,*
*If care she not for friendly warning,*
*Her destiny a nervous wreck.*

*Oh! Mighty oak, for now you rise*
*My coat-tail willingly embrace.*
*Now due, your family tree's demise,*
*Forswear and join the privileged race.*

*At your service proud Lord Thunder,*
*Tread you not; white lightning's toes*
*Huff nor puff will split asunder,*
*You're doomed to clap, where'er she goes.*

*To clash with fierce consuming flame,*
*My deadly adversary seek,*
*No puny flesh may play this game,*
*Fire and wind cannot be beat.*

*I am the everlasting wind!*
*To all the deadly enemy without,*
*Arm in arm with what's 'is name?*
*Strange bedfellows make without a doubt…*

Charlotte Munro

# 10

## PORTSOY PETER

Three miles down the road we pulled onto a lay-by to wait on two things: Daddy and Nicky finishing the painting job and Portsoy coming back on Thursday.

You may find it difficult to understand how we later coped with our experience. I cannot say, except that time pushes memories into a smaller piece of a traveller's mind. Our precarious existence in temporary abodes may also have made us accept it, or maybe it was our outlook on life itself. In other words 'tomorrow has its own worries, be they natural or unnatural, face each day like there's no other and that's final.'

Daddy must have been doing a fine job at the painting, because no sooner had he finished one farmer's barns than he started another.

Menmuir, a few miles down the road, saw our next stop. First, though, I would like to share one last snippet from Kirrie with you.

I hope you remember when I said that the bold boy, Portsoy Peter, would be a subject of conversation? Well, if the tea's in the cup and the bum's in the chair, then just you listen to this.

Thursday morning, and as promised, Portsoy arrived safe and sound. I use those words carefully, because he had a strange way of living on the edge of a knife. I was getting ready to go into Kirrie for some messages, Mammy had a few cottar housewives to fortune-tell and the lassies were going with Nicky and Daddy to help do easy chores at the painting. Portsoy said he'd come with me, and dearie me, I can feel the shiver run up and down my spine at the mere mention of that day.

In Kirriemuir town there was in those days a very reputable establishment where one could purchase whatever one wished (my companion's words). I will not name the fine store, instead let's call it Kirrie's Harrods.

When we came into the main street something so beautiful caught my eye that it held me in awe. There, in the window of Kirrie's Harrods, draped over a slender, white-faced, rouged-cheeked dummy doll was the most beautiful garment I had ever seen—a pink cashmere duffle coat with jet-black toggles. My heart louped somersaults in my young breast: never had I seen such a beauty, what a garment! I stood there transfixed, completely forgetting the groceries I had to buy for the family's supper.

'You see something you like, Jessie?' whispered Portsoy.

'Oh aye, man, take a deek at that, I have never seen such a coat. Would you look at it, man, could you see me in that pink?'

'Aye, lassie, that I could, dae ye want it?'

'Dae I want it, ha, that's a laugh, dae ye see how much they're asking for it?'

A price tag for some enormous amount hung from the cuff— don't ask me how much; I can't remember what it was, but so outrageous was it I knew in a million years I'd never afford it. But so lovely was that coat, that for a poor wee travelling girl just to look upon it was more than enough. Old Portsoy pushed an arm through mine and said, 'if you want something bad enough you should have it, now watch and learn, my girl.'

With those words still ringing in my head, my escort walked me into the department store, and proceeded to charm the staff with a born wit of the highest degree.

'Now, Jess', he whispered, 'don't speak unless I touch the pinkie of your left hand, and talk like a toff!'

'I cannae talk like a toff, all that marbles in the mouth stuff,' I told him adamantly.

But he convinced me I could and that was that.

Portsoy then approached a slender middle-aged lady smelling of roses and bade her good-day. She smiled, and with one hand sitting gently in the other asked if we needed assistance. My companion went for the jugular. 'We, that is my niece Gwendolyn and I, are visiting my cousin the Laird for a day or two, and we were passing this magnificent shop. Gwenny has taken a liking to the cashmere piece in the window. Do you have it in blue? Blue's her colour, you see. Well, do you?'

I froze as Portsoy made out he was thoroughbred, and an English one at that! Worse, he implied I was his niece!

The rose-smelling lady, who by now was smiling from earlobe to pearl-studded earlobe, approached me with a swirl of measuring tape and called to a girl no older than myself to bring a size-12 in blue. This she did. It was gorgeous. Portsoy Pete knew, however, it was the pink one I wanted, and said, 'oh, dimples, my darling, I know blue's your colour, but that shade does nothing for Gwenny's lovely eyes. No dear, best try on the pink, mmn?'

By now sweat buds I never knew I possessed were erupting over my body like mini-volcanoes. Portsoy touched the small finger of my left-hand, meaning it was time I spoke. The mother of all nerve battles took place in my dry throat and I squeezed out the minutest 'yesssss'. The battle was then lost, closing my lips forever as trickling beads of sweat ran from below my hairline, down my back and disappeared under my breasts. Not even the Banashen herself had the power to bring such fear. I wanted to run out the door, not stopping till the trailers on the lay-by came in view, but something halted me in my tracks—a pink, cashmere, jet-black-toggled duffle coat was being draped across my shoulders by the girl. I slipped one arm in, then the other, and as if in a dream gently fastened each shiny toggle. Portsoy came behind me and lifted the hood over my head. Then swiftly turned me to gaze at my reflection in the full-length gilt-edged mirror.

I was absolutely beautiful. For the very first time in my entire life I wore a coat no ordinary traveller girl had ever worn. I felt like the Queen of the travelling people.

'Portsoy,' I whispered, 'I know full well you and the whole of Kirriemuir don't have the lowie tae pay for this coat.'

'Shsst. I never touched yer pinkie, wait and watch.'

So, whilst the young lassie folded my new purchase into a gold-coloured box, Portsoy conned, to the highest standard of his profession, the rose-smelling manageress.

'Now, where, oh where, did I leave that blasted wallet of mine?' he turned to me.

Obviously his pinkie-touching technique was still applicable and I stayed silent.

He pretended to search through his pockets for a wallet that never existed, saying, to humour the lady, 'I have a shoot this afternoon, my man must have popped the pocket contents into my tweeds. So, sorry Gwenny, but we'll have to leave this coat of yours here, can't be helped, lovey.' Then he turned to the lady, apologised and summoned me to leave.

'What in heavens name is he up to?' I thought. The idea that he'd taken cold feet, and wasn't conning the dear lady as he'd first thought to do, was a relief to me, but I was sad I'd lost the coat. I had misjudged him, however, because Portsoy knew exactly what he was doing. His plan was still ongoing.

'That will not be necessary, sir,' the manageress said, as she pushed the boxed garment into my hands, smiling broadly. 'Feel free to settle the purchase any time you're in town.'

'If you think that will be alright,' he said, adding, 'I tell you what, just in case I'm called prematurely back to Harley Street, better pop it onto the Laird's account.'

'Certainly sir!'

I can say this to you, reader, in all honesty: when we walked from that store I felt like every law-enforcer on the entire planet was about to pounce. I was terrified.

'Happy with your purchase, Jessie?' asked my wily companion, as we headed back to our fancy mobile apartment nestling on the Kirriemuir lay-by.

Honestly, words failed me, I didn't know whether to scream out loud, throw the boxed coat over a dyke or hide beneath a boulder. 'How do I explain this coat to Mammy?' I asked him.

'Your wonderful mother has no idea how much a coat from that shop costs, and if you don't tell her, then where is the harm?'

Little did he know he'd asked the impossible of me—to lie to my Mother: not Death himself could force me to do that. I fell silent and knew that this beautiful pink coat would never be mine. Next day I'd give it back, even if it meant going to jail.

Strange, though, how our best intentions can be waylaid.

When I entered the trailer Mammy said a dear relative was nearing his end and she and Daddy had to go to him. We were to stay with Nicky and Portsoy Peter until they came back. That very night Nicky pulled our trailer over to Menmuir, then went back for his mate's. I never told anybody about my pink cashmere coat, nor did I show it to them, because whilst they slept away the night I ventured into the dark, found a soft piece of ground and buried it like a corpse. Portsoy's venture, although a terrifying experience for me and my conscience, was an everyday laugh for him. So, no surprise that he wondered why I was never seen wearing the coat of many lies!

Menmuir and its neighbouring area seemed to be full of farms and outbuildings. Daddy was certainly going to be a busy man. Mammy and I did a lot of hawking. One day we went up an old track road, hopefully to make a bob or two at some cottar houses snuggled in behind a heather moor, when we came upon a really nasty young woman seriously abusing one of her children. A sad wean, a lassie of no more than ten if she was a day, was getting a beating for dropping her baby brother. Her mother with all her strength was using a heavy stick across the lassie's back. Mammy saw red, took the stick off her and broke it in pieces. 'Never you do that to your own bairn or the Lord will take a heavier stick across your back, shame on ye.' My mother, as wee as she was, could wield quite a power when she came upon injustice.

'I tell her till I'm blue in the face, but ever since my man left me that quine has turned as wild as a schnell north wind.'

The young woman, along with her brood, hurried away down the road, and Mammy said, 'God alone knows what thon lassie has to put up with, her no having a man, but there's nae excuse for cruelty tae children.'

That night, while the family enjoyed a sing-song with some local folks who'd joined our fire, I stayed inside the trailer and remembered this story Mac told me. And given the day's events it holds a lot of weight.

# 11

## FAIR EXCHANGE

'That lassie o' yours, Anya—well, what can I say?'

Anya gathered her apron into a tightened fist at her side and bit her lip.

'Will you put down that poor wee bird or I'll lay intae ye wi' a stick!'

The impudent, unruly child stared at her mother and the neighbour, spat in their direction, then sealed the fate of the unfortunate bird by twisting its thin neck and threw it at their feet, before running off laughing loudly.

'The devil's in your wean, she needs a priest!'

Anya watched her friend walk off, those sickening words swimming round inside her head made all the more forceful by her daughter's actions. Yet to look at her she was such a pretty thing, with big blue eyes, blonde curls which cascaded down her back in golden ringlets and a smile of an angel.

The badness was in her right enough however, because as far back as Anya could remember her little Maura was wicked to the core. The time she delighted in biting her newly-born brother's finger until he turned blue with the pain; and the relish she took in leaving tiny creatures like spiders legless as she slowly removed their spindly legs one by one. Nothing was safe from her fiendishness.

Anya's heart had been broken many times in Maura's seven years of life, and she wandered how long the village folks, kindly as they were, would suffer this 'child of Satan'—their words, not hers. So often a gentle soul would pop in through her door and offer help, but nothing worked. She even wished that she was a convert of their faith, but this was never to be. Anya was of Romany lineage and her beliefs were in Mother Earth and Father Sky. Her teaching lay in fire, water and air. She believed that if Maura was disturbed that this came from disturbance in the elements at her birth and not from some unseen force that possessed her being. She was mistress of her own self.

Her other four children were of a quiet good-nature and gave her much happiness, but Maura was disruptive, the opposite of her siblings, and they loathed her greatly.

Anya saw humans as a vast field of flowers, of many colours, shapes and sizes, all swaying in the winds of life. If a weed was among them, then it had to be removed. Little Maura was a weed and it was up to her to destroy it! After all, was it not she and her late husband Daniel who planted the offending flower? Yes, it was time for a terrible decision.

That night as she lay in bed, fingers of silver moonlight dancing on her tear-streaked face, she made a dire decision. She would give back to Mother Nature her weed of wildness and ask her to take Maura home. It was the Gypsy way.

By early morning she had risen, fed and clothed the little ones, telling Maura she was going away with mummy.

'Oh dear Lord, lass, you cannot do such a thing,' pleaded her friend when Anya told her what had to be done. 'It's God's hands that seek the lost souls, even bairns can be taken away by the dark, but only he can save them.'

'This may be your way,' Anya said, 'but we gypsies have our ain beliefs. Now, can I ask you tae watch over my other children while I'm gone?'

The kindly woman nodded, and as she watched the young widow walk away over the horizon, she inwardly prayed that her heavenly Father would intervene and save the life and soul of the child.

'Come now, Maura, let's me and you away for a long walk,' she said, grasping her daughter's hand tightly.

'Where do you take us, Mither? And why?' The youngster was suspicious. Anya knew this, so her answer had to be convincing.

'The old wife, our dear neighbour, has need of herbs, you know the ones she uses to heal open sores.' She went on, 'It seems all the ones growing by the hedge have withered and died. I know of a field many miles from here where there is an abundance.'

'I don't want to go with you. Why can't I stay with the rest? My feet will swell.'

'Now Maura, be still with the tongue.' Anya could hardly bear to look at her child, given the awful task which lay ahead, and changed the subject. Her heart was beating loudly in her chest with every step.

Soon the girl tired and glanced backwards, saying, 'I want to go home. I hate all this walking through thistles and nettles. My legs sting, and I hate you too.'

Anya slowed her pace, realising she was forcing the child to go faster than her small legs were able. 'We'll be there in a while, bairn, I can smell the lavender.' Little Maura, knowing how the healing herb grew sporadically amidst lavender fields, was convinced, and settled her otherwise rebellious mind to gaze at her steps, before deliberately stamping on her mother's toes. Any other time Anya would have scolded her, but not today.

Soon it was time. The summer sun had lost its heat and began to sink slowly into the westerly horizon. Anya sat her child down on soft grassy clover, surrounded by fern and buttercups. Maura wondered where the herbs were and asked her mother. She lied, saying they grew over by the hedge. It was Anya's plan to feed Maura deadly belladonna poison disguised within a piece of bread. The hungry child found no reason not to eat and did so until every crumb was devoured. Within no time Maura's eyes rolled upwards in her little head and soon the poison had done its deadly task. Anya, through blinding tears, arranged a deathbed for her child of soft clover heads and lavender blossoms, all the time calling upon Mother Earth to take care of her baby. Unable to look upon the still features of Maura, she ran and ran until all her strength was gone, then fell and lay hidden amidst deep undergrowth. Her terrible task completed, she lay on the root-filled ground crying, until a troubled sleep overcame her exhausted body.

It was a muffled sound from within the deep undergrowth that awakened her, a strange noise not unlike someone whispering. She sat her stiffened frame up and stretched her neck to see. There was smoke from a small fire. A simmering kettle hung from a blackened tripod. Then she saw him, the old man. He was outstretched on the ground, covered by a thin grey blanket of coarse wool.

She was certain he couldn't see her. How could he, as she was completely camouflaged by hawthorn bushes? Yet, without turning or opening his eyes, he beckoned her to join him.

As she gingerly stepped forward it became clear that this was no ordinary situation. Laid on the ground in a neat pile was a penknife, a hat, a small book, 'perhaps one of those bibles,' she thought, and a chipped cup, all his worldly goods. She'd seen this arrangement before when an elderly man died in the village.

It seemed as if Death would follow her this day, and a cold shiver that ran through her whole being left her frightened. Bending down she quietly enquired if there was anything he needed. 'No,' was his whispered reply, 'but you, lass, whatever ails you? I sense a heavy-burdened heart.'

Anya knew when Father Time is on his way, folks see things. Perhaps this dying man could see that the loss of little Maura had left a scar on her. It may have been this or maybe that his own life would soon be extinguished. Her burden was so heavy she felt the sharing of it would lessen the terrible pain tearing at her heart.

Soon he heard it all, the evil of Maura, Anya's beliefs, everything. When she had finished she lowered her guilty face to the welcoming soil and sobbed an ocean of tears. The old man said nothing. The only gesture he made to this grieving mother was a gentle stroke of her hair before he pushed his chin upwards, breathing a final gasp, and then he was gone. She covered his face and sat watching and wondering who he was, and what manner of life he had led.

Darkness had engulfed their little clearing, and as she lay lost in time and silence, watching the flickering lights from the small fire entwine and dance with each other, a strange light came from the body of her companion and spread from head to toe. Suddenly it took on the form of thin, spindly, swaying hands. Fingers of light ran over his frame as if feverishly playing an invisible piano. Anya, unable to move, shook with terror.

All night long the fiendish fingers ran up and down, back and forth, never missing one inch of this old man. And all Anya could do was sit and watch spellbound. Then, as silently as it began, the haunting was over. His body, which had been raised in the air, was gently lowered back onto the now cold ground. Anya did not go near him until the thought of the old lady caring at home for her other children brought a gleam of sanity back to her mind. Dawn had brought a welcome light. She decided to gaze briefly upon the face of her dead companion, perhaps to fix his face and this weird memory in her mind, so she peeled back the grey cover. And lying there, staring up with sleepy eyes, was the living, breathing body of her very own child—Maura!

Anya, unable to grasp the meaning of this miraculous situation, did not speak, just gave a grateful thanks to whoever or whatever had given her this second chance. Not only was she given back her child, but the evil nature that was once so apparent in Maura was gone. In its place was a gentle, caring child. Was this the miracle of her neighbour's God, or a gift from Mother Earth, who could say?

Anya would never forget that night she spent with a stranger not of this world.

That was just another tale from traveller folklore for you, reader, and I hope you enjoyed it. Most of the ancient stories were told as moralistic warnings, to teach travelling bairns the ways of right and wrong. It was a great way to learn, I thought, and better than shouting the rules at little ones. A story would remain in a child's head long after a shout or slap had lost its meaning.

# 12

## THE BLACK PEARL

When we got back to the campsite between Menmuir and Montrose, Daddy was having a crack with some lads who were passing by; travellers, they were, and I believe related to the Stewarts of Blair. Grand men, and they told me (when I nosed at what they did) that they were 'pearl fishers'. After a cuppy one showed me a wee silver snuffbox. I gently peeped inside the opened box to see, nestling in cotton-wool, three of the largest pearls I had ever been privileged to see. Beauties!

With this in mind I now share an ancient folk-tale with you, and I do hope it's to your liking. Here, then, reader, is the story of The Black Pearl.

As you wander up the road towards Glen Turret you will come to a small waterworks sub-station that overlooks a deep ravine. Stop awhile and glance over to your left. Do you see a castle surrounded by high walls, with two massive pillars upholding heavy oak gates? No! Well, if you'd taken the same route several hundred years ago, then you would certainly have seen such an ominous building.[1] The castle was home to Toshach, early chief of the Macintosh Clan. And an evil man was he!

Toshach was known the countrywide for his wickedness towards his neighbours. He would rather cut off their hand than take it in

1 The remains of Toshach Castle were dismantled as late as the early nineteenth century under the supervision of the Murrays of Ochtertyre.

friendship. Although he was only twenty-five years in age and of handsome features, no father would offer his daughter's hand in marriage to such a fiend. So one day, Toshach, raging with the want of a wife to breed him sons, stole a pretty country girl from her duty of gathering in the flax. Her parents tried to save her being carried off and forfeited their lives in the attempt.

Unknown to Toshach, however, was the fact that the pretty maid had previously been promised to a pearl fisher from the Earnside. Between Templemill and Strathgeath flowed a precious oyster burn with beds thick with pearls. It was there he lived, preparing the cottage for his soon-to-be-bride.

Now, when the pearl fisher discovered that the tyrant of Turret had carried off his beloved, he turned to the Fairies for help.

'Do I live my life with my beautiful Meera, or will she be lost forever to Toshach?' he asked the invisible fairies, whom he believed danced upon the mussel shells and turned their pearls to silver. They answered by telling him to leave a handful of pearls lying on the grass overnight, as was the way. Now, if in the morning the pearls had been strung together, he would know that Meera would be his. If, on the other hand, the pearls were scattered, then that meant she would be lost to him forever. Needless to say the poor lad had a sleepless night ahead of him.

Meanwhile, back at the castle, Toshach's cousin Bregha, who had always thought he would choose her as his bride, was fuming with anger at the vision of loveliness who had stolen her chances away. She had to find a way of discrediting Meera in Toshach's eyes.

On the coming of the next dawn the pearl fisher found to his great satisfaction that the fairies had strung the pearls together—but one of them was black. He knew only too well what this signified: his beloved would be disfigured, afflicted in some way.

Never matter, he would love and protect her whatever the affliction. What was more important was, how was he to rescue her?

The castle walls were impenetrable; water cascaded from great heights by either entrance to the place. There seemed no way in. Nevertheless he had to try, so that morning he set off. On approaching the giant pillars at the lower end, he was met by two fierce guards. Finding himself without an explanation to give, a gentle whisper in his ear told him what to do—'give the pearls to the chief's new bride-to-be as a wedding present.' This he did, before swiftly walking away.

The guards took the gift intended for the girl and gave it to Bregha, who saw an opportunity in this gift to discredit Toshach's choice of bride.

'Look,' she told him, holding the pearls, 'see, your beloved has chosen a husband already. He brought her favourite jewels for her to wear; she is unclean.'

When he heard those words anger grew within him, and he screamed at his own stupidity for choosing an unclean thing.

'Take her to the dungeon, I shall slit her throat in the morning,' he ordered his guard.

Bregha was overjoyed by this turn of events, and instructed the servants to serve their master a supper of venison and mead.

That night after both had feasted and were asleep in each other's arms, the fairies set to work rescuing the maiden from the dark deep dungeons. Loosing her shackles, they hurried Meera away out of the castle by a concealed underground passage which was entered through a cave opposite the Turret Falls and reappeared beneath the Barvick Falls.

The moment she fell into her beloved's arms the thunderous roar of an earth tremor shook the ground beneath their feet. The castle of Toshach and all that lived therein were destroyed.

The significance of the black pearl was soon apparent, as the fairies removed the girl's sight—no one had ever seen the fairies as she had done and lived to tell of it. But she had suffered enough, so they took her sight instead of her life. The love between the girl and the pearl-fisher was stronger than ever, and he became her eyes.

The souls of Toshach and his evil cousin Bregha were given over to the Boorak spirits of the forest, and to this day there are two trees in the wood that have an uncanny resemblance to a man and a woman. Would you like to cast your eye upon them? If you're ever up the bonny glen, then why not take a look for yourself?

Those lads had a way with the old ballads, and when one produced a set of bagpipes then it was a certainty they were for staying the night. We laughed at their jokes and cried at their songs: what a talented bunch of men indeed. If any of you have ever had the privilege to know and perhaps hear the great 'Stewarts of Blair' in concert, then you'll know what I mean. 'Tradition bearers' amongst the travelling people, that is what those talented folks were. I have been privileged to share a stage with the last of those bearers—the great Sheila Stewart herself—and may I say in all honesty, it was indeed an honour.

At breakfast, along with a wee nip of October frost, came a parting tale from one of those lads. Here, why not have it yourself with a scone and a cup of your favourite.

§

This was how he told it.

'Ma Daddy's cousin, an I cannae tell ye his name, said one night while he wis heading hame frae a real busy day ahent the scythe he lost the path and ended up at a burn-side.

This is whit he telt me:

"Noo, as ma wee fingers were awfy sair and rid raw, I bent doon tae wash ma hands in the burn. Noo thon water wis as frezzin cauld as the frost on a January morning, and wi ma palms blistered I lay doon fur a whiley, keepin ma hands in the braw cauld watter. As I was only ten-year-auld I fell asleep richt easy. It was a hootin hoolit that opened ma een tae a bright yella moon. Thinkin Mammy an Daddy wid be frantic lookin fur me I jumped to ma feet. As I turned tae git ma directions I noticed three trees over on the horizon brow. Now can ye jist imagine whit went through ma young head, whin hingin frae the middle yin wis a rope an hingin frae it wis a skeleton—aye, man, a puckle ae bones, an they were rattlin an rollin as if the divil himsel wis gieing them life. Lord roast me if I tell a lie!"'

I split my sides laughing, but the teller said he thought the story might have a bit of truth, because when his father's cousin asked around the locals it seemed a certain gent was hung between trees at the burnside. When he enquired further he discovered that two young men had fought over a bonny lassie they both loved. When the winner took the girl's hand in marriage, the loser, unable to live without the fair maid, hung himself from the lonely spot. Maybe the youngster did see something, but, come on, a skeleton? Still, I didn't want to appear disrespectful, so stopped laughing and told him our tale of haunting back at Kirrie. At this my listener burst his sides laughing and thanked me for cheering him up—huh!

Menmuir saw Daddy and Nicky work from sunrise to its westerly setting. Mammy worried he was taxing the old lungs, but he reassured her he was fine. He added that the money he was accumulating would stand us in good stead during the winter. Now, reader, what's that old saying again? Oh yes, I know—'Don't count your chickens before they hatch.' Yes indeed.

Daddy was on top of the world. Of course he was: a bulging bundle of notes tied with two elastic bands was payment for one of the big jobs. 'Look, Jeannie, we're rich!' he told her as he met us in the town of Montrose. We were in getting messages, and he thought because he desperately needed new trousers he'd get a pair. As Mammy and I went for food, he popped into a menswear shop to buy the trews. Now don't ask me why, what or when, but whilst my father was undressing to try on those new flannels, someone slipped a nasty hand into Daddy's old trouser pocket and removed the bundle of notes! The thief managed to steal all our winter money, a total of over three hundred pounds. I am aware by today's standards that isn't a vast sum, but believe you me, to a travelling family in the early sixties that was a fortune.

We searched the shop from top to bottom. Daddy even accused the manager of having a hand in it, but nothing doing: our father's money had walked and it would never be spent by us. The thief, I am positive, would certainly not have spent that hard-earned cash with any enjoyment, not with all the curses we hung over his or her head that day.

Fate wasn't finished with us either, because when Daddy completed his final job, the farmer didn't have any cash to pay him. It seems that the sad man was hoping to sell his farm and emigrate. Daddy, however, had been seriously hurt by the trouser thief, and would have payment in kind. Well, this came in the way of a 3.4 Jaguar saloon.

Mammy near had his face in the soup pot, but when he said he could fetch plenty money by selling the motor, she softened up. Now, I expect you're thinking everything turned out all right then. No, sorry reader, but he fell in love with the car and hadn't the heart to sell it. I mean, a wee traveller man with a car like that, could you blame him? What a brilliant status symbol. Silver grey with that famous 'cat' perched sleekly on its long nose. Nicky also had his eye on the vehicle, thinking on the classy bints he could pull. He'd have to stay with us, though, and that pleased Mammy because she'd grown so fond of her sister's boy. We kind of liked having him around too.

74

Well, winter wasn't that far round the corner, so after three weeks of back-breaking tattie-lifting we experienced a monumental change. Daddy had decided to go back to Manchester. For Perthshire's agricultural travellers, a trip over the border meant going far away from home. Still, I suppose with us being big-league paint-sprayers, a few hundred miles was not to be grumbled at.

Now, you remember from my first journey how our winter in the smoggy city left Mammy at the door of death. This time there was a different peril. On this journey the long arm of the law tried to snatch away Daddy's liberty. Now, folks, for a travelling man that's a big liberty! It served him right for showing off with his Stirling Moss drive through the city centre in the fancy wheels.

However, we'll leave this story until a few more tales have been the better of sharing with your good selves.

## 13

### JEANNIE GORDON

We were on the road again and on the way we stopped for a while amidst the lowland gypsies. Here is my all-time favourite story from the Border counties.

In the time of upheaval at the end of the Seventeenth Century, while Scotland blew war trumpets between the north and the south, a small band of gypsies lived in perfect peace and harmony to the south of the bonny town of Hawick. In this group lived a woman by the name of Jeannie Gordon. Quite a tall lass, not awfy bonny but well respected by all who knew her. She had once been the proud wife of big Johnny Young, but had seen him killed during a fight with a fellow basket-seller at Selkirk.

Our tale opens one sleepy late afternoon in the month of July. The lassies washing clothes in the river were startled by a deep-throated gurgling sound from the water's depth. Unbeknown to any of them an underground stream at the head of the town had taken all it could after weeks of torrential rain, and like a great geyser suddenly spurted up through the ground with a velocity never before seen by even the oldest inhabitants.

Thirty, forty, fifty, aye, maybe a hundred feet it spouted into the air to fall back upon the poor unsuspecting folks of Hawick. They didn't stand a chance as it cascaded in and through their houses, taking every movable object that lay in its surging path. Baths, brushes, basins, tables, chairs, dishes, wee dogs, nothing escaped. Those who were able to clung like grim death to whatever offered a hold, it was too bad for those who didn't. It was a nightmare for those Hawick folks right enough, but not so the gypsies. Oh no, they looked upon the river's bounty with rubbed hands and gleeful eyes. Never had they seen so many free goods. Every able-bodied gypsy was waist deep into the water, pulling out whatever they could grab hold of. Jeannie was no exception, until she saw something bobbing furiously in the raging torrent. Of all things, it was a baby's cradle. 'The babby,' she screamed, 'get the wee babby, look—it's in the crib.' Now any travelling body will tell you, no matter how rich the plunder, if a baby is in trouble then drop you drop it all and rescue the innocent. The men and women linked arms to span the rushing water and reach the little mariner. Just in time Jeannie, standing the last in the line, stretched her body as far as humanly possible and from the brink saved the tiny bundle, which was completely unaware of its almost certain doom. The infant, a boy of several months, snuggled into Jeannie's bosom and was now stirring for milk.

'Who's to go into Hawick with me and return this babby to its natural mother?' she asked the band. An old man approached her shaking his head.

'Nobody, Jeannie,' he said, 'because if any one of us goes near the toon then we'll be flung in jail for stealing. You know that, woman.'

'Aye, but for the love of God, will this wee mite no dee if it bides away frae its mither?'

'Leave it here, then. If a mither is fretting then she'll come a-looking. Now come on, Jeannie, we'll have tae uproot and go from here. It's the safety of us all that matters.'

Jeannie knew full well that if she left such a vulnerable bundle at the mercy of the woods then a fox would feast before long. No, there was only one thing to do, take him with them. That she did, weaning him on goat's milk and giving him her family name of Gordon.

Now, this might be the best time to tell you that Jeannie had a daughter, who when she took on Gordon, was only a yearling. Jeannie never lied to him about her not being his true mother. However she did lie and say he was abandoned at birth, and his real parents were now dead. Her daughter, whom she named Rosy, grew up at Gordon's side, and it was a known fact amongst the gypsies that the pair would one day wed, such was their obvious love for each other.

Now our tale takes its characters on a troublesome and dangerous journey in which old Fate himself takes a fiery hand.

It so happened that as our band of gypsies was going from one place to another, they met a colourful regiment of Irish Dragoons who were marching to take up arms with Argyle against the Earl of Mar. Gordon was instantly struck by the uniforms and manners of the soldiers and had to enquire of them where they were going. Now, since this particular regiment was renowned for enlisting any able-bodied male who just happened by, the sergeant was quick to work his charm on the innocent Gordon. He regaled him with tales of daring exploits and battles and soon had our laddie wanting a bite of this cherry. The wily sergeant asked Gordon to repeat an oath of allegiance, then handed him the King's shilling, his payment as a serving soldier of King James.

'Rosy, you away hame an tell ma mither I'm awa tae fight a battle. Tell her when I'm done I'll be back.' That said, and grasping the silver shilling tightly in his hand, he hugged the sobbing Rosy and was gone. Back at the campsite Jeannie was beside herself with grief, and believed this was the Lord's punishment for keeping him all those years ago. At once she donned black garb and took to her closed tent, uttering not a single word. Poor wee Rosy did the same. They were of the same mind: their beloved Gordon was lost to them forever.

Soon the Dragoons along with the new recruit arrived at Stirling to join Argyle, who'd had word that the Highlanders' champion, Mar, was rapidly heading towards them to engage them in battle. They met at Sherriffmuir, and oh, my, the terror of old death spread itself evenly over the field of blood. In the midst of the battle young Gordon fought, not for Lowland or Highland, but struck out for his very own life. For it soon dawned on his good self that, victor or loser, his kind would be treated the same, as all gypsies were. After he had felled more than six big Highlanders he made the decision—to throw down his weapon and make tracks for home. Suddenly, however, a young officer was thrown from his horse in front of him. A heavy broadsword rose in the air wielded by yet another wild warrior from the north. Gordon had no stomach for this fight, but he felt duty bound to save this young calvaryman. Just as the enemy was about to drop his sword on the neck of his victim, Gordon ran him through with his bayonet. The Highlander fell like a stone, and Gordon had saved the young man's life.

With that he fled from the field of murder and mayhem, running until night and exhaustion engulfed him. After weeks' living rough, he eventually found his way to the quiet serenity of his campsite, and collapsed. Rosy and Jeannie were as overjoyed as if heaven itself had opened.

'Ye're hame, ma boy, God has, this day, been too kind.' Jeannie's face was streaked with tears that she'd held back for so long. 'Promise me you'll never go away from us again, please, laddie.'

'Mother, thon soldiering is bad doings right enough, and it's not for a gypsy laddie. Aye, ye'll never see me take arms agin ony man, it's my promise to ye and the guid Lord. We gypsies have nae enemies, mother,' he added. Then he turned to Rosy and said, 'I was hardly thinking of ever seeing your bonny wee face again, sweet lassie. Soon we'll be wed, if it's yer aim.'

'Gordon, nothing in this earth could guide me away from a lifetime with you. Oh aye, its ma aim right enough—yes, yes, and a thousand times yes!'

The band of gypsies felled a tree, chopped it up, then piled the grandest fire and celebrated until the moorcock went hoarse. Later, when all was still, Jeannie asked God not to take Gordon from her but instead to grant her the strength and the right moment to disclose the old truth about her adopted son. She would pick her moment, but not yet. For now, his happiness was enough to soothe her troubled breast.

Soon life as a wandering band took on its familiar duties. Cutting river reeds, drying them and working hard producing baskets. It was while selling those baskets that the hand of fate was to once again hold Gordon in its tight grip. At Jedburgh it was, in the town square where two soldiers just happened to be passing a quiet hour when they recognised him. 'Hey lad,' called one, 'you took arms for the King at Sherriffmuir?'

Thinking no harm in answering, Gordon replied, 'I did indeed'.

'Then you're a deserter, come with us.' Those words had hardly left their lips when our bold lad was shackled and marched away. Struggling, he called back to the completely dumbfounded Rosy, 'Tell ma mither, but God help me, I love ye baith, an ye'll be my last thoughts on this earth, Rosy.'

Now when poor Jeannie heard this, she was convinced her God had not forgiven her and was determined to punish her for keeping the wee cradled baby all those years ago. Again she and Rosy donned black and went into the darkened tent to console each other, thinking Gordon was now lost forever!

In no time Gordon had been marched into Edinburgh Castle and tried for desertion, and next we find him standing prepared to meet his doom on the sands of Portobello.

'Here,' said the head of the execution party, handing him a hood, 'this will help the shock o' seeing whit's coming.'

'I'll see whit ever ye have. It's a gypsy I am and we see the setting sun and the rising moon, so you can put that black demon o' a hat away.' As the sergeant walked away, Gordon filled his thoughts with his bonny Rosy and old Jeannie who had carried him through snow and wild blizzards, without help or care from any other body. Then he waited on the order to fire.

Now it was normal for Argyle to take his horse onto the sands to see that his men carried out their duties properly. And this he just happened to do on that fateful day.

As he approached Gordon he noticed something familiar about the condemned man.

Before the firearms were raised he dismounted and went over to Gordon. 'Did you take arms with me on the bloody field at Sherriffmuir?' he asked.

'Aye, I was there,' answered Gordon, wishing to God this task was done.

'Do you remember a cavalryman falling from his steed and nearly run through by a Highlander?'

'If ye dinnae mind, man, but thon bullets are waiting in their barrels and I'm feeling the fear o' things.'

'Yes, no doubting you are, but tell me quickly, were you the man who saved the cavalryman?'

'Yes, my bayonet came between the two.'

At that Argyle ordered Gordon's execution to be halted, then turned and said, 'I was that man whom you saved, I owe you my life.'

When Argyle discovered Gordon had been enlisted without properly understanding a soldier's lot he had him pardoned. To add to our lad's astonishment, the gent gave him, for his trouble, a bag of sovereigns. And, snatched once again from the jaws of fate, our lad made his way home. I'll leave it to your imagination, reader, as to the welcome he received. Now all that remained was for him to marry Rosy and, perhaps, to build a strong tent for his mother's old age. But before that, let's see what the wily old hand of fate unleashes.

It was a beautiful morning. After weeks of rain the band of gypsies found themselves, as they were at the opening of my tale, just outside Hawick. Rosy and Gordon were quietly watching the fast-flowing river curl and turn in her natural contours. A gentleman fishing in a salmon-cobble waved to them as the water took him downstream. Inside her tent, Jeannie had taken the decision to tell Gordon the truth, and what better place, aye, reader!

Suddenly, though, a shout from the fisherman that he had lost his paddles sent Gordon diving into the river to save the man, who was becoming more distressed by the moment. Rosy ran as fast as her legs could stretch to summon help from her fellow travellers. Jeannie heard the commotion and made toward the riverbank. When her eyes fell upon the distressed gentleman the memory of that day came flooding back. 'God and not fate shows his hand this day,' she thought. What did she mean?

In no time Gordon had reached the swirling cobble and was soon guiding it into shallow water. Two men helped the mariner from his wobbly boat as Rosy wrapped her lad with a blanket. Jeannie brought the man into her tent, Gordon and Rosy followed. 'Madam,' said the gratified fisherman, 'is this your son? For he has the thanks of a stupid old man, and although I am that, and no doubting it, I am also of considerable wealth and I will put no limit on the purse he will receive as thanks.'

Jeannie stared at her guest for a few lingering moments, then said, 'you have no need to give Gordon anything, sir, but if you sit down I shall give you a gift.'

Bewildered at the old gypsy's words he sat back on a meagre but comfortable seat, and asked her to continue.

'Gordon and Rosy, what I now tell this man is for your ears too.' She beckoned them also to sit down. When all were seated, old Jeannie Gordon began. 'I recognise you, sir, to be the Honourable Mr Riddle, the Provost of Hawick. Is that right?'

'Yes, madam, that I am.'

'Do you have a son?'

'If you know of me, madam, then you know also that the raging river that almost ended me this day took my only son from me.'

'How long ago, Provost, did that dreadful deed take place?'

'If you know of me, woman, then you will also be aware my dearest baby was swallowed by the water some twenty year gone. Now I must be home. How much reward, young man, do you require?'

Gordon said that none was necessary.

'Sir,' Jeannie continued, 'this day God has brought your child home to you!'

'What evil spirit has hold o' ye wife, for you to utter such terrible words to an old suffering man?'

'See yer boy, Riddle, the lad who pulled ye from the river stands beside ye!'

Jeannie sank to her knees, and at long last the pain of concealing the truth left her in great waves of relief, as she told them of the water-cradled Gordon. Old Provost Riddle was shaking as he moved closer to Gordon and examined his features. 'Yes, ye have yer mither's eyes and my very ain father's high cheekbones, is this my son standing here? God, woman, a thousand curses on ye if this is a lie.'

'I am from the gypsy, sir, and if you know anything about us then you will know we cannot lie.'

All the time Gordon and Rosy stood silently, holding tightly onto each other's hands.

Gordon spoke first: 'Mither, have I saved the life of my father this day?'

Jeannie hung her head, for she knew that if he accepted the truth then she had lost him. Still, better living without him than living with him always haunted by the past.

'Yes,' she whispered. 'Embrace your father, son, for many years has he done without you. Come, Rosy, let us leave them to their joyous reunion.' That said, she took Rosy's hand and stooped from the tent.

'Father,' said the young man, 'I am unable tae think straight on these matters. Only I feel I must ask what ye would have me do.'

'Son, my dear, dear son, you must leave this hovel and come home to your rightful place. I have a grand house where you shall live as intended, as a blue-blooded gentleman. Clothes of the finest cloth shall you wear. Now say your farewells and let's be away home. Oh, what a wondrous day indeed this is.'

Gordon knew that no matter what happened from then on, his dutiful place must be at his father's side. He found Rosy and his mother standing sadly by the riverbank and told them what he had to do. Rosy, unable to bear being without her man, ran off in floods of tears, but old Jeannie had suffered before and would do so again. 'It's glad I am that I cared for you, ma laddie, because things have turned out fine. Now away with you, I'll see tae Rosy.'

Now, nothing of material wealth was spared for Gordon, or should I say 'the Honourable Gordon Riddle, son of the Provost of Hawick'. He wanted for nothing, but strangely, a rich heart is not always a happy one. Something was missing. He knew what it was and told his dear father. 'It's my Rosy, father, ye see, me and her, we're betrothed.'

'Son, there is something you must understand, the gypsy has no rights. It matters perhaps to them if promises are kept and broken, but not to a gentleman like yourself. Now go and tell her. Anyway, the broom yellows, soon they will have moved on—surely you know this.'

'Aye, father, that I do.' Gordon had duties now, the life of one who would soon run the Provost's office, and he had to break with the past. Still, that did not mean it would be easy. He found Rosy amongst the river reeds, singing a sad song. He heard the same pain in her voice as was in his heart. When she saw him, all her love and longing wrapped itself around his broad chest as she clung desperately to him, kissing every inch of his face. 'Oh Gordon my love, its been a while but I knew ye'd come back, I telt Mammy.'

Gordon pushed her gently from him and told her their love was impossible, they had to say farewell. Rosy ran off, unable to listen further, while he went to the campsite to say goodbye to Jeannie and tell her he'd to lose Rosy.

'Why dae ye have tae lose Rosy, son? Surely you two are as in love as the merle that sings tae its ain love in the dusky night.'

Gordon then went on to say his father would not allow the mixing of gypsy blood with his line. 'Now, what makes you think a mixing would take place?' she enquired impishly.

'Mother Jeannie, what is it ye're saying?'

'Well, son, perhaps the guid Lord wishes me to disclose a final truth. Ye see many years a go a terrible wicked nursemaid was employed by Lord and Lady Uphall to take care of their new baby, a girl. Now the maid got entangled wi' a rogue who made her steal the baby, hide it, then ask a pretty sum for its safe return. Lord Uphall, though, was enraged to such an extent that, before he knew where the baby was hid, he ran her through with his dirk. Every able body then set out to find the newborn child, but she was not found. It was around this time I was passing along nearby, and as I passed a few wild rose bushes, did I not hear the weakest cry. When I parted the thorny branches, there was your beloved Rosy lying there minutes from death. Thankfully a nursing lassie was on the green and gave the baby milk. Of course, as with yourself, if we, the dreaded gypsies, had taken the baby home, we would have been killed for even laying a finger on such a royal child. No, son, it was take the baby and run as it was with you. So we called her Rosy because of where she was found. So go and find her and take her to Uphall with my blessing.'

So, reader, there you have it, except to say that the wedding of Lady Uphall took place shortly after that time to Gordon, the Honourable son of the Provost of Hawick. I would also like to add, it was the only wedding of such high esteem that ever invited a band of roving gypsies as guests.

Jessie's father (right) aged 15 with his boyhood friend,
Wullie Donaldson

Jessie's mother and father in 1942 (Pitlochry)

Jessie's mother holding Babsy (Aberfeldy)

Jessie (right) and her sister, Renie

Jessie aged 14 with her mother, Jeannie, in Kirkcaldy

Jessie aged 14 with her father, Charlie, in Kirkcaldy

Jessie's mother fooling around in Lennie's Yard, Kirkcaldy

Jessie's sister, Janey, in front of the bus

Sandy Stewart, the 'Cock o' the North' (*Picture reproduced by kind permission of David Cowan*)

Tiny the dog

Jessie and Davey on their wedding day in Perth, Hogmanay 1966

Jessie with her daughter, Barbara

Jessie's children—Barbara, Stephen and Johnnie

Jessie with Johnnie (left) and Stephen in 1983

Jessie (back) with two of her sisters, Charlotte and Janey, and her mother

# 14

## THE BORDER GYPSIES

Well, my friend, did you enjoy that age-old love story? It never fails to give me the greatest pleasure. But I'm forever a romantic. I was asked not that long ago by the wonderful Robbie Shepherd of Radio Scotland, did I think our country held a romance for me? My answer was easy—'Yes'. With its vast heather moorlands, through which you can picture lovers running. The rolling waves of the west coast shoreline, where a parting forever takes place as sweethearts say farewell. One watches the little boat fade into a sun-kissed horizon. Oh dear, there I go again, lost in my thoughts. But I'd better get back to the past. Where were we? Oh aye, among the Border gypsies.

The town of Melrose saw our next stop; well, a mile outside it in a wood that was regarded at that time as no-man's-land, to be precise. Daddy was walking the talk with the fancy motor amongst all the travelling men, and I'm sure he had a permanent sore head keeping it above his neck. Mammy never was a status follower because she had hawking to do. She asked me to do the washing while she was gone. Now, it's amazing, so it is, what one hears when bent-backit over a metal bath scrubbing dirty clothes.

Two old dears sat by their fire and had this conversation. It was about wars and foreigners and humour. It went like this: 'I wonner why the Breetish aye beat thon French in a' the battlin' they done the gither?' said one.

'Och, I ken fine well,' answered the other wife, looking upwards towards the heavens. 'It's because afore going intae fechtin the Breetish say their prayers.'

'Aye, but surely yon Frenchmen dae the same.'

The other lady thought for a minute, then said, 'ach noo, lass, ah'm thinkin yer richt, but hoo wid the guid Lord unnerstaun yon French gibberin tongue?'

How indeed!

After I spent the morning washing and scrubbing I stood proudly back, watching my finished articles blowing in a north-westerly. Up and up they went, with gallons of water spraying into the atmosphere from soaked cuffs, collars and towels. I must say there is a deep sense of satisfaction after slogging hard at a job (although it was damned hard avoiding the stinging blister popping up on my knuckles), one that my washing machine of the present day has robbed me of (what a liar).

Still, unlike the lass in my next wee tale I could take laundry or leave it (preferably the latter). See what you think of this.

Travelling folks are no different from anybody else when it comes to 'phobias'. Even though we live closer to the earth than many others there are still certain things that can be seen as obsessive. Take the woman who is terrified of grass, she wears three pairs of socks under her wellies rather than risk touching it with her toes. Then there's Maggie Blains; she has a phobia to butterflies. Now I ask you, how can anyone be afraid of such beautiful creatures? Well, a relative informed me that the poor wife swallowed one in a piece of bread and jam. The worse case I heard of was Tommy Macintyre, who sneezes for Scotland around trees, and him a woodcutter. Please!

Here is the lass I mentioned. Her phobia was of grimy earth, and her living in a tent of all places. This happened on my campsite that day. Like me she was washing her fingers into blistered bubbles. And although it was a big moan for me, she wasn't aware of them. Earlier her man had fixed a washing line between two sturdy oaks. All morning she sang happily, hanging one item after the other until there was not so much as an inch left for a holy sock. Now, as it happens when men are busy, they don't always do what their good lady asks them to do with certainty. In this case it was the fixing of the washing rope. My fellow washerwoman's line began to unfasten and slip from its tree. Without warning her spotless clean clothes slipped from the rope and rose into the air. Up and away went socks, knickers, woolly waistcoats, babies' nappies, headscarves, trousers, shirts. And the rest was gone before I could tell you what it was. The woman let out the wildest scream I'd ever heard as she helplessly watched her newly laundered clothes join the hoodie crows gliding in the blue yonder. Inconsolable she was, as she lay prostrate on the ground. When she eventually raised herself she stood up, pushed a fist to the heavens and said 'God! God! Pairt me if ye must frae ma bonny bairnies, aye, even ma guid man. Take if ye want the breeth frae ma body, but God in yer mercy dinna pairt me frae ma new-washed clean claithes!'

I swear that that wife, if she had had enough soap, would have removed the tent pegs and scrubbed her very abode. What a fixation with cleaning she had.

Just thought I'd share that with you, folks.

Thinking of my father showing off and bragging about the fancy car, here's something else that might interest you. If you have ever been over the high road to Applecross, then you will be well aware of its precipitous dangers. Those bends and almost vertical braes are, even with today's technically advanced cars, a wild hazard. And many a nerve-wracked passenger has begged the driver to stop just in case brakes might fail. Imagine what like it must have been some sixty-odd years ago, when the road had a mere scraping of coarse gravel on it. That would have been a frightening journey for a goat, never mind a young man driving a big shiny black Buick.

Yes, if you've jumped ahead of me then you're right enough. Daddy drove the first car over into Applecross. There are folks who will argue with me about this and say it was a Postie. However it was in the coastal town I met the very policeman, now a very old man, who remembered welcoming my father as he drove in.

When Daddy jumped out of the car the whole village clapped and cheered. The bobby, who was all business-like, approached Daddy and enquired if he had a license to drive 'this here vehicle?' When Daddy said 'no, I don't,' then the policeman offered to sell him one!

What I noticed at this time more than I would ever have done before was the vast number of hunting dogs the Border gypsies had. We may have pulled onto four or more sites heading south, and every family had at least six dogs apiece.

There were reasons why dogs were important to the traveller. The main ones were hunting for food and guarding. Another reason, and may I say one not to my taste, was for 'sport'. But no matter what the reasons, if a good dog was for being sold, then men could go on for days dealing and bargaining a price.

Our wee Tiny could rabbit and rat better than any ferret, but he was simply a family pet. If he missed his natural goal in life then he never let on, especially when Mammy filled his bowl with cooked mince or some Lorne sausage.

Many travellers, however, took their dogs far more seriously than we did, and I know of a man who left his wife because she took a dislike to his lurcher.

My friend Bob Dawson, an extremely dedicated follower of all of Britain's travelling people and their ways, wrote a book on travellers' dogs, and I now, with his permission, print a piece from it to tell you all the things you may have wondered about them but never found out. Understandably, travelling folk keep a lot to themselves about their ways, including their dogs, but here, through Bob's writings, is something about a traveller's best friend—his dog.

## SIGHT HOUND LURCHER CROSSES

There are 11 officially recognised Lurchers formed by crosses with sight hounds, but such dogs are unusual with travellers because although the Greyhound gives speed, and some sight hound blood line courage, they are very difficult to train because, so it's said, of their lack of intelligence. My old friend Nelson—dead these many years—had the best such cross I had ever come across, a mix of Greyhound and Wolfhound. It was hopeless with hares, but extremely effective with rabbits which hardly ever got away. The only traveller I ever knew to use a Greyhound/Saluki cross found the dog so stubborn, refusing to chase when it should, and refusing to come back when called, that he tried to 'train' the dog by starving it, in the mistaken belief that it would be more inclined to eat when very hungry. The experiment failed, and the poor dog was too weak even to concentrate and use the little intelligence it had. I felt very sorry for it, though I accept that, from a traveller point of view, it was a useless animal. Since this incident, several travellers have told me that they like a Saluki cross because of the animal's good looks, which seems to me a spurious reason to have a dog, but travellers accept that it does not make a good Lurcher. (Ginge's comment is 'brain-dead. I wouldn't waste a collar on one.')

Deerhound/Greyhound crossed Lurchers are often used as show dogs, but as few travellers are into show dog breeding, I do not think it is a common animal amongst travellers, but Deerhound/Greyhound cross with Greyhound is a little commoner, as this increases the Greyhound blood in the animal.

Amongst old-style travellers, dogs had to earn their keep, so some crosses of Lurchers were favoured in particular areas because of the lay of the land. In Cambridgeshire and Lincolnshire for instance, dogs need to be large with staying power. In the Midlands, smaller fields need smaller but faster dogs to catch rabbits—rabbits are faster than hares over short distances.

## FARM DOG CROSSES

The purist sometimes claims that the only proper Lurcher is a cross between a Greyhound and a farm dog, especially a Bearded Collie, Border Collie, Rough Collie, Alsatian, Old English Sheepdog or (historically) a Smithfield Collie, this last being a dog once used to drive cattle and sheep to and from Smithfield Market in London.

Such crossed dogs are quite frequently seen with travellers, though the Border Collie/Greyhound cross is probably the commonest and the Old English sheepdog the most unusual. Alsatian/Greyhound Lurchers are good for deer, but not for hare, and tend to be unreliable near children. Generally, however, the farm-dog Lurcher has the advantage of being good with the kids, reliable, hard-working, intelligent, with a good jaw and staying power. They are also easy to train, I'm told. That said, such Lurchers are less common amongst travellers than others, though whippet/Border collie crosses are somewhat commoner. As they are easy to train, they are often good dogs for new Lurcher-people to learn on. One of the attributes Ginge looks for is a dog with a thick coat to protect it from injury and weather. His preference is a tall Collie/cross Greyhound. He regards them as easy to train, alert, sensible and loyal.

## TERRIER CROSSES

Almost every terrier breed has been crossed with Greyhounds to produce Lurchers, though the only one recognised by the official Lurcher clubs are Airedales.

Bedlingtons, Bull Terriers, Wheaten, Kerry Blues, Irish and Jack Russell's, and such dogs often show great courage and guile, though they can be stubborn. The commonest Lurchers are Greyhound crosses with Bedlingtons, Kerry Blues, Airedales, Staffordshire Bulls, Jack Russell's and Irish. Ginge remains sceptical about such dogs.

## BEDLINGTON/GREYHOUND CROSSES

A good Bedlington/Greyhound cross is said by many travellers to be one of the best Lurchers available—if you can get one. The difficulty is that very selective breeding by the specialists has produced a Bedlington which is no longer as effective for work as its predecessors and, therefore, when crossed it often lacks many of the characteristics which once made it such a superb dog. This is also Ginge's experience.

It was once an exceptionally common dog with travellers in the North. The original was a cross with colossal stamina, able to take any game (rabbit, pheasant, hare or deer). Its thick coat gave protection against bad weather and against thorns and barbed wire; it was a very hard worker with a good nose, but its disadvantage was that it was not a bright dog, and so needed careful training as it did not easily think for itself. Although there are times when a dog needs to act by instinct training, it can be a disadvantage not to think for itself.

## STAFFORDSHIRE/GREYHOUND CROSSES

Not a common Lurcher amongst travellers, though Welsh Romanies sometimes have one. I have never seen one at work, but am told they are courageous and have considerable stamina but are bad tempered with other dogs and can see that as a more desirable activity than the coursing itself. Their use is almost entirely limited to rabbits.

## ODDS AND SODS

Only eight other crosses are recognised as Lurchers—Foxhound, Beagle, Golden Retriever, Spaniel, Setter, Rottweiler, Doberman and Labrador. Perhaps it's a little unjust to put all other Lurchers into this category but, in my experience, there are very few to be found other than those listed above. I have seen Greyhound/Labrador crosses, which appear to be intelligent dogs, and once a Greyhound/ Setter Lurcher, but I have no idea how these dogs performed. I have also heard of Rottweiler crosses which purport to take an elephant (well, a slight exaggeration here) but the experts tell me that with the Rottweiler's nature, such Lurchers would be unlikely to be much good. Similarly, I am told that Lurcher/Lurcher progeny are often pretty useless. Ginge says that there is a lot of waste with such dogs, and good ones are hard to find.

So now, friends, when you hear stories of travellers who allow dogs to roam wild and also of tales about sheep killing, then you will know that the owners of these pets have not prepared their background with enough responsibility.

Thanks to Bob for that insight into the travelling man's favourite dogs, which now leads me into this next tale. Another one of Mac's.

# 15

## THE LAST WOLF

Midway between the Highland villages of Brora and Helmsdale there stands a stone. Inscribed on it are these words:

> *To mark the place near which (according to Scrope's 'Art of Deerstalking') the last wolf in Sutherland was killed by the hunter Polson, in or about the year 1700. This stone was erected by His Grace The Duke of Portland, K.C., A.D. 1924.*

This commemorates the tale of how the said hunter went into Glen Loth with two youngsters, one his son, the other a herds boy. In a rocky mountain gully around the burn of Sledale they came upon a narrow fissure in the rocks. The laddies squeezed down and found a small cavern and in among the debris of bones and feathers there were six wee wolf cubs. Polson instructed the boys to kill the cubs. Now, when she heard her cubs screaming, the tormented mother, not seeing the concealed hunter, tried to rescue her young. Polson dived forward, and holding her by the long bushy tail, was able to stab her to death. In those days Polson was considered a hero, today he would have been marched into a court of law and prosecuted for animal cruelty.

Here then is Mac's tale of a wolf.

§

It was when the twentieth century was at its start that a young travelling couple found themselves in the valley of the Tweed.

Many miles of cart road without stopping had left them footsore and belly-weary. She was in labour with a first-born, and desperately needed a birth-bed.

Rachel bit hard upon her bottom lip; her pains were more powerful now than earlier and still they had not found a place to stop for the night. 'God help me, Jimmy, but if I don't lie down somewhere this baby will drop out onto the hard road.'

Her much-suffering husband had tried all day to find a suitable spot, but whenever he pulled the horse off the road a landowner appeared at the roadside and threatened him, each more menacing than the one before.

The last man came brandishing a hunting rifle. Jimmy practically begged on bended knee. 'My wife is near her time: surely you can find it in your heart to allow us this small corner of a field?' But nothing doing. So it was with great reluctance that Rachel and Jimmy found their journey's end in the depth of a thick forest. The forest of Glentress. 'I know these woods,' he told his wife, 'I remember coming here several times with my father's family when I was a boy. We'll be safe now, I know we will.' Soon the tent was erected and Rachel lay on her birth-bed of soft fern and green mosses.

As the first streaks of early dawn sunshine crept over the skyline a tiny cry filled the forest. Those weary travellers now had a son; their first born. Jimmy drew water from the burn and set light to a few sticks, then boiled a brew for his exhausted wife. Rachel was hungry, but the previous day's long arduous walk had left her so tired she could hardly lift her head. So after a gentle wash she and her new-born snuggled up inside the rounded canvas tent and both slept away the morning, while her man set off into the comforting shelter of the thick trees to find food.

It was peaceful at the small campsite and Jimmy knew his wife and child would be safe from harm. No need to concern himself about landowners, because they seldom ventured deeper than the perimeter dykes, usually sending foresters in to check instead. Jimmy knew the old man who patrolled this place and had gone with his father and gamed with him several times. 'No, they'll be safe,' he convinced himself. After a few hours and two rabbits later he set off back to their temporary abode. A good distance from home a terrible scream, that sent dozens of wood pigeons fleeing skyward, had Jimmy, heart beating faster than a hare's, leaping burn and bush to his family's side. Soon, breathless and panting he was at Rachel's bed. She and the baby, thank God, were unharmed, but something had frightened her. 'So help me, I'll swing for the beast that put this fear intae ye, Rachel,' he cried, convinced that some so-called gentleman had found the tiny campsite in the clearing.

'It was no man, my husband, an' I wish tae all that is sacred that it was. No, it was a hound! One as big as any I have ever set eyes on. It had the eyes of a devil, and Lord roast me if I lie tae ye, husband, but it wanted the baby, I swear, it was our child it wanted.' Poor Rachel, she cradled her child so tightly Jimmy though she might smother him.

'Give me the bairn, Rachel, I'll check him to see there's no marks on him.' Jimmy didn't wish to seem unconcerned, but a hound—well, relief spread through him; his wife must have been dreaming. However, Rachel knew that no fever or fright could make her imagine things. She had seen something and had no wish to spend another minute in that forest because of it.

'I'll fill a heart intae the fire, lass, while you feed the little yin, then we'll eat this gift from God.' He moistened a flannel, then wiped the sweat from her brow. 'Bonnie lassie, I know these parts, but if you think you saw a big dog then I'll visit up on Braeside cottage and speak with Ian the keeper, he'll put me right.' That seemed to quieten her, allowing him to skin and cook the rabbits.

Later it was a stunned Jimmy that heard what the old keeper had to say.

'Well, well, she's still there, I thought Sir Colin took her out last winter.'

The said gent was a relative of the estate's owner and had spent some time in the Canadian Rockies, said old Ian. He was there shooting; his favourite hobby was killing anything that moved. To add to his sport he was supposed to have smuggled over to Scotland—of all things—a wolf.

'A wolf!' Jimmy felt his bottom jaw drop, 'what in the name o' hell was he planning to dae wi' a wolf?'

'Aye, ye may well ask. Seems he had the idea o' filling the woods wi' the creatures. Bring in his buddies and have wolf shoots. Nothing doing wi' that stupid idea because every sheep farmer for hundreds of miles would have put paid to his wolf before he could bring in breeders. However he had the good sense to kennel the bitch, but did she not chew her way out. I scoured the ground for the poor cratur, never seen hide nor hair of her though. We breathed easy, thinking a dog fox might have killed her, until a young travelling laddie told me he heard puppy yelps coming from a hole in the forest. I told Sir Colin and we found seven pups. The only explanation to that must have been that a mating took place with the traveller's Alsatian dog, they have a wolf-like way.'

Jimmy sat heavily down and thought on his wife and child, then excused himself and was gone. 'I'll pack and go this very day. If Rachel sees yon beast again she'll go oot her senses.' Jimmy was soon striding for home. He checked to see no one was near before climbing the dyke and disappearing back into the trees, but oh my, a shout from the hillside had him rear his head. It was the man with the gun, the one they encountered the previous day.

Old Ian however had meant to give Jimmy a bit of salmon, and chased after him just in time to stop Sir Colin shooting the travelling laddie stone dead.

'Put that gun away, sir, for Jimmy here is the son of a friend o' mine!'

'What would you be doing mixing hands with the likes of rodents, Ian?' asked the angry man.

'Well, I ken o' nane other than the travellers for keeping a trim on vermin. Everybody has their uses, Sir Colin, you know.' Old Ian obviously was held in high esteem, because not many would get leave to speak like that to the landed gentry.

Jimmy, though, had been held back from being with his family and if it wasn't for the scream Rachel sent through the forest that moment, he would have grabbed Sir Colin by the throat. Instead, ignoring him, Jimmy and old Ian ran to Rachel's aid.

What a terrible sight met their eyes: the small canvas tent was flattened, firewood lay scattered. Rachel stood motionless, arms hung limp at her side. Worst of all, Jimmy's baby son was nowhere to be seen. He grabbed his stunned wife and, shaking her, shouted, 'what has happened to the wee yin? Rachel, the bairn, tell me!'

Rachel slid onto the forest floor, and holding a tiny white shawl toward the heavens screamed, 'It took him, came back and took ma babby! I told you it wanted our bairn. Oh, why did you leave me?' From then on she would not be consoled, such was her torment of despair. Jimmy turned to old Ian for help, but all seemed lost. A hungry wolf, what did they know of such things? No one knew anything of North American timber wolves in Scotland. Suddenly Sir Colin forced a way through the gorse and when he saw what had happened immediately apologised. 'I had better tell you both,' he said, 'I found out that those travellers had returned, the ones who came last year. They spent a few weeks over on the other side of the forest. They had dogs, I think one must have been the Alsatian. I found a lair with more young and killed them. I know where it is; perhaps I can make amends and take you there. Maybe the she-wolf will be resting and feeding on…'. Quickly he stopped his tongue and walked off, old Ian and Jimmy at his heel. They left poor Rachel swaying from side to side, beating her breast and mumbling in the ancient mourning tongue of her ancestors. Jimmy caught the sleeve of Sir Colin's jacket and threatened revenge for the disaster he was responsible for.

The gent wasn't listening, however, because suddenly a sight rose up in front of the threesome. Jimmy and old Ian had never seen such a vision. A great grey form barred their way, standing its ground; dropping its head and with curled lip it flashed pure white fangs. Sir Colin slipped his hand down to where a ready-loaded rifle hung and lifted it to shoot. The big she-wolf charged, slashing with her mighty jaws, and landed on Sir Colin just as he fired. Both fell upon the mossy floor of the forest, blood pouring from the mighty beast. At last her torment was over, but she did not go alone. Sir Colin, for all his sins, also lay dead, having fallen upon a jagged tree stump. It all happened so fast that old Ian and Jimmy hardly had time to draw breath. Suddenly from a small opening beneath them, a cry was heard. Jimmy pushed his head inside a cave-like place, and there, lying on a bed of crushed dry leaves, was the living, breathing form of a baby—his own child. The mother wolf had substituted their newborn puppy for her lost ones. That was the only explanation they could think of. Jimmy and Rachel (who believed God had looked after her baby) left Glentress Forest the next day, and went on to have seven more children. Their precious first child was christened Ian. But he was seldom called by that name. Travelling people, however, will tell you the nickname he goes by—Wolfie!

I shall be hard pushed to forget Mac's parting words on the wolf of Glentress. 'A lassie a wee bit "gyte" was yon timber wolf,' he told me, meaning she had been broken and did not fit.

Deary me, the ways of the world.

Still, no time to dwell, because we're on the road again, a long road at that. Manchester looms, she of the thousands of people—all kinds of folks, different colours and creeds. However, very few of them were Scottish travellers, so let's tell you how we fared during the winter of 1963, ten years after our last visit.

Before we settle there for the winter I'll part with another tale for your attentive eyes. This wee story I now slip in was from an elderly Welsh traveller. His name was Eddy Blue Boy the Third. Sorry I can't elaborate on the title, but he made me laugh and that is why this story stays in my mind.

I had seldom heard the ancient worthies until then, and although he parted with several tales it was this one that stuck firmly in my head.

# 16

## DAVIE BOY AND THE DEVIL

Time and place have no meaning to the characters of our tale, so just say it happened a while ago in this place and that.

Davie was a traveller boy who had, after many years, come wearily home from a seafaring life looking for his family. When he at last arrived at the campsite where they'd last met, he was sad to see it empty, void of old and young, dog and pony. Sitting down on a stone, head in hand, he looked around the place where many had played and he felt heart-heavy. Scanning the quiet place before heading off, he noticed that where his camp usually stood was a mound of perhaps only a foot wide. As he began to scrape away the small handful of sand he recalled his father saying to him as a little boy, 'if I have a message for you I'll bury it.' Yes, this was a message from his father, because in the hollow he uncovered lay a box. In it were three biscuits and a note. The note read: 'If you be hungry, my son, don't eat these biscuits until you have shared them.' What a strange thing for his father to say, he thought. Still, his father was a wise man, and he had taken the time to conceal the box for Davie, who by the way was beginning to feel a mite hungry. However, he would abstain from a morsel until he met someone hungrier than himself. This was just around the corner because there he found an old back-bent woman who asked him for a small crumb of food. 'I only have three biscuits old hag,' he told her, 'but you are welcome to share one with me.' The wizened wife thanked him, ate the half biscuit then went at a snail's pace away. Soon he came upon another old lady and she too asked him for food. 'There are two biscuits in my bag but I'll share one with you.' Again the elderly soul thanked him for his kindness and crawled off.

Two days later his hunger had taken on a life of its own, gnawing at his innards. 'I must eat this last biscuit,' he thought in desperation, scanning the skyline for someone to appear. Just as he was putting the biscuit to his lips a sound from the roadside reached his ears. 'Help me, please, I am starving to death.' Davie made over to a clumpy grassy patch to find, lying in a dreadful state, another ancient woman. This one was even more sickly than the others. 'Help me to sit up, young man,' she begged, 'I have no strength in these bones.' Davie bent down and gently seated her against a tree trunk.

'Here, old wife, I have only one biscuit left, but you can have it all.'

'Thank you, my good man', she said, handing him a woven sack. 'You deserve much more than a biscuit.' Davie thought the old woman was perhaps missing her marbles, for what good was an empty sack to one who was in the last throes of hunger?

'When I am gone down that road, you open the sack and ask it for whatever you desire, but never a thing of badness or greed.' Those parting words left Davie totally confused. He scratched his head and sat down upon the same patch of grass she had sat on no more than minutes before. The hunger returned with a vengeance, eating steadily deep into his gut. He peered inside the sack, and making sure no one should see him and think his actions those of a madman, whispered, 'Can I please have food?'

And did he have food? Did he ever! For there, to astonish his eyes, was a table bigger than one set in a banqueting hall, of every kind of eatables one could wish for. And for one who had the merest crumbs of shared biscuits in his belly, then was that not a feast! Davie ate until the last bite swelled in his throat and nearly choked the once-hungry lad.

Then, like a babe, he lay within a sun-warmed grass field and slept, slept and dreamt of steak and vegetables, puddings and creams, salmon and fruits, all produced from an old hessian sack. Yes, if ever there was a happy traveller man then he'd be hard pushed to beat our Davie.

Awakened and refreshed he carefully folded the magic sack and tied it over his shoulder. Little knowing or caring where his wandering footsteps would lead him, Davie set off down and over the road that led to somewhere or nowhere. By the day's end he'd arrived at a town snuggled within high stone walls in the middle of which was a castle. 'This is a strange place,' he thought, noticing an obvious lack of inhabitants. As he looked all over for a place to shelter for the night, it soon became apparent not a single house had a light or open shutters to its name. Finding no one he went and knocked loudly at the castle gate. He waited some time before at last the gate creaked open, and standing peering out from behind the heavy wooden gate was an old man who asked Davie his business. 'I need digs for the night, where can I lodge?'

The elderly gent told Davie that he would find nothing in this place because the ancient one had eaten most folks. The rest had taken to the hills in fear that they too would be feasted upon.

'Ancient one,' asked our visitor, 'and who might he be? And can he not eat food like the rest of us?'

The old man was a bit taken aback by Davie's response and asked him where he had been for the last ten years and more. After realising Davie had been on the high seas, the old man beckoned to him to come in and share his supper. Davie didn't feel the need for food, having eaten enough to choke a horse, but thought it best not to offend the man and said a drink of tea would be fine. They drank down tea and then Davie discovered what was happening to the people.

He drew upon his pipe, did the old man, stared into the fire and said, 'One night when her Majesty the Queen was alone in her chambers, she made a wish that the King's dungeon was filled stapped full with gold. Suddenly she turned to see a tiny man dancing in the flames of her fireplace. He said that if she wanted her wish to come true, then she had to bring two handmaidens over to the fire for his Master. Without question the greedy monarch did as requested. The most terrible thing happened next—a dozen tiny little men just like the first grabbed the two innocent maidens and drew them into the fire, never to be seen again. The King, on hearing this, was horrified at the evil greed of his wife, scolding her for dealing with the underworld. She said that before he judged her, why did they not see if the tiny man kept his part of the bargain. So down into the dungeon they went, and yes, there it was, a mountain of sun-kissed gold filled every corner. But the King was not impressed, and went into his wife's chamber to see if the magic forces could be summoned. At once the little man appeared to him and said, if he wanted things to be as they used to be, then he must bring the Queen over to the fire. This he did, and in an instant she too was seized and swallowed up by the fiery imps. Then the rooms began to shake. Flames shot forth from the fire to curl and slither up the wall. The fireplace was glowing like a furnace. Then he of all terror, of all horror, of the most grotesque form, the Devil himself, shot out and held his Majesty by the throat. 'You will bring me and mine food—living, screaming, kicking food—do you hear me, mortal?'

The quivering King nodded his head vigorously. The Devil, as suddenly as he had come, was gone, leaving a cold fireplace and a wreck of a king.

'So now you see where the townsfolk have gone,' the old man concluded.

Davie thought long and hard before saying that he might be able to help. He asked to see the King. After climbing several flights of winding stairs the pair were ushered in to sit before a bent-backed and sad-faced man. He was not old, yet he had the appearance of one who had lived a dreadful existence. 'I have a young man here, who thinks he may be of assistance, your eminence, sire,' said Davie's companion, with an air of despair in his croaky voice. The King hardly lifted his head to look at Davie, but bade him sit anyway. Davie said that he too had a powerful magic, not to be used for greed or evil but only for deeds of goodness.

'Take him away to do what he wishes,' said the King to his faithful old servant, though neither of them had the slightest belief in Davie or anyone else for that matter.

Davie was taken into the Royal Chambers and soon had the fire kindled, spreading a warming yet menacing heat throughout the room. He didn't have long to wait before the tiny man he had heard of came slithering over the flames. 'Have you food for my master?' he enquired. 'Yes, I have,' answered Davie. 'Then give it here,' squealed the demon. Davie shook his head several times before saying he had to see the ancient one first. The last word had no sooner left his mouth when the ruler of demons whooshed up and hovered in the room like a tower of solid flame. Davie felt his toes curl inside his boots and his tongue swell with fear.

'Where is my meal,' roared the earth-shattering one. 'I need fed!'

'Sire, I have a meal better than any living, scrawny person—would you like to taste it?' Before the Devil could do to him what he'd done to all the other mortals, Davie spread his sack on the floor, peered inside and summoned its best. It did not disappoint: the whole room began to fill up with every possible edible morsel. 'Come eat, fill yourselves,' he called to the demons, who were pushing and shoving to be able to feast upon Davie's gifts. The Devil was the first to gorge, spewing and slushing his way through fruits, beef stews, fishes and fry-ups until not a single crumb was left. He liked these new delights and ordered Davie to be there again next night. Davie came again as he was told and the next night also.

After a week, when he was certain he'd gained the trust of the king of the demons, he set about his plan. 'Keep all the doors open leading from the chambers and down the stairs, and also open the castle gate,' he told the old guard. 'This night we will see the end of the ancient one and his family of gargoyles. Trust me, old man.'

That evening, as was now usual, when the fire was lit those wicked vipers from the pits of hell came forth to feast. With drooling slavery lips they waited impatiently, scratching at Davie and then at the sack. The Devil ordered him to provide food or else they'd eat him instead.

'Now, listen here, you lot,' said the bold hero, 'why do you wait night after night for a feasting when you can enjoy the pleasures of the sack all the time?'

'Well, tell us more, then, Davie boy, please come closer and tell us more.' The Devil pushed aside his family of ghouls in anticipation, curling long fiendish fingers round Davie's neck.

'It's easy, my lord of the underworld—jump inside!' The drooling band gathered in a tight circle and peered inside the sack, 'I see nothing,' said one, 'nor I,' hissed another.

'Of course you can't see anything, because you must all jump deep inside. Only then can the sack work its magic.' Davie felt the Devil's bony fingers loosen their grasp as he bent down to sniff and gaze within the blackness of the sack. His followers, as if waiting on his orders, gathered round. 'Let's try this, my wiry little worshippers,' he cried then leapt into the sack. In an instant his band did the same. Davie waited until the last cloven foot had disappeared from view before whipping a strong band of rope around the opening. 'Look out,' he screamed, 'I'm coming through, I've the devil on ma back!' Out of the chambers and down the stairs he darted, with the bag of hell on his back. Out through the main door, out through the courtyard, out through the castle gate, on to the street he ran and ran with all the demons of hell scraping and screaming on his shoulders. The King, who heard the commotion, was standing on his castle wall shouting from the high turrets, 'Haste on Davie, haste on my man, you'll do it!' His old guard was doing the same.

Davie went round the bend in the cobbled street, and with one last dash began emptying hell's cargo down into the town's well. Down, down they went, tumbling and rolling and screeching, never to escape the blessed water of the well.

Davie had used his sack as was asked of him by the old sick lady—'never ask for greed, only need!' Well, folks, if ever a sack was used for need, then it certainly was this one.

Before long word spread that the Devil was defeated, and soon the townsfolk came home to their houses. The King began to do his duty, and soon found a worthier Queen than his last one. And as for brave Davie, well, one day while washing at a quiet river, he met and was reunited with his family and never needed to ask his magic sack for anything again. (He keeps it safe, however, just in case.)

The tale I have just shared with you is part of the 'Seven Deadly Sins'. Travelling people used these stories to teach their children about what in the world was right and wrong. As in the Bible the Devil, that timeless serpent who represents all sin, was always the main baddie, while a mere human of low birth was the hero.

# 17

## WINTER IN MANCHESTER

W e were back on the road now, and as we planned our winter in Manchester I stirred up quite a storm. If you need a cuppy, then go on, fill yourself one, then settle back and we'll have this blether.

Lancaster loomed on our horizons. Mammy asked Daddy if he remembered where her old chum Lizzie Gaskins lived. He said somewhere to the north of the city, but that we didn't have time to visit because it was getting late.

'I'd like to see her again, Charlie, we didnae half hae a guid auld laugh when we were weans.' As we sprawled in the leather luxury of our Jaguar cruising down the English highway with our caravan yoked up behind, Mammy told us that Lizzie was a traveller from Stirling who had married an English lad. They had made a good living on the antiques and settled in Lancaster, only occasionally popping south to the hop-picking in Kent.

Daddy promised that when we'd found a winter stopping place then he'd take her to visit with her friend. But 'best laid plans' and all that, because I put the spoke in Daddy's wheel before that day wasted away.

I felt a jaggy pain in my right side as we ate breakfast, but thought nothing of it because I was aware the dreaded monthers were on the skyline of my teenage years, and us girls didn't mention such embarrassments. Bloody monthers—why in the entire world did Mother Nature send those cursed times upon the female form beats me. Knots like invisible fists twist and turn away deep inside the gut, accompanied by drum-beating headaches; black moods when you could quite happily fling hot oil at anyone, and then those blasted rivers of red, yuck! Who in their right mind would want to talk about such a curse? Yes, God must have been in some helluva mood when issuing the monthers. And what was the reason—babies! Yes, all that just to reproduce ourselves. I promise you this, reader, when I stand outside those pearly gates He'll hear me, I can put hand on heart to that.

Anyway, there I was with knots getting tighter and running up and down my right side with knuckle-dusters on. It was more than I could stand. 'Mammy, I've a bugger of a pain in my side,' I cried out. Before my mother could answer I felt a bolt of flaming pain shoot under my ribs, pushing every mouthful of porridge up my gullet and covering Daddy's head and neck. Mary, Renie and Babsy began boking, forcing Daddy to pull off the road. In seconds we were all leaning over the fence, retching. Mammy felt my head, which in her words was 'on fire'. 'I think we had better get Jessie to a hospital, Charlie, she's not well. Come on, darling, let's get you lying down in the trailer.' She lovingly helped me into the caravan, while the rest of the family cleaned themselves of my vomit. 'Can you think of what it was you ate, pet?' she enquired. I couldn't think of anything other than what we'd all eaten that morning. She thought it might be appendicitis until I told her my beasties were visiting.

'Never in all my time did I see a lassie with a reaction like this,' she told me. 'No, you need seeing to.' Nicky and Portsoy, who were following behind, pulled over and said they'd wait on a nearby lay-by until our return. We sped off to the Royal Lancaster Infirmary. By the time we eventually arrived I was delirious, with a temperature to fry on. In no time I was poked, prodded, X-rayed, injected and eventually bedded. 'We can't seem to find a reason for your daughter's condition, but we'll keep her in overnight for more tests.' I screamed that it was only the monthers and to let me out. But nothing doing, hospital it was and that was that.

While they were in Lancaster, my family sought out Mammy's old friend, who was overjoyed to see her.

Next morning the family arrived to find me thankfully recovered, sitting in the waiting room. The doctor told them he believed

I had a condition known as grumbling appendicitis, and might one day need it removed. I had a reprieve on that occasion, folks, but I would have gladly parted with a dozen back teeth to have seen the bugger staring at me from a glass jar than living in the knowledge that my grumbler was still snuggling into my wee intestines. Still, as the Good Book tells us, 'sufficient unto the day is the trouble thereof.' And thereof it certainly was, because when we arrived back at the lay-by where Nicky and dear old Portsoy Peter were supposed to be waiting for us, the polis had shifted them, over four times. The poor souls spent the night yoking up from one lay-by to another before going back to wait for us in the first one. That, however, wasn't the trouble I am referring to, oh that it was. No, Portsoy had been arrested by the cops who just happened to be on the look-out for him. We did not know it at the time, but there was a warrant out for his arrest regarding a toff's missing something or other. I can't say what it was, but it had enough value to send the hornies south to find and arrest him. So off we went, minus our pal, to winter stop between a car garage and, just as on our previous visit, a piece of waste ground.

November, with its touch of nippy morning frost and foggy nights, had us searching through the ragbags for woolly jerseys with high necklines. If you didn't read *Jessie's Journey*, to which this book is the follow-up, then share with me now what I mean by the 'rag-bags'. These were large brown paper bags, each containing six washing pegs and a small sample packet of washing powder, along with a note which read 'Please accept these in return for any old clothes, preferably woollens, many thanks.'

Most folks on finding these bags on their doorsteps were happy to part with unwanted rags and in return to have something back, especially useful objects. However I have to say the odd one would be happy to pocket the goods and replace them with the contents of their bowels, filthy pigs! Still, only rarely did we encounter such low life. If we did we usually pushed the bag back through their letterbox to allow them a moment of reflection before they cursed us to the depths of damnation. In complete contrast, one day we began our cold street hiking by starting off in a well-to-do area. Hardly had we placed one bag when a lady called to us. When we went back to her house she beckoned us round to the rear entrance, to find, sitting there, dozens of hessian sacks filled to bursting with woollens.

By the time Nicky and I had the last one piled into the Big Fordy there wasn't an inch to spare. What a great day that turned out to be. The gentle lady didn't ask a penny, she was only too grateful to get rid of all her old clothes. I saw lots of nice cardigans, but when she told us that her sister and husband had died I thought it best to leave things in the sacks. Travellers are very superstitious and later on I will share more of this with you.

Our day would begin with the frost biting into the tips of our fingers. I say 'our' meaning, on this Manchester visit, Nicky and I. Mammy stayed at home while the lassies went to school. Daddy, being the mechanically-minded chap that he was, had found an odd hour helping in the garage, and this was of great benefit. It covered our rent, although I have to admit we certainly found him coming in many times covered in oil from burrowing into the guts of cars. Still, it was a labour of love to my old Dad without a doubt.

So I hope you've got the picture, folks, as to our abode in the Rosy City. I'd like to tell you now about our neighbours. Opposite the waste ground, to our north, there sat a large smelly waterproof factory. I don't know its name, just that it made raincoats. Once a week, a massive lorry-load of cuttings was dumped onto the waste ground. Believe me if you can, reader, but under that smouldering mountain of material lived the city's vagabonds. Almost like an army of vampires they emerged onto the night skyline to forage hotel and restaurant back-entrances for scraps of food.

For me they represented a menacing, heaving mass of life's un-wanted, the dregs of society, but to my mother (God love her) they were sad, unfortunate individuals who had fallen from life's hard road and never found the way back. She always smiled and greeted them, as she would do anyone. They in turn would remove their crumpled bunnets, click heels together and greet her with as much politeness. 'Mammy,' I remember saying, 'thon lads could just as easy slit our throats while we slept for whatever we had, and here's you smiling and giving them the time of day.'

She took my hand, answering me by saying, 'lassie, a beggar disnae steal, he begs.'

I, with my blindness to adult knowledge, shrugged my shoulders and asked my mother where was the sense in her words. To this day I see her eyes twinkling with a tear in each. 'They have already been robbed, Jessie, of all dignity and honour. Nothing left for thon poor souls than to live within the cess-pit of nature, surviving on the likes of folks who have a little heart left in them to show the compassion this world seriously lacks.' She then scolded me and reminded me that we travelling people should understand that better than others. She finished with these words. 'After all, who do you think taught tramps the ways of begging if not us?' Mammy had a way of painting pictures with her well-chosen words, and this is why, to this day, I can share them with you, my friend.

Within a fortnight of us settling into the secluded spot within the Cheetam Hill area, the only other person who came into our midst was a young policeman called Jim. He took to us because he came from Fife; he was another Scot living and working in the heart of England and needed perhaps to hear familiar Scottish voices. Mammy enjoyed his visits when he was on street duty. She'd whistle him in for a hot mug of tea; this was a godsend to a street bobby, especially one who had to walk the lonely nights away with eyes in the back of his head. At first he said, 'Och, you're no needing tae be giving me tea, Mrs Riley,'—then, after a while, he'd appear with a bag of scones or a packet of biscuits expecting our hospitality as if he were one of the family. Daddy, who mainly eyed the law with mistrust, soon dropped his guard to Jim, the young friendly bobby from Fife, and treated him like an old pal.

After November had passed we got ready for the deep dark winter ahead, and I certainly felt that the ragging was taking a chunk from my pretty feminine fingers. Nicky said it left him shattered in the evenings, and gave him no time to 'check oot the bints' (look for talent of the female kind). This had me scratching my head, I must say: you'd think there were more than enough 'bints' sharing his breakfast with him every morning. Yes, I know, folks, he had the sowing to do, I know, I know.

So, with Daddy's permission, Nicky and I went job-hunting. He found one in demolition while I settled for work in a lampshade factory. It sticks vividly in my mind, does this factory, because it was tightly sandwiched between Gallaghers' Tobacco factory and Strangeways Prison. Quite a thought that, don't you think, folks?

My boss, a wee round fat guy by the name of Swift, positioned himself in a podium above the workforce. He was a bit like a stern minister glued to his pulpit, fearful to leave lest he falls from grace. I must say, however, my boss was a gentle little man who smiled and nodded and seldom gave orders. He just liked sitting and doing his business from a high viewpoint, leaving the day-to-day running of the place to a tall, thin, one might even go so far as to say ghostly-faced woman. In spite of her appearance she was the nicest, kindliest soul you could ever hope to meet and spoiled me rotten. Why, you ask. Well, once she and her late husband spent two weeks in Rothesay, and now loved all of Scotland's hantel because of it. If I were late she'd touch my hand and say, 'did Mr Frost keep you awake, pet, that sleep found you late?' Or something just as caring. Yes, a nice cratur she was, but for the love of me I can't remember her name. (If you are reading this, gentle lady, then get in touch.)

I loved my job making lampshades in that place, perhaps because I enjoyed seeing the finished object. The job was simplicity itself, though. All I did was take the wire frame and wind different-coloured plastic ribbons round and round until the frame was covered. Downstairs they had a far more delicate job to do. The people who worked there were intricate painters. It was their job to paint flower-designs and suchlike onto hard-canvassed shades. I knew within myself I could have flourished in that studio environment. But one had to be six months on the ribbon job before venturing downstairs, because once a design was applied to the skin-shade it had to be perfect. Only proper artists were allowed a brush in hand there. Still, I think I could have done 'no bad'.

Remember I told you Daddy wanted me to be the 'bide at hame' daughter? Well I couldn't let him know that a certain young artist had given me more than a fleeting glance during canteen visits. His name was Ian Campbell, and he was three years older than me with the most gentle nature and sparkling white teeth thrown in for good measure. We talked ourselves silly and found we had so much in common it was uncanny. My nights were filled with dreams that had us running along sun-kissed beaches, kicking soft warm sand through our toes, then falling into warm embraces and smouldering kisses. Oh yes, dreams were made for times like those. I kept our day meetings secret, telling no one. However, it soon became apparent we were a duo. One day he, not me, decided to put a more permanent seal on our sneaky, feely-touchy romance.

'Jessie, would you like to come home and meet my parents?' he asked cautiously.

'Of course I would, but I can't ask you to meet my folks because my father doesn't want me involved with boys, I hope you understand.' He did without question, and went ahead to introduce me to his folks. It happened on the Friday. And you will understand why this particular incident stays forever in my mind.

I was a nervous wreck with all manner of thoughts swirling through my mind; would they like me? Did he tell them I was a gypsy? And how would they take it? By the time we reached his front door the small amount of lipstick applied to my dry mouth was gone, leaving a vague pink line instead. I had taken a lot of time with my clothes, pressing my hemline until it resembled a sharp knife. Mammy kept saying she needed the gas ring to boil the kettle, so would I please hurry and remove the iron. Daddy was obviously suspicious, but accepted my excuse about going to see Clark Gable in 'Gone with the Wind.' I'd have gone with the clouds to see Clark, never mind the wind, but not that night. I lied to my father just as every other teenager does who sneaks around. It was not my fault, though, because if Daddy had left things to Mother Nature, I know I'd have been as honest as the day was long.

So, as I was saying, there we were, me and Ian, standing with fingers entwined on his frosty doorstep. And talk about frost! His mother, the queen of freeze, opened the door. Fairly tall she was, with a straight back, and sporting short curly black hair. I smiled gingerly and stepped inside an immaculate hallway. Ian started to remove my coat when suddenly she stopped him with a raised hand. 'I cannot allow you in my house,' she said through clenched teeth. Ian tried in vain to quieten things; the poor laddie didn't know where to look. I did though, right into his mother's face. Our eyes met with steely stares. 'I suppose you think I'm not the right kind for your son!' I shouted, standing there in the pristine lobby of this complete stranger's house.

She turned and walked away without an answer, leaving Ian dumbstruck and bumstuck on a small chair. It was his father who helped me understand. 'I must apologise for my wife, but she doesn't believe in mixing the blood. It's not a personal thing with her, my dear girl, but it wouldn't be right, you see.' He too walked off, leaving me in total confusion.

But me being an 'intae-the-face-wi'-all-things buddy' I had to have my say. 'Listen to me, you bloody English, jumped-up, would-be toffs! I'm just as good as you if no' better, who dae ye think you are anyway!' Ian held my hand and said, more to shut me up than anything else, 'Jessie, it has nothing to do with you being Scottish or even being a Gypsy. It's our colour! My parents want me to marry a black girl like myself!'

After telling the wimp not to open his mouth to me on the coming Monday, or any other day of the working week, I pushed open the door to storm off down the road like all spurned females. My poor hips and thighs were scadded red raw with the speed I shifted myself. But not as red as my face, I bet.

Another dead-in-the-water romance then, folks. Do you think my Da had put the evil eye on that side of my life? I wonder. Anyway, what did I know about skin colours? Hell, I fancied the bloke, is that not enough? Apparently not!

When I got home no one bothered where I had been or why I came home early, because we had had a visitor while I was gone. Of all people, it was our wee con man, Portsoy Peter, who had arrived back to finish the winter with us. I must say I for one had missed him and his wee Alfred Hitchcock face. No one told me where he had been. However, when the opportunity offered I asked him. This was his reply: 'You know how much I enjoy the company of toffs and their expensive lifestyles, Jess? Of course you do. Well, when her Majesty asked me to spend some time in one of her confinement homes with all expenses paid, I just couldn't refuse.'

That's my Portsoy for you, and I will always remember him. It's not proper, I know, to encourage a conman, but he never to my knowledge took a penny from the folks without money, only from the folks with plenty. We've a while in his company yet, folks, before there is a parting; and the winter in Manchester still had a wee sting in its tail for us.

## 18

### KING RUAN AND THE WITCH

W hy don't we have a blether now about another ancient tale without time, reader? I'm feeling the need for a visit home to bonny Scotland, so let's us, you and me, travel north to a field skirting Bankfoot, not far from Tullybelton in Perthshire.

Here we'll drift back before the days of recorded history and hear the story of 'King Ruan and the Witch's Promise'.

Once upon a long time, back before the rising of millions of tides, there lived a young King. He was called Ruan, and he was not a bad fellow. His entire kingdom, which spread from the Tay's birth spout to its entry into the northern sea, was filled with good, kindly people. However, they had a problem. I don't say, and God forbid if I do, that their King was the cause of it, but in a way, I suppose he was. You see, he wasn't a pretty boy, in fact he was the very opposite. He was so ugly, nobody would look upon his face without feeling a wee heave from his or her guts. How could their King with a face like a hew-haw ever find love? And no one was more aware of this problem than Ruan himself. He rose from his bed each day with the heaviest of hearts, longing to be cuddled, but no matter where he searched, not a single female would spend a moment too long gazing at his ugly face. If by chance they had noticed the sad unhappy eyes staring from within that face then it might have been a different story. He might have melted them somewhat. His longing had him search everywhere but to no avail. He might have searched in the forests and found a pretty nut-gatherer, but he had a terrible fear of trees and was never found anywhere near them.

Such was the pain in his heart he decided to visit the ancient field witch who, they say, knew all things.

Gathering his people round him, he told them what he intended to do.

'No, sire, please don't, it is folly.' The people knew her evil ways would indeed lure their beloved King away, and they pleaded for a week with him to change his mind. No, he'd made his decision, the witch it was: there was no other choice.

His dearest friend, an old soldier who had fought for his late father when he was king, asked Ruan to stay and be patient. One day the right girl would win his heart. But it was no use, he'd made up his mind.

Now, although folks knew of the wizened woman from the green grass, they had never set eyes on her, it was enough to know that she was a demon who stalked the country when the moon was full.

Ruan set off to find her, looking in caves, calling from hilltops, searching in undergrowth, but after a week and some more he was no further forward. At the end of each day he would find a quiet secluded spot and lie down. One night, while he was in the deepest slumber, a voice calling in the wind awakened him. 'Help me, Ruan!' it cried out. He jumped from his bed of rushes and stared around at the cold damp ground. The spreading moonlight gave the merest glimpse of trees in the night. He called out to the forest, 'I am here, what do you want from me, stranger?'

'Ruan, I am the witch of the fields. I hear you calling my name, but before I help, you must free me from the trees.' Ruan thought he was being haunted by the evil beast, and called back that he didn't need her help after all, he was on his way home. It was with the fastest legs he ran all the way back, not looking in caves, or calling from hilltops, or peering into undergrowth. Completely exhausted, King Ruan fell into the arms of his anxious friend, the old soldier. 'I knew she would try to spellbind you, sire,' he warned him, adding, 'don't you be a-going looking for her kind no more. Sooner or later a lass will be to your liking, just be patient. Thon demon knows your mind and would hide in the dreaded trees for you.'

And so it was that not a single night passed without the sad voice calling into his slumber, 'Help me, Ruan, help me.' Unable to resist his dreams a minute more, he called his faithful followers to his side and told them he had to go and find the field witch or else he'd surely go mad. 'You don't want me to be a mad king as well as an ugly one, now do you?' he asked them.

'Sire, it is not your ugliness that bothers us, rather it be the sadness that it brings to your heart,' said his friend. 'We love you too much to see an evil auld biddy steal you away from us.'

However he knew that peace would never be his until he found the field witch.

Again he called from hilltop and undergrowth and caves, 'where are you, woman?'

Weeks passed with no sound from the demon, until one night a storm of nightmarish proportions forced him to hap on the boundary line of a thick forest. All night long he lay staring into the deep dark branches. Like giant fingers they slapped and flapped against each other. Ruan became so frightened he could not move.

As quick as it began the storm winds dropped, and the moon like a flower within the darkened sky spread her light in streams of shadows. 'I must go from this place or else the trees will surely have me.' He shivered with a deep fear and speedily rolled up his bed. No sooner had he taken a step, when from out of the forest came the voice he'd waited so long to hear. 'Ruan, help me, they are closing in. I have little time left.'

Without a moment's thought he turned in his fear and as before ran and ran and ran. Not a breath of extra air did he inhale until his almost dead body lay once more on the lap of his old friend.

'This time, sire, I will not allow you to go out of my care again,' he sternly said.

Next day the old soldier called on as many people as he could and told them that under no circumstances were they to allow King Ruan out of their sight, because 'she of the fields' had bewitched him and would certainly kill their monarch if she could. From then on, wherever he went, a shadow of stern faithfulness followed. Yet still rest evaded him, as each night that oh so haunting voice beckoned him, 'Ruan, my life drains, please, I beg you, come.'

Unable to contain himself another minute he dressed before the sun yawned over a sleepy horizon, but this time however his faithful friend would go with him. Before long the pair were on the skirts of the vast forest that held Ruan in a grip of fear, and there they waited. The old soldier had come armed for a fight with the she-devil, for he would rid his master of her spell or die. Late afternoon saw a thundery sky spread out to meet a dark and fearful night. Together the two waited and soon they heard, through peals of thunder and flashes of jagged lightning, a gentle voice calling. This time his heart froze as he heard the witch say, 'Ruan, I am slipping away, I fear you're too late.'

'Stay here, I must go into the forest, old friend. Do not worry, I have a feeling she means me no harm.'

'Master, it's a folly you do this night, for the forest will strangle you. She knows what you are afraid of, I beg on my old painful joints, dear King, do not venture forth.'

However nothing would relieve his anxiety but to meet with the witch, and striding into those dreaded trees our brave lad went to meet not just his fear of trees but the witch herself. All night long the old soldier stood in the place his master had bid him stay and waited like a faithful dog. He stayed there until all the storm's power had abated and then he saw him. Coming forth hand in hand from those terrible trees was brave Ruan with his witch: a beautiful young girl. 'Master, what form of evil spell has she been under?' asked his bewildered companion. Ruan told him to sit down and he would explain.

'When I was born, an evil witch of the fields took my love stone from my crib and hid it in this forest. If ever a maiden fell in love with me, then the wicked one would steal her away and hide her in the trees of which she had given me a deep inborn fear. The only way I could release my love was to conquer the fear and rescue her. But I only had two chances. You see, old friend, if I failed a third time then the spell would never be broken. I would live in my ugly form and happiness would forever flee from me.'

His old friend turned to the girl and asked her how she came to love his master who was so abhorrent to the eye?

'When passing the castle to gather nuts one day I saw my belov⸱
he was sleeping by the burn. When I leaned down to ⸱
his face I did not see a thing of ugliness. I saw a te⸱
with a hidden depth of blossoming love. I ⸱
face came to me. So I whispered his⸱

however, the witch who stole his love stone heard me. She captured my spirit and hid it in the trees, thinking Ruan would never have the courage to rescue me. Please, soldier, put down your weapon, I tell the truth.'

The old man lowered his sword and he saw the love shining between his master and the girl. 'Yes, this is indeed the way of things,' he thought as he followed behind his master and the young woman who had brought the love his heart had so desired.

The wedding was a day of wonder for all to enjoy. The couple lived a long and happy life, giving to the place by the Tay many wonderful children. And as for the witch of the fields, well, she was never seen or heard of by anyone.

Now, reader, as was the way of ancient Scotland, two large standing stones have been placed side by side in a field twixt Tulleybelton and Bankfoot, and they are to this day a prominent feature for all eyes to see. One is square and misshapen, resembling, some might think, a donkey, while the other is pointed and slender—they represent Ruan and his Queen, the nut gatherer.

I wondered about the crib 'love stone' mentioned in this tale, and through research found that crib stones were four tiny pebbles blessed with Mother Nature's kisses and arranged round the head of a new-born royal. They represented: 1st—love; 2nd—health; 3rd—wealth; 4th—wisdom. I can't say for certain, but during the time of the Druids it is thought they used stones a lot.

The late father of my friend Mamie Carson, Keith Macpherson, who had a gift for verse, wrote the following poem about a Standing Stone and I thought this a fine place to slip it in. For your pleasure now, folks, I give you—

# The Muckle Big Stane

*Oh ken ye Mcleod frae the muckle big Stane,*
*It stands in the field at the fit o' his lane,*
*A link wi' the Romans wi' cup and wi' mark*
*Their ghosts gethir roond every nicht efter dark,*
*And Andra, guid man, maks it one of his rules*
*Tae join in their crack on his way fae the bools.*

*But ae nicht this winter, no many weeks gein,*
*He passed without stoppin at the muckle big Stane,*
*Wi' his chin on his chest, and sae doon at the moo,*
*The ghosts thocht at first sicht that Andra was fou,*
*And they agreed that strong drink maks the best o' men fools;*
*Then they heard Andra mutter 'I'm bate at the bools.'*

*So they bade him come ower just like one o' their ane,*
*And they sat themselves doon by the muckle big Stane.*
*Andra spoke oot—and his heart it grew sairer—*
*He jist couldn't thole bein licket by Crerar,*
*A buddie gey handie wi' blacksmithin tools,*
*But no in a class wi' himsel at the bools.*

*Noo the ghosts made a ring, each the ither hand taen,*
*And they swore by the marks in the muckle big Stane,*
*That Crerar the smith they would visit that nicht,*
*And leave the puir buddie half dein wi' fricht;*
*They swore by the elves wha bide under toadstools,*
*He'd never again bate their man at the bools.*

*Noo Andra McLeod, be it sleet, snow or rain,*
*Aye stops when he's passin the muckle big Stane,*
*Since that fearfu nicht, when he gain them his crack*
*The whole Roman Empire he'd had at his back.*
*So long as the Stane, Andra's destiny rules,*
*He'll no lose tae Crerar again at the bools.*

Keith Macpherson

# 19

## HELENA'S STORY

I am going to shock you with this next story, but I hope that when we've shared this, my friend, you will understand that, of all the evils in the world, beating a pregnant woman must rate one of the worst.

Yet it's sadly a common picture today, as it was then, a battered wife. Nowadays it is referred to as domestic abuse. Traveller folks loathe a man who beats his wife. It is regarded as the despicable act of a coward. For a man to lift a hand and strike a woman is, in their eyes, the same as an Alsatian attacking a Westy.

Here is Helena's story.

Bonny Helena adored Robert. Everybody knew it. Her family idolised him and his folks thought the world of her. Since the youngest age both were inseparable, and when old enough they married. For a few years he worked hard to give her a nice caravan and a good sizeable lorry for himself. Night after night he'd drive home after long hours breaking and collecting scrap metal, fall into her welcoming arms and sit down to a warm meal. Then one day Robert received his call-up papers. This meant his dreams of wealth and building a grand house for Helena were to be put on hold, for the duration of his national service of two years.

But suddenly a crack in the world appeared. A violent war was taking place in Korea, and Robert was thrown into a battle of, as we all now know, massive proportions. When it was finished he came home, like many of his comrades, a different man. Not so as one could visibly notice, but the smile had been replaced with a serious frown. Fewer people came calling on the couple because of his rudeness and lack of civility. He began to drink more and more, and worse was his treatment of Helena. He'd been seen hitting her, although she at first denied it and then made excuses blaming her nagging. It didn't take long for his business to slip downhill, so one night after a bad bout of 'supping wi' the De'il' he came home and beat her so badly she was taken into hospital. That was enough for her family to intervene and remove her from the scene. Her heart, though, was with Robert, and it didn't take long for Helena to pack her bags and go back. This happened three times after that, with even the police arresting him; something seldom done in those days because wife-beating was looked upon as a triviality and usually solved over a cup of sobriety and tea.

They finally parted. Helena went away to live in the south of England where he would never find her. This seemed to sober him up, and he set about rebuilding his shattered business, turning away from the demon drink. After a teetotal year, Robert eventually persuaded her family to get her to write, and said he was trying to make amends. In spite of all that had passed she still loved and forgave him. In a short time he set about courting his estranged wife and this time he promised 'no more tears'. Well, things went from fine, to good and better. He had indeed changed. A nice house came along, the business blossomed, and soon the happy couple awaited the arrival of their first baby. A lovely boy put the icing on the cake. Tragically, however, he only survived a week.

This sent Robert back into the so-called solace of drink, and Helena's nightmare began all over again. Still, he had the good sense to draw back and not tip over the edge. They tried again and soon another baby was nestled in the womb. But Robert began to fall into deep black moods, and only a drink would help. Helena found his heavy hands were again finding their mark on her tender frame. One night, after his business had gone to the wall and their home was facing repossession, he set off to spend another drink-fuelled night with the amber spirit.

She was asleep when early morning brought him home. The final beating was horrendous! This was the final straw, the one that broke the camel's back. I will tell what happened in the form of a poem.

## Water of Life

*As the demon from the bottle flows,*
*The spirit deep within him grows:*
*It tells him this, it tells him that,*
*'Angry young man, go kick the cat.'*

*His blue eyes turn a fiery red,*
*While she sleeps soundly in her bed*
*He hears the amber spirit say,*
*'Pack your cowardly soul away.*

*Wear the mantle formed for you,*
*Demand another drink or two.*
*Now see him standing by the door,*
*Hit him till he tastes the floor.'*

*The barman shouts,*
*'Get out, listen here.'*
*While the demon whispers in his ear,*
*'What you need is a knife, my dear.'*

*Out in the street, his money spent*
*He staggers home, head hung, back bent.*
*The spirit mutters, 'She's to blame,*
*When you get back show her some pain.*

*Never mind that pregnant bitch,*
*She's the reason you're not rich.*
*You don't need me to tell you so,*
*You're the boss, she should know.'*

*He kicks the door, bounds up the stair,*
*Grabs her long, soft, brown hair,*
*'Look at you, fat, ugly cow,*
*I'm starving, woman, feed me now.'*

*'You let her off, you're much too soft*
*You will regret this at your cost*
*Before she rises from that floor,*
*Kick her, go on, once more!*

*Good lad! I'm glad you understood,*
*Now let her lie, enjoy the food.'*
*Shivering she watches till he sleeps*
*Then tiptoes out on darkened street.*

*The skin across her face grows tight,*
*He didn't miss his mark tonight;*
*From head to toe she's wracked with pain,*
*She knows he'll swear, 'never again!'*

*But she's had enough, just can't go on,*
*The sharing love has all but gone.*
*The stone bridge wall is a dark, cold place,*
*Water sprays her tear-stained face.*

*She whispers to her child unborn,*
*'With life anew we'll meet the morn.*
*He beats me black, he beats me blue,*
*But he won't hurt you, my baby new,*
*I promise this, he won't get you.'*

*The bell wakes him from drunken sleep,*
*Makes to the door on shuffled feet.*
*Policeman, helmet in his hand,*
*'Can I come in' he asks, 'young man?*
*I have grave news for you,' he said.*
*'I'm sorry but your wife is dead!'*

# 20

## MANCHESTER HOGMANAY

Do you know, reader, sometimes if we could see what future lies before us we might take another road—but we don't, do we?

Back on the waste ground in our cosy caravan I find myself sitting staring into the darkness, with more than a few monsters haunting the darkened recesses of my young mind. Mammy had, as usual, been blethering with the earth creepers, and I told her she was becoming far too familiar with them. She laughed as she always did, and said that the poor craturs were telling her they were becoming colder as winter stiffened on the city. What did she do? Well, she toddled off to the corner shop and bought a bag of kindling. Then she got Nicky to take the van and collect two bags of coal. Over she went, poking and prodding at the mounds of discarded plastic and calling their names because, yes, she'd even found out what some of them were called. 'Mr Weatherspoon, Mr Delifario, Mr What-dae-ye-call-yerself?' Oh, and better not forget, Major Something. Those were only a few. I think the fact she identified them as individuals mattered more to them than if the names were correct.

Right away they shed the vast humps of waste material they were under and began helping Mammy and Nicky build the grandest fire they'd ever seen. Earlier in the day my dear mother had made a batch of treacle scones, and as the tramps sat on makeshift seats of old boxes and the likes, the glow from the blazing fire on those craggy faces was a picture to capture forever in the mind. They never asked for seconds, nor did they say a word, the contented stare of warmth said it all. Mammy and Nicky left them to their thoughts and went to bed. I sat up for ages, peering through a slit in my caravan curtain, watching the vagabonds chatting and sharing some liquid concoction from a tin heating the deep bits while the fire did the same to their outer regions. I was young, and knew that as far as the men of the night were concerned they'd never have my total trust as they had Mammy's, but it was nice to fall asleep knowing they had found one night of relative comfort. However I will now retract that, because you'll never guess what those stupid creepy-crawly idiots did? They went and got drunk as skunks and set fire to their mound houses! I thought Martians were dropping on top of us from the skies when the fire sirens descended with flashing blue lights and hissing hoses. What a night to remember. Daddy called Mammy everything under the sun, while she swore never to help the drunken old bastards again. Yes, I must say, folks, it was a night when the Keystone Cops, Flash Gordon and Dante's Inferno all rolled into one. And, I'll add, there was a tramp the spit of Charlie Chaplin who took off into the dark with a yellow flame spurting from his rear end. What a delightful spectacle!

You will be thinking 'she's a heartless swine', but don't worry, no one got hurt and after a wee clean up next day there was as many wee humps to sleep under as before. Only difference was that my Mammy was forbidden to help the tramps again—strict orders from the 'high heed yin', my Daddy.

Now, maybe after I share this next episode with you, you'll be thinking Daddy should have kept his trap shut.

It was all to do with his fancy Jaguar.

Mammy and Portsoy went into town on that busy Saturday to do a bit of shopping. As Christmas was round the corner we were all in a grand mood. Nicky had a few bob to spend, Mammy too was flush with a regular stream of woman clients needing their fortunes told, and as for me, well, Mr Swift served on all his staff a generous bonus. Aye, we were not a bad bunch of happy Scottish travellers on that particular December Saturday. Trust my Da to go and spoil it!

'I'll be here waiting, Charlie, at four o'clock', Mammy told Daddy outside the *Daily Express* building, adding that he was not to be late, for she didn't like hanging about with a pile of Christmas presents. Portsoy said he'd find his own way home. Daddy set off, and I do not have any information as to his whereabouts, folks, only that he was away the best part of five hours.

Mammy was waiting dead on four outside the newspaper office, when suddenly the air filled with police bells clanking like mad. The whole of Manchester's Piccadilly froze at the screeching of brakes and peep-peeping of horns. Then, to her absolute horror, who should come tearing along, polis at his back? My Dad! His eyes were standing on their stalks as he darted a quick glance at Mammy, who by the way had turned to stone with a dropped bottom lip. If a lay preacher had laid eyes on my Mother he'd have thought she'd seen Sodom and Gomorrah tumble.

She arrived home in a taxi still struck dumb. What in heaven's name had he done?

Thankfully, Nicky and Portsoy were home and immediately went along to the nearest stardy. They seemed to be away for ages, and when at long last they arrived back they had no news for my anxious mother. 'What in the name o' hell is yon daft faither o' yours up tae?' she said, glancing at my sisters and me. No sooner had she uttered those words when there was a loud knock at the door. It was our friend Jim, the Fife polisman. He'd brought the news we were all desperate to hear.

It happened during our stay in Manchester that certain villains (big-time bank robbers by the sounds of it) were using grey Jaguar cars as getaway vehicles. While Daddy was minding his own business and driving to pick up Mammy, a right Al Capone style robbery was in progress. In all the getaway carry on, Daddy's car got mistaken for the one the robbers had. When he heard and saw all the shiny black polis cars descending on him he panicked and put the foot down.

'So, if you can settle your mind, Mrs Riley, Charlie will soon be back home with you.'

Jim's reassuring smile told us everything would be all right, and it was. What was Daddy's response? He painted his status symbol—Gold! Yep! Even the cat!

Well, there you have it, folks, our quiet stance behind the garage had so far been anything but. Och, what's the point of living if one can't bite on a bullet once in a while?

From then on our existence went on an even keel. Christmas came and went, but not until New Year's Eve did we realise that guid auld Scotia was the place to be. England just shines at Christmas with everybody having a richt braw time, but if it's celebration time, well, us Scots certainly take all awards at Hogmanay. Mammy bought in the drink, stout for herself, whisky for the boys and blackcurrant cordial for us. Lots of black bun and shortbread with bricks of fruit cake found our wee bunch celebrating up to the gong of midnight. Somehow or other, things didn't have the same ring to 'A guid New Year' as it might have done over the tartan border, and by two o' clock we were sound asleep. Next morning, apart from Jim the horny coming to first foot us, the day had an empty, hollow sound to it. Still, we hadn't reckoned on our neighbours—the creepy-crawlies. Mammy noticed that, apart from our empty bottle of blackcurrant cordial, the drink box was full. She had had her stout but Daddy didn't fancy a whisky and Nicky only sampled the beer. Portsoy had his own supply and God alone knows how much of that the old lad drank. He certainly found it difficult giving his face a wash, so I reckon he'd opened another bottle. He always said 'never buy the one, it might get lonely.'

'I can't abide keeping drink in the place after the bells,' Mammy told us all at dinner. Oh, this only meant one thing, she was going to visit the earthworms again.

Daddy told her just to leave the box sitting some place, for they'd surely find it. 'Smell it more like,' I mused.

She and I carried the booze-box over as near them as possible, and while I dived home for fear of slipping and falling into a gungy hole Mammy whispered to them: 'Mr Weatherspoon, hello, Mr Delifario, you there? Major, also Mr What-dae-ye-call-yerself.' The ground rippled and she knew things would be fine.

That evening as we settled in for what was forecast on the wireless as a change in the weather, there was a tapping on the caravan door. Daddy as always answered it.

'Jeannie,' he said, 'there's a few blokes out here need to speak tae ye.' Mammy gingerly stepped outside, and out there, shivering in the first covering of snow stood (and I kid you not) every bloody tramp in the whole of Manchester and maybe beyond!

The Major came forward, rolled a crumpled cap between black and orange fingers, and said, 'Madam, we'd be glad if you'd allow us to toast you and your family's good health.' With that, a horde of jam-jars, broken cups and containers of every sort, holding Mammy's offering of the 'cratur', rose into the cold January sky to fall back and slide down those sadly-abused throats.

'Men, please step inside.' Mammy pushed open our narrow door, and one by one the creepy-crawlers stepped into our spotless clean caravan until there was standing room only. I felt my dinner heave inside my belly as the smell hit the back of my throat, but that was only a temporary thing—after all I'd smelt worse from a dung-field. And as the night pushed onwards we were entertained to mouth-organs, singers (with beautiful voices even although half the teeth were absent), jokers, magicians and, my favourite pastime—story-tellers. Amazing fun was the only way to describe the first night of 1964. That was the best New Year's party we'd ever had, and we've never since seen its likes.

I wonder now if you may want to hear the story one of the city tramps told us that night. I'm glad you do. So get the kettle boiled up, pour your favourite cuppy and share this with me.

## 21

### THE LETTER

Young Johnny rose on that memorable day from a cosy bed, washed and went down stairs. His dear, sweet mother as always greeted him with a kiss and said there was a plate of his favourite hot oats waiting for him, then handed him a letter that had arrived by the early post. Before enjoying his breakfast he opened his mail, only to find it was written in a foreign tongue. 'Mother, be a dear and read this for me, you have a flair for languages and I don't know what it says.'

His mother obliged and sat down to read. What happened next was unbelievable. He watched his mother turn from a gentle, loving lady into a furious, foaming-at-the-mouth monster. 'Argghh, you beast, you horrible evil creature, get out of my house this instant and don't ever come back here again!' she screamed, throwing his letter at his feet, then grabbing his collar she heaved her son from the house. Johnny stood there in the cold street flabbergasted. Without a moment to lose he picked up the offending letter and set off to ask his vicar why its contents had turned his mother mad.

The vicar, as always politeness itself, ushered him into the parlour. 'Hello lad,' he said, 'what brings you to my door this early?'

'Well, vicar, I received this morning a letter.' He removed it from his pocket and handed it to the vicar. 'Please, could you explain, if you can, why it has turned my dear, sweet mother against me?' The vicar smiled, reassuring his visitor that his mother had obviously read it wrongly. 'No mother would do such a thing, especially yours.'

He unfolded the page and sat down, popping a pair of one-legged glasses over his nose. For a minute he paused, then without warning reached into an umbrella stand, retrieved a golf-brolly and started thumping the poor lad over the shoulders. 'Get out and take that, that thing, with you.' Johnny gathered up his letter and dashed for the safety of the front door. Once outside he thought 'nothing, no matter what, would make the old, gentle vicar react in such a fashion, some one just has to explain what is in this letter.'

How, though, could he show it to people? He needed a plan. Soon the paper with its demonic contents was folded safely in a leather wallet, only to be shown to whomever he deemed completely trustworthy. For a while he lived a quiet existence, living in a tiny flat high up in a tall tenement building, speaking to no one. He got a job in the bucket lorries, working very hard and deliberately keeping his letter a secret.

Then one morning, during a torrential downpour, he met Sally; he was sheltering in the café doorway where she worked as a waitress. Seeing how wet he was, she invited him in for a warm cup of coffee. They immediately fell head-over-heels in love. Within six months they were wed, but not once during that time did Johnny tell Sally about the letter eating away at his heart. Then one night he asked her a question: 'do you love me more than anything?'

'Yes, of course I do, darling, you should never have any doubts.'

'If I show you something, will you solemnly promise me not to let our love rule your head?'

'Nothing could spoil our life together, absolutely nothing, now what is it?'

Johnny sat his love down on their bed and very carefully unfolded the letter from its wallet. Not taking his eyes off her face, he handed Sally the tormenting document. 'Perhaps like me she won't be able to read it,' he prayed.

That night with his torn cheek and blackened eyes Johnny again found himself wandering the streets, destitute and alone. Would he ever know the true contents of the letter?

Next morning, along with other street tramps, he was rounded up and moved on by the local police. One policeman spoke to him and enquired why he had ended up on the streets? Frightened to speak to anybody, let alone the law, Johnny turned and ran as fast as he could down an alleyway. The policeman, thinking he was a criminal, gave chase. It was easy catching poor Johnny, with him being hungry and battered. Soon he was sitting in a prison cell, a shattered man, and he hadn't a clue why. 'Look,' he screamed at four other men sharing his cell, 'see what I have. Do you want to kill me or hang me from the ceiling by your shoelaces? Come on then, tell me what is in this letter first.' Poor unfortunate thing, he would rather have died than never to have known why this awful letter plagued him so. An old man stood up and took the letter from Johnny's fingers. He sat down, took a pair of heavy-rimmed glasses from his shirt pocket and began to read.

'Please don't hit me, I beg you,' Johnny wriggled on the floor like a cowed dog. 'Please, mister, just tell me what it says.'

Slowly, with fire raging in his eyes, the old man leaned down and said, 'why, do you not know what this says?'

Johnny cried into his jacket sleeve that he just hadn't a clue.

'When you get out of here, go and visit this old Chinaman, he will tell you what to do.' The man handed Johnny a piece of paper with an address scribbled on it.

Soon, address firmly clasped in the desperate man's hand, he set off to find the wise Chinaman. At long last they faced each other, with Johnny's existence depending on what he'd be told, please God.

The same scenario unfolded with the Chinaman threatening to cut off his head with a Chinese War sword and Johnny begging for his life. He told him that the man in the prison cell had said he would help him. The slightly-built little man thought for a moment, then said, 'Before I copy this into English you must solemnly promise to follow my instructions to the very last letter.'

'As I live and breathe, old man, I will do all you say.'

'When I copy this I will seal it inside an envelope, then inside a metal box, and you must take yourself to a far-off shore. Find a boat and row miles and miles until you are completely alone, remember no one must be anywhere near you. Then, and only then, remove the letter and read it.'

Johnny gave his word, hand on heart, thanked the small man and did all he asked.

In mid-Atlantic we now find him bobbing alone in his little skiff, miles from anything remotely human. Beads of sweat begin to trickle down his face into a dry hot body. His breath now comes in short pants. He opens the metal box, a seagull screeches high above him and he dives under a tarpaulin. The sky is once again clear, there is nothing further to delay him. Hands quiver, as inch by inch he unfolds the letter. He holds it up, then opens sunburnt eyelids and, and, and—swoosh! A GUST OF WIND BLOWS IT OUT OF HIS HANDS.

If you feel like hitting me, folks, then that's exactly how I felt when first hearing this. Sorry, but some you win and some you lose.

Not very nice to you, am I? Still, after spending all this time with me, I'm sure you'll forgive and forget.

## 22

### BACK ON THE ROAD

$B$ack to Manchester now, and we find a cold January has passed without much happening, except for one thing, though, a job for Saturdays. To make a wee bit extra I took a job at the open market selling outsized shoes for an old Jewish gent called Jeremiah. He owned several shoe stalls at the Cheetam Hill Road market.

For a whole day from eight in the morning until four in the dark afternoon I stood trying my utmost to sell the ugliest shoes I'd ever set eyes on. There were size nines and tens, aye, even elevens of every colour of the rainbow, white patent boat-like things and the most horrible black shiny ones. Believe it or not, my friends, but those shoes of various extremes were made to adorn the female foot! Jeremiah insisted that everything could be sold, it wasn't the item, it was the seller. So he, that wily old bent-backed gent, who instantly reminded you of a character from a Dickens novel, taught me how to charm those chuckit shoes onto female feet. The customers, those sadly misinformed ladies, purchased shoes that, I'm sorry to say, made them look more like shoed penguins than anything else. I can still to this day see them smile when I lied and said they were a perfect fit, and that they didn't half go with their outfits, or hair or eyes. I even sold deliberately, as pairs, one size nine and one ten. Old Jeremiah swore we all have one foot larger than the other. For all that hard sell I earned a measly ten shillings. However I must be honest, and say it was a grand way to learn how to duck when a woman of over six feet threw a pair of bad fitting shoes at you!

Well, folks, at long last winter is over. Mammy is whistling while sewing bonny tartan curtains for the trailer, and Daddy has purchased, for the coming months' spray-painting season, a new compressor. Although he went through the last few months bronchitis-free, little did he know how much it was to plague him in the future, and all because of his unhealthy way of making a living. Nicky said his goodbyes to the 'bints' he'd befriended, although come to think of it, I only ever met one. I'd say by looking at her the blonde wasn't real and she'd not see forty again, but who was I to judge?

Portsoy said that once he was over the border he'd go another road from us, but would make his way to the 'berries' in July. My young sisters, like me, were becoming more restless with each sighting of daffodils. All our talk was of who we'd see first when home again in the Perthshire glens, or anywhere over the border, come to think of it, as long as it smelt like shortbread and had the seal of Scotland set upon it.

It was sad, I must say, seeing those unfortunate creepy-crawlers sharing goodbyes with my mother. What would they do now for the free booze and hot treacle scones she so lovingly baked for them? They'd go back to lying by day under the mountain of plastic cuttings, and spend nights raking food buckets at the rear of hotels and restaurants. So farewell, you Brasso braggarts, may the guid God show you a healthier road to walk upon.

Before we parted from the bustling city our friend Jim, the Fife policeman, had to have his dram. That night he came in as always and we toasted his health, me and my sisters with blackcurrant cordial, Daddy and Mammy, Portsoy and Nicky with the amber spirit. I swear, when big Jim left our caravan that night, his eyes were meeting in the middle. I hope to God he didn't come across any crimes taking place.

Daddy swithered before leaving about whether to head south for the hop-picking, but I think Mammy was hankering to see the older girls, after all she was a Granny now, and like grannies the world over she needed a cuddling at the wee yins.

On the road we settled down until Carlisle came into view. We stopped off here for a day or two while Mammy did a bit of hawking. The day before we left, Daddy took me into the town and surprised me to tears. Without a word he guided me into a posh jewellery shop and asked the assistant to show a tray of their best gold hoops—gypsy-style. I picked the cheapest: he put them back and chose the dearest. 'Happy birthday, ma lassie,' he said, draping an arm round my shoulder. I felt like a queen with my thick gold hoops dangling from my now sixteen-years-old lugs.

As we drove back to the field outside Carlisle, no words were spoken, and to this day I remember the purity of those silent moments. The love between a daughter and her father can sometimes bridge an unseen river that, no matter the drought, never runs dry.

### Memories

*An oasis in a hostile world shared in silence,*
*Twigs dancing in boiling water,*
*Through the smoke our glances meet,*
*And his dark eyes smile at me.*
*No other movement, no spoken word,*
*The glow comes not from the fire,*
*But from deep within me, and I know no fear,*
*He is my Dad—dark, still, strong.*
*I am his child—safe, happy, protected.*
*We drink our tea.*

### Janet Keet Black

Before we re-join the road, let me share the memory of one fateful summer's afternoon. The time my dear mother stuck me with a darning needle.

It was in Crieff while we were staying along the Broich road. This was an area where the Ministry of Defence used to barrack prisoners of war during WW2. Several Nissan huts and hangers had been left *in situ*. For a while a local farmer housed his pigs there. Many travellers, not having the canvas for tents, moved the pigs out and moved themselves in. I was only six years old when, with an envious eye, I noticed the pretty travelling girls with hooped earrings.

Mammy was washing her usual mountain of clothes when Daddy's auntie, old Jess Johnstone, came visiting. She was a sprightly old biddy who dressed totally in black, even covering her grey head with a thick, black, coarse head-square, tied tightly beneath a pointed chin. As she never failed to do during our stay in that field by the River Earn she eased her narrow frame into Mammy's favourite seat next to the bus door and demanded a cup of tea. My mother, who by now was sweating like an Irish navvy, told Jess, 'in a minute, auntie, in a minute.'

This was when I made my big move: 'Mammy, can I have my ears pierced?'

'Lassie, can ye no see how busy I am? Later on, when I've time.'

Old Jess by now was getting a bit thirsty, and her constant demands for tea had Mammy scrubbing Daddy's thick woolly socks with a vigour to make the Irish navvy envious.

'But Mammy, I deeked the barry hoopit chats the gouries a' hud in their lugs, an please, Mammy dear, kin I nae have them tae?'

'Jessie, shut your bloody mouth about hoops, or as sure as hell's fire I'll leather ye sore! Now clear off and play.' Mammy was getting fair roused, but it wasn't me who prompted her next act, oh no, it was that crabbit auld woman.

'Kin an auld bent woman who's brought up a dozen weans no git a drap tea fur her crackit throat in this place?' Jess was by now constantly tapping her feet on the bus floor, adding that if Daddy were there he'd give her a cup o' tea.

Mammy lifted the corner of her damp apron, half-dried her soap-sudded hands, and with the force of a force ten gale threw the ribbed scrubbing board a mile in the air. Thud! It walloped off a big thick oak and fell to the ground, before bouncing several times and settling next to a pail of rinsing water. With enormous strides for a wee woman five feet one inch in height, my mother stooped under her seat, the very one old Jess was perched on, and hauled out her sowing basket. Purns of threads, darning-wool cards, yards of laces, thimbles and an assortment of gaily-coloured buttons were tossed up and over old Jess until Mammy found what she was looking for—her biggest needle, the Darner. 'You, luggy, here!' I didn't stand a chance as she threw me over her wet knees and thrust the darner, dripping with Dettol, into one ear-lobe and then the other. Blood spurted down my neck as Mammy removed her own small, thinning gold hoops and pushed them into my newly-bored holes. I was too sore to scream and too shocked to think. I got what I wanted, but, by God, at what cost.

Old Jess got such a shock she leapt from the bus, threw a handful of tea-leaves into the pot, and for the remainder of my mother's washing day, cup followed cup of fresh tea. Folks who'd witnessed my mother's heechy that warm summer's day said not even a pig could squeal like me. I thought I'd never uttered a word, but according to them I was rending the air with my cries. It just goes to show what a fright can do to a buddy. It was a heavy price to pay for it, but in a few days my red ears had calmed down and I joined the rest of the hoopies. Daddy replaced Mammy's earrings with a brand new pair. Those worn old battered rings she rammed into my ears all those years ago I keep in a wee silver box, as a reminder to a lassie who had learned what it was like to push a mother with the strength of an Irish navvy too far!

Thought you might enjoy that wee bit of nostalgia, reader.

When Daddy asked us all to vote on the way we should take from there, whether east or west, it was unanimous for going via the west coast with its rugged beauty and warmer sea. I felt the lump rise in my throat at the thought. To me there is no place more picturesque than my Scotland's western coastline, and we knew every hidden bay and Atlantic inlet. I could taste the salt in my mouth.

At Gretna we headed west along the A75 until Annan. Here we left the main road and travelled to Clarencefield, a tiny village where some travellers were camped further down beside the shore. Daddy knew them and was rare pleased to see that one in particular, a boyhood mate of his, was there. They were part of the Boswell Border folks, a grand lot. It was a delight to see the campfire burning bright and to hear the cant tongue flowing freely again.

Another great treat for me was when an old tramp of the road joined us, who pulled a jew's harp from his pocket, and while he and Mammy did a duet we all had a wild sing-song. I'll just add this about why I have a lasting admiration for the gents of the road: it is because they were fuelled by the spirit of Mother Nature and not by allowing the evil demon lurking in a bottle to enter and demoralise their inner selves. You will understand why, because of this, I had little respect for the crawlers who softened my Mother's heart in Manchester. Now, I should add, I have softened with age, and have learned never to judge my fellow man.

As the remnant of the day gave way to the creeping of the night and angelic voices grew hoarse, we partook of my favourite pastime—storytelling.

# 23

## THE KELPIE

Many tales are told of the evil beast that haunts the ghostly gloaming in the Highlands, emerging from a deep loch or pool to bring an end to some poor unsuspecting soul. In the northeast the water horse, unlike in the west, never changes colour, staying a golden yellow whereas his western counterpart goes from black to light brown. There are also, in some parts, those who can change form to deceive. Then there are the 'water wraiths', tall, green-dressed females, all withered and scowling to herald one's doom. However, folk tales of such a beast are not predominately told in the north. Galloway is where there is a dreadful creature, and here he is: the water kelpie.

§

It was dark, and she knew fine well it was not a time for one as young as herself to be out. Had her parents not often warned her, 'Lassie, if he sets on ye, then ne'er will he stop until you are his.' Her heart beat faster with every step, for darkness was moving quicker than her feet. Shadows melted into the ground to become giant trees and bushes, wherein lurked the eyes of ever-seeing owls. What a relief for her to see, far down the valley, her parents' house, and one of them waving a lantern of reassurance that she'd soon be home. Suddenly, while passing a deep pool in the river's bend, from the corner of her eye she saw a flash of white. Startled, she turned to see a handsome young man alight from a beautiful, pure silver-coloured horse. Without saying a word, he gestured with an outstretched hand for her to come. For a moment she felt her head swoon and her slender body sway. Then a whistle brought reality spinning back, it was her father. Knowing what she did about the water kelpie that could shape-change, she turned and ran faster this time into the waiting arms of her anxious father. That night, unable to sleep, she sat staring into the darkness, watching him galloping back and forth, from hillock to glen to river.

Come morning, her parents realised only too well that once the water kelpie has set eyes upon his prey he will stop at nothing until she is his. The lassie was packed off to live with an aunt, and there she lived, finding romance in the arms of a handsome young soldier who was not without a title or two.

The day was set for their wedding, and as tradition has it they were to be wed in her hometown. People came from miles to see the pretty Galloway lassie marry her Duke. She was a picture of pure beauty standing at the altar of the flower-decked church.

However, just before the exchanging of rings the sound of horse's hooves was heard from outside the church. No sooner did the wedding guests turn their heads when the door flew open, and there, for all eyes to see, was a great silver-white horse, with wet flowing mane, galloping towards the terrified bride. On its back sat the demon who had marked her for his own. He leaned down, and with one scoop had her onto the horse before a hand was raised in her rescue. Her heartbroken husband searched high and low but never saw his lovely bride again. Unable to live without her, he died of a broken heart. After that, some folks swore that if one stared into the pool near that fateful spot where she first met the demon, a sad white face could be seen beneath the water's surface.

# 24

## HEADING NORTH

Let's you and I share a wee bit of history from the Border country now, folks.

The Border country, what a historic place. Kings and Queens with mighty armies came through it to conquer the North or to hide in Scotia's mountains. But what about the inhabitants who lived there, those hardy Borderers? If ever a phrase had meaning for them, then this is it: *passing through*. If the south was at war with Scotland, they were the ones who first took the brunt of an incoming army fresh for a kill. And if the shoe was on the other foot, then again the Border saw the sword of the Highlander before the English did. Yes a 'stuck-in-the-middle folk' I'll say. Perhaps that is why the lads are bigger and stronger than the rest of us. Good at the rugby too, they recently informed me.

My kin also have found a home in this lovely part of Scotland. From as far back as the sixteenth century gypsies have settled here.

They were a colourful people, and like other nations had their monarchs. I was brought up on tales of the 'Lord of Little Egypt', who was known to people in general simply as Johnny Faa, but to his own folks he was a blue-blooded king. Historians of gypsy culture tell me it is nigh on impossible to track the Faa succession, because so many ended on the gallows or were sent away on prison ships, but there are folks today who claim they are descended from the King and can show a legal and true genealogy.

The village of Kirk Yetholm became a settlement for gypsies around the year 1690. Faas intermarried with Youngs, Blythes, Gordons and Rutherfords amongst others.

Queens and Kings continued to be crowned but the last I know of was Charles Faa Blythe Rutherford, born in 1825 and crowned in 1898 in his seventy-third year. His reign was a short one because he died in 1902. And like all the other monarchs Scotland has crowned, he was not followed by issue or otherwise. My old Granny Riley, who hailed from Ayrshire, told me many times about the 'wee broon-skinned King wha had richt green een'. She claimed her mother, maiden name Annie O'Connor, told her the real monarch should have been a woman by the name of Esther. However I have no proof to set before you on this one, reader.

My father claims to be descended from royal gypsy lineage, and the way he used to demand half a cup of fresh cream mashed into his chappit tatties, I don't doubt it. And another thing, I wonder why Granny called him Charles?

Saying our goodbyes to the Boswells, we set off in the early morning heading north. For a while we meandered into this bay and that inlet, and gently followed the contours of Scotland's west coast. Some days we were blown inside out, while others brought a gentle warm gulf breeze that sent woolly jumpers to the back of the drawers. One thing we found a great asset was the endless heap of driftwood strung out along beaches to fuel our campfires. I, for one, found not having to carry heavy piles of wood from bramble-floored forests a treat, leaving me more free time to beachcomb. As I mentioned in my last book this pastime of mine was more like an obsession that could fill my whole day. One day, I believed, a treasure would reveal itself to me and I would be rich; until then I'd gather scrap metal to fill a tattie bag. The scrap-metal man for all my humping and heaving would pay me two to three pounds sterling. (As a little lassie I dreamt that I'd be the richest scrappy in Scotland, with a fleet of lorries emblazoned with Her Majesty's coat-of-arms on the doors.) However it wasn't the filling of that bag that was the main thing, rather the freedom of wandering hour upon hour along a deserted beach, throwing sea-shells at screeching gulls and pushing bare feet into green and brown kelp. Finding caves and imagining a wild pirate instantly stealing my heart and whisking me off to find treasures of the mind. Then Mammy's whistle to tell me that the dishes needed washing would dash all my daydreams.

I missed sharing those latter years on the road with my cousins. They'd long since left the old ways, settling into houses. My young sisters were pestering our parents to find a house as well. Not me, though, I was a tinker, gypsy, vagabond, road tramp, gad-about. Every day found me stretching it out to milk the life for all it was worth. However, it pains me greatly to say the worth of travellers was being whittled down; soon my sisters would have their wish and I, though I little knew it, was seeing the demise of Scotland's true travelling folk.

We'll come to that another time, my friend, because for now I'll share a tale with you about a funeral, and by all that's holy, what a burial it was.

## 25

### WULL'S LAST DIG

*Think, passenger, as you pass by,*
*And on my tombstone cast an eye.*
*As you are now so once was I,*
*As I am now you soon must be,*
*Therefore prepare to follow me!*

Plain enough are those words so wisely engraved on the kirkyard wall at Aberfoyle, that bonny wee village nestling in Scotland's Trossachs. And oh so true!

We, however, are not setting sights in that part of the land. Instead our attention is diverted to the sleepy village of Collbrae, wrapped around an idyllic peninsula on the west. Hope it's a nice day, my friend, while you read, and nicer if the west wind is flitting through the pages, just to put a bit of atmosphere in for you.

When Father Padraig O'Duffus wasn't doing the baptising, burying and ringing the church bell he'd be found in the Crypt. This place of seclusion he called his 'resting place', and what better a name. Only his closest friends were allowed access into the secret chamber, they being his auld mates Dr Peter Macpherson and the undertaker-cum-gravedigger, Wull Blair.

The hardy threesome, who'd inherited an old tinker's recipe for 'the making o' the brew', had set to work many years past and now had a grand supply from their very own still.

'Down here, boys,' assured the priest, 'we can sup the liquid peat and suck the pipe without hindrance from any living soul.'

Padraig, Peter and Wull had it made, and, to quote the priest, had found 'a heaven on earth'.

Yes, an idyllic place indeed, and nobody else was supposed to know a thing about it. But who could keep such a secret from the busybodies of a Scottish village? Everybody knew, of course they did, but the knowledge that it was located under the remains of the dear departed kept folks well away. The good women of the village believed auld Nick himself supped from the still. Many a time the manse housekeeper mentioned, in no uncertain terms, that she feared for their very souls. She was a grand, upstanding Irish woman, who had been Padraig's blessed bidey-in cleaner for as many years as he cared to remember.

As we open our tale he'd been left to fend for himself for two weeks while she tended her sister's girl. The lass, who lived in Donegal, was having her ninth child, and the priest's housekeeper never missed a birth.

So with those formalities out of the road, let's go back to the supping and puffing Crypt.

Padraig stared with those half-open slits for eyes like a prize cock who'd just beat off the others for the best hen, and said, 'Give me another fill o' the brew, Wull, me dear old mate, an' I'll be showin you ma winning hand.'

Wull, as always, saw his pastoral mate get the better of him at cards, and began to feel the red anger above his frayed collar. 'Och, ye've the deevil himself wi' ye the day, Padraig, for that's four in a row.'

'When a man wins at pontoon it's neither him above or him below has a hand in it, but only sweet Lady Luck—now pay up.'

Old Peter, the village doctor, and always the soberest of the three-some, gathered loose cards from off the cold slab table and popped them in his waistcoat pocket, saying, 'when you reach this level of conversation it aye ends in blows, so no more of the game, I think.'

Padraig was far from pleased, and told him, 'Hell blazes, man, I was feeling a winning streak resting on me there, why dae ye need tae spoil things?'

'Because we're here tae celebrate Wull laying down the spade and folding his box tools, have you forgotten this is his retirement? We should be rejoicing an' no fighting over a card game.'

The priest laughed, displaying a toothless mouth, slapped Wull on the back and said, 'Aye, my old mate, you're a hard act to follow right enough. I don't know a single soul for miles who can carve a box and dig a grave like yourself. Total precision, that's what it is. You'll be missed on the sacred ground, I ken that for certain.'

That was a plain statement of fact, describing a man who laid low the dear departed and returned earth to earth. To him death was a job, a simple task he'd undertaken for fifty years. It was his Uncle Tam who did the job before him, and he was long since gone, lying beneath the soil at the far end of the graveyard behind Mrs Baird's rose-garden wall.

Wull gulped down the homemade 'breath o' life' that Padraig had distilled from God alone knew what. Partly to disguise the lump of emotion rising in his throat and partly the fact that his companion had more cards hidden in his cassock than rosary beads. To him, cheating at cards was normal and expected, and when playing only for penny stakes, why cause bother? After all, with a friend like the priest, a man who had the kindest heart beating under that old faded vestment, Wull had a lot to be grateful for. To be totally truthful, the three old lads between them couldn't be surpassed in good-hearted kindness.

Still, they did keep a secret from the outside world and another one they did share with the villagers.

You see, Collbrae being the most peaceful place in all the west coastline, meant that more than one tramp came passing through, to sit, rest and slumber a while. And many times these quiet folks just happened to forget to wake up from that deep sleep. Tinklers of metal, tramps of the road, wandering minstrels and others found in wee Collbrae their last resting-place. Was it the gentle sea breezes, or the way the sun's rays danced and glittered upon the green water? Or perhaps it was those friendly village folk, who'd sit a while and pass the time of day?

What better place, then, to finish life's journey, than with those folks who never closed a shutter or locked a door? Only Death himself knew why.

However, in the cold reality of Death, who does his business then goes, thon visitors were always lacking a penny to fill a pocket. So without question their demise and disposal became the responsibility of the three men: Doctor Macpherson to state time of death, Father Padraig O' Duffus to give God's blessings and old Wull to fit them with a coffin coat and find a spot for them beneath the earth.

Let's leave the lads to their enjoyment for five minutes, reader, and see the housekeeper Mrs Macallister arriving home a day early; and, by googily golly, it's as well she does!

'No doubt the place will be like a bomb hit it,' she says to herself as she scuttles up towards the manse door, knowing a sinkful of dishes and floors covered with dust will meet her. A sideways glance at the half-opened curtains made her cringe. However, she was well aware that this was the day of Wull's retirement, and that a certain threesome would be tucked under the graveyard supping away, so at least she'd be left in peace to get on with her housework.

Coats draped themselves over chair-backs, while a pair of welly boots lay discarded where the priest had left them. A bladderful cat dashed between her open legs to disappear in a puddle of bliss. As she rushed through to a usually spotless kitchen, removing her neat black coat at the same time, the sight she saw filled her Irish heart with fury. 'I'll have a cup of tea before I start this pile of greasy-coated grime,' she thought, then went back to the hall to hang up her coat, muttering under her breath, 'how in God's name does this excuse for a holy man think heaven's gates will open for him? Surely the Recording Angel will have filled half the book with him alone. What a lazy, gambling, liquor-loving...' suddenly she noticed, lying among unopened mail on the hall table, a rather rich-looking beige-coloured envelope. Instantly, with trembling hands, she lifted it. Edged in black it was—and not just black paper but cloth—velvet!

'Oh my, I don't like the look of this, better let himself see it.' Now, although Padraig feared his housekeeper to a degree, one thing he'd never allow her to do was enter his Crypt. She knew this, but there was something powerful about this letter, something mighty important; she had to risk it. Clenching it in a knuckle-tight grip, she made her way towards the priest's leisure hole, blessing herself at the passing of each gravestone.

'Father, are ye down there? I'm coming in whether it pleases the three of ye or not, I've a letter.'

'Quick lads, hide the whisky, it's Macallister home early! What the hell, woman, ye know Wull here is parting with his tools and shovels. Can't we ask for a bit peace from your prying nose?'

'Never you mind my nose, here, take a look at that, it might be from the Bishop or some one in a position, here, take it.' She shoved the envelope into his hands, then sat down on a cold slab stone, rising immediately when aware of what lay beneath it.

'Och, it's only a funeral letter, you open it and stop panicking, then away and see tae the hoose. I thought the cat was half ways down yer throat there for a minute, wi' the noise out of ye, woman!'

Mrs Macallister had a feeling, and nothing under the sun would shift it until she knew what the envelope held. 'Feel the paper, Father, it's thick and silk-like, and look here at the edges, they're velvet black. I tell you, man, whoever sent it has a wealthy way o' doing. Please, Father, open the thing before I go mad.'

Padraig thought to himself, as he took the letter and opened it, that his old housekeeper was already there, but he was too much the gentleman to tell her.

'I can't read the blasted thing, it's in a fine waving scroll and I don't have my glasses anyroad.' He handed it to Wull, who said he'd never the need of writing and reading, and passed it to Peter.

The doctor slipped two fingers into his shirt pocket; retrieved thin-rimmed spectacles, popped them on his nose tip, took a deep breath and began to read.

*For the immediate attention of Father Padraig O' Duffus, The Manse, Collbrae.*

*Dear Father,*

*It is my solemn duty to inform you my husband, 'The Duke of Domchester', passed away on the tenth day of June 1904.*

*It was his dying wish that he be laid to rest in the graveyard at Collbrae.*

*He often came as a young man to holiday in that peaceful part of Scotland where he'd quietly fish and enjoy the company of the village inhabitants.*

*His funeral cortège will arrive in Collbrae from Glasgow on Friday, the fifteenth day of June. Please make the necessary arrangements. I have informed the Bishop as to my husband's wishes and he kindly promised to accompany me on Friday.*

*I hope this meets favourably with you.*

*With kind regards*

*Duchess of Domchester.*

Mrs Macallister wiped a tear from her eye as she did when hearing of the departed, then said, 'ah well, that's alright then.'

'Alright! Alright! How can it be alright, woman? Are you thinking straight? This is Thursday—they're coming tomorrow!' Padraig had never sobered up so quickly before.

Peter reassured him by saying they'd get everything ready and told him not to panic so much.

However the old priest looked across at the retiring undertaker/gravedigger, who had gone very pale, and said, 'Wull, will you tell them or will I?'

Old Wull shook his head and said, 'There's not an inch left in the graveyard for a toad, never mind a Duke, the bloody place is full up.'

'Holy Mother of God, we're all finished when this gets out that Collbrae refused to bury a Duke because it was full to bursting with tinkers and tramps. Give me a drink o' that firewater before I have a heart attack.' Mrs Macallister helped herself to a cupful, not realising the power it held. Instantly she started choking, and if Peter hadn't brought his fists hard down between her shoulder-blades then it would have been two funerals instead of one they'd be worried about. Finding her breath returned, she began a hysterical tirade of curses. 'We'll be plagued by boils and beetles, God will surely send the locusts and frogs! Oh my, what a terrible day for us all—we are doomed, doomed I tell you!' Peter, thinking the only way to shut her up was another swig, filled a cup, held her nose and instantly poured it down. Her face turned red, then blue, and it was decided to let her find her own breath this time.

The threesome had to think of a plan, and fast.

'Mrs Baird has the only available plot. If we ask her, aye, even pay her, surely she'll allow a Duke a burial.' By plot, the good doctor meant her rose and azalea garden.

Padraig shook his head, 'no, no, lad, thon woman swears her ancestors fought and died alongside the "White Cockade"—she'd set fire to the Duke in his coffin before she'd allow an Englishman to rest within a hundred miles, never mind right outside her kitchen window.'

As a doctor it was supposed he was more of an authority, so Padraig and Wull turned to Peter.

'What we have to do is get her away for the day and help ourselves to the garden. I'm sure the village can get heads together to come up with a plan,' said Peter, glancing with concern at Mrs Mac, who was laying on a stone slab singing the Londonderry Air, with two eyes focussed on the point of her nose.

Wull said that his replacement to be, young Skiff Smith, had a way of charming women, and might be able to persuade her to visit her sister over on Millintroch Island. 'He's got a good excuse he can use,' sniggered Wull, 'the Ferryman brought news that she's sick.'

'How can he do that, then, Wull? She's as sharp as a fish-knife and hates all men.'

The gravedigger's eyes twinkled: 'I've been informed by the lassies that Skiff can charm the whelk from its shell. I'll go and fetch him.'

Mrs Macallister sobered fairly quickly and dashed off in clouds of embarrassment to scour the manse with bleach, broom and boiling soapy water. She was more concerned about the Bishop than the Duchess, and feared for her job.

Soon the secret chamber was filling with the hardy folk of Collbrae, determined to bury a Duke and be the envy of the West Coast. Along with young Skiff there was Angus and Malky, two hardy creel fishermen, Dod the polisman, Mrs Mackinley the village postmistress, Big Annie, herself a one-woman telephone exchange, Jock and Jenny who ran the pub, and plenty more besides.

After toasting the plan to bury His Grandness the Duke of Downchester, every hand set about preparing Collbrae for its VIPs. But everything depended on Skiff charming a certain crabbit old woman from her hard shell.

Young Skiff, with hands behind his back and fingers crossed, began his part of the plan.

'Mrs Baird, the ferryman has brought bad news from Millintroch. It's your dear sister, she's fallen with a sickness.'

'My sister Phemie? Ill, ye say? She's niver had a day's sickness in her life, and how wid thon big useless ferryman ken?'

'Oh, Mrs Baird, I heard him say she had been gathering in the sheep when the poor soul keeled over. Everybody from one end of the island to tither is thinking she might not make the morn. Please come now, just in case. Look, if ye want I'll come with you, hold yer hand if ye want.' Skiff held out a hand and softly touched her arm and waited. For ages she stared at him with those wee, sea-green eyes.

His stomach was turning somersaults, and for a moment he thought she didn't believe him, when at last she lowered her gaze and said, 'I'll fetch my coat an' lock the door. You can stay here, young Skiff. I've reached this age without help from men, I'm sure I can manage. Now, is thon ferryman sober?'

Yes he was, and thank God she didn't need Skiff, because there were more important things needing done. Still, it was best he see her well and truly off the peninsula, so he escorted the wee green-fingered lady away, making doubly sure with the ferryman that he'd been paid enough. There was a sound reason for paying him, because before an oar went to water on the return journey, the bold lad would surely spend every penny in Millintroch pub, and he would need a day to sober up.

With her well and truly out of the way, the hardy villagers, working under makeshift lights, demolished Mrs Baird's garden wall. Every plant and bush was replanted in and around granite and marble grave-stones. On and on through the night they toiled, stopping now and then to sup from that handy, never-ending supply of home-brew.

A bright orange dawn saw them gathered to eye their hard work. Yes, it looked just like a quiet, tenderly cared-for resting-place, just the kind of graveyard to lay a Duke in. Would all go well? According to Mrs Macallister the Bishop would have no complaints, even the cat was gleaming. Yes, it might just work. What about Mrs Baird, however, when she arrived home to find His Grandness' grave inches from her kitchen window? Well, by the time she was due back, the villagers hoped to relocate the Duke, rebuild her wall, and re-plant the flowers back in their own wee resting holes.

So after a quick spruce up, combs through hair, black garments put on, they lined up on the quayside and waited. Peter felt his pulse to see how much faster it was pumping. Wull wiped the sweat that was building up between his fingers and hoped the shovel wouldn't slip, thanking the Almighty them grand undertakers in Glasgow had got the Duke ready for burial. Finally Padraig, well, if his throat dried up then it wasn't for the want of lubricating.

Skiff stood out on the point, watching and waiting for the royal barge. Suddenly his signalling whistle sent them all rigid; the royal barge was sailing round by Dougal's cave and would soon be upon them.

'Well now, would ye tak a look at that,' whispered somebody. Every eye was on the black-bedecked sailing vessel, long and narrow, with all manner of dignitaries lined upon its decks. The bishop stood alongside a tall veiled lady dressed in the finest fox-furred coat. She raised her head and nodded to the villagers, then lowered it again. The funeral boat gently docked. Peter's pulse was visibly leaping beneath his collar, while Wull had a permanent wet streak down the side of his jacket. Padraig began clearing a nervous throat, as everybody uttered a silent prayer.

The hearse carriage led by four regal greys had arrived in the village an hour earlier and was waiting. Six large gentlemen carried the Duke's oak coffin, adorned with brass handles and gold-threaded tassels, off the boat and onto the hearse. The sun slipped behind some clouds and the faintest smir of sea mist added to the heavy atmosphere funerals can bring with them.

It was only a few hundred yards to the graveyard gates, and soon all were in their places. Wull had done a grand job as usual—six feet deep, eight feet long and three wide. He thought of the times he'd dug that familiar trench, his 'masterpiece', with his lasting thought always, 'ye'll no git oot o' that so easy.'

The women folk had done a fine job arranging Mrs Baird's flowers. Yes, all was going to plan. The Duke's coffin was lowered; a single rose was gently placed on it, then he was settled into his place for eternity. Padraig said the usual blessings under scrutiny of the bishop's gaze.

All seemed to go well. Peter winked at Wull, he in turn winked at Padraig.

Then, just as the sun pushed aside the ribbons of greyish clouds, a crack began to appear around the shiny black shoes of the mourners. Two granite headstones headed in slow motion towards each other, then rested with their points together. There was another crack, and more headstones began to wobble as several faint-hearted guests took to their frightened heels like hounded hares. Then it happened: without any further warning the earth, including the plot containing the Duke's coffin gave way. Now, the villagers knew exactly why this catastrophic event was happening, but to the Duchess, the Bishop and friends it was as if hell had invited them in. Down went the Bishop, up went his frock. Down went the fox-furred Duchess, followed by guest after screaming guest. You see, during all the previous night's digging and preparations, no one had taken stock of what couried beneath the ground.

The Crypt lay directly beneath Mrs Baird's garden wall. Only a few feet separated the Crypt and the garden. Every single guest, including His Grandness the Duke, was now collapsing on top of Padraig, Peter and Wull's homemade still several feet below in the secret chamber. Broken fingers brought screams along with bruised bums and heads. Hats, gloves and feathers joined the handbags and hankies to float and bob in the last drops of the 'Tinker's Brew'. What a blooming disaster for the village of Collbrae!

Mrs Macallister had to be carried back to the manse and no one saw hide nor hair of her for a week.

I will now leave it up to you, reader, to imagine the fate of all concerned. Just in case you can't, please allow me to tell you.

Peter had been village doctor far too long, so when a suitable more able-bodied younger man was found then the responsibility of the villagers' health was handed over to him.

The bishop never found it in his heart (despite what the bible says) to forgive Padraig, so he was defrocked, sacked and kicked out. Mrs Macallister refused to clean for anyone else so went with him to his new house.

As for Wull, well, he put his shovels and spades into the capable hands of young Skiff Smith, who became the proud keeper of a brand new graveyard situated a half-mile down the road. Oh, and in case I forget, he did the undertaking as well. Because of the old graveyard being in such a dangerous state, a group of architectural planners had came up from Glasgow and measured out a new one. Big Annie swore she had overheard a telephone conversation between the Bishop and one of the architects instructing him that a special plot had to be landscaped for the Duke.

Regarding Mrs Baird, the strange thing was her sister Phemie really had fallen sick, so rather than leave her to fend for herself she moved in.

Which takes me back to Padraig's new house. It was Mrs Baird's place he bought, since it had such a bonny garden. 'Rubbish,' said Malky and Angus, 'it is the smell of the auld still wafting up his nostrils when a westerly blows, and not a row o' rid roses.'

A last word on Mrs Baird. Folks said she never said a word about that day when an English Duke was buried in her garden. But the women of the village would have loved to be flies on Phemie's wall, I bet.

So if, one fine day, it's the village of Collbrae you find yourself in reader, then why not take a walk round to Dougal's Point. To the cave to be precise. If you do, you might find a grand welcome. For in there are three mates puffing on their pipes and supping from a hidden still filled with a 'tinker's brew'.

I hope you enjoyed the farce of Collbrae, then, reader.

# 26

## TRUE ROMANCE

$B$ack to the road now, folks, and we drift into May with its extra hour of daytime, flowery trees and hearts searching for love. However with my 'love-seeking' never to be, I settled into a future already decided for me. When I give more thought to this subject it makes me wonder about arranged marriages. In many parts of the Asian world, brides and grooms are joined even before they are born. Now, here was I with no such luck, because I'd been chosen not to be joined to anyone. No fear then of me being mated to a gadgie with a guffy's face—or, on the other hand, of hitching with an Adonis. Oh no, as I told you earlier, I would spend my life taking care of Mammy and Daddy in their old age. But I suppose when you consider what a great set of parents I had I should have been grateful.

We had pulled onto a deserted beach well up the coast. Nicky left us to visit his folks and with Portsoy out of the picture it was a quiet and serene place. Quiet serenity puts me into a thoughtful mood even to this day, and one morning after finishing my chores, my feet went walkabout for miles through slipping leathery seaweed and powdery sands. I had no recollection of tide or time as I succumbed to a perfect sunshine. Hollywood would have killed for such an atmosphere: it was heavenly, or, as we travellers say, 'a truly barry day, chavie, just kushtie!'

To those who sought Cupid's arrow it was a perfect day. I had no thoughts in that direction until I saw him...

He seemed almost Lowry-like upon the skyline, the young lad. And like the artist he too was a painter, sitting in front of an easel, sketching white fluffy clouds touching a green ocean. Not wanting to appear nosy, I walked slowly as if to go around him. His brush-tip was applied to the canvas so I stopped, not wanting to distract the lad. Obviously, though, with only the two of us sharing miles of deserted sands, he was aware of my gaze and turned. 'Hiya,' he smiled, and I wished I had had a canvas to paint such a perfectly handsome face.

'Hiya,' was all I managed. It was enough, he popped his brush into a jar half-filled with coloured water and asked me to join him. 'Do you bide here?' I asked.

'Bide, what kind of word is that?'

I felt my face grow red and redder, until I'm sure it glowed. 'Do you live in this area?' Repeating the question would not, under different circumstances, have brought a feeling of discomfort, after all the word was Scots and not cant.

He stood up, pushed hands into baggy-pocketed trousers and stretched a strong-muscled neck toward the sun, 'No, but I wish I did. My name is Rod, and I come from London with loads of cars and people and buildings. Do you "bide" here?'

We both laughed and suddenly a voice in my head said, 'don't tell him you're a traveller.' I responded to this feeling of shame and for the first time in my life I lied about my status. I could feel them, the old ancient ones, turning cold in my heart. Here was I, a proud travelling girl, denying my roots: how could I do such a thing?

Then I caught his gaze, melting blue eyes shaded from the sun's glare by a tanned hand, and blatantly lied. 'My name is Jilly, I'm from Edinburgh here on a few days' break from University.' (I had once heard someone say that all the rich and best-bred folks came from there, and called their girls, or their horses, Jilly. I was doing fine until he asked what I was studying and the year, and everything else a student at university would know.

'Gosh almighty, why did I dig such a hole for myself?' I thought, then ran off to pick up a mother-of-pearl shell glinting in the sunshine, while he went back to his easel. But like a magnet he drew me back to him, and doe-eyed and captivated I watched him silently paint. Whatever was happening to me had never happened before, even my stomach had little creatures bouncing about in it with tackity boots on. No words could explain why I felt this way, was it love at first sight, perhaps?

Rod painted, I watched, I talked, we laughed as hour followed hour. Lunchtime came and went, but what did I need with food? I had all the nourishment I wanted from my beach companion's smile, and from thoughts of us walking off into the sunset to who cares where. As we wandered through the pages of Mills and Boon I even imagined giving myself to him completely. You know what I mean by that, reader, and I thought that vivid dream would soon be realised when we became better acquainted.

Firstly I'd come clean and tell him who I really was: 'Jessie from the campsite over across the dunes, and not Jilly from the home of Arthur's Seat'. But before I got the chance, I saw, coming toward us, a young woman. I wondered why she was smiling. I didn't know her and surely my Heathcliff didn't either. She was a right bonny lass, and when Rod saw her I was left standing while he ran and scooped her up in his arms. She held onto a floppy hat trimmed with a long chiffon scarf. A long, almost see-through dress, the same colour as her headscarf, hugged slender hips and trailed upon the sand. She was beautiful, and I was gutted, deflated, dowdy and scunnered tae the hilt.

'Darling this is… sorry, what did you say your name was, again?'

Of all the bloody rotten Rods—he hadn't been listening to a word I'd said!

Picking up the thin cardy I had left lying by a rock, I said, 'Hiya, I'm Jessie.'

My stupid blind eyes filled to the rim with painful tears as I turned on my heel and waved goodbye. Another heart-sore lesson for me. When would I ever learn?

As I reached our campsite I noticed Daddy had been watching me running up the beach. He asked if I was all right. Not wanting him to see my tear-stained face, I nodded, then went into the caravan. Mammy, who'd been away hawking with my three sisters, smiled and asked me what I'd done with the day. When she heard about the artist, and me lying about my roots, she touched my face and said, 'lassie, if I'd a penny for every wee white lie that slipped from my tongue, then we'd be living in Inveraray Castle by now.' That was enough to abolish my fear of passing over at life's end and meeting the wrath of the ancient ones. Still, there was a slight heaviness on me that night as we sat round our campfire, and it left me feeling a wee bit ashamed of myself. I cringed at the easiness in me towards a complete stranger. I may have gained a slightly bruised ego but what if I had allowed my heart to rule my head? What if I had given my most precious gift freely? It wasn't the ancient ones who haunted my innermost thoughts that night, it was the fact that I had nearly done an unthinkable thing before marriage. Sleep only came after I had wrestled with the reality that my future didn't include marriage anyway, so the only disappointment would have been mine.

Goodness gracious me, folks, nearly an X-rated one there!

This wee story I share with you now was one my father heard at a tender age. He said, 'I was as high as my auld spaniel's left lug, and never forgot the night after a snake bit me, mother told me this wee story.' While he was playing in a heathery moor up and round by Ballachulish an angry old adder gave him a bite like no other. To quiet him, Granny told this wee tale.

## 27

### ROSY'S BABY

Rosy was a city lass and didn't know a single thing about the countryside. Her mother hated it. But Daddy lost his job as a shoemaker and was forced to move into the old dilapidated farm his uncle had left him. Into a month, and already Mother was nagging: she didn't like the awful place, not one bit. Poor Daddy tried his best. He rebuilt the old dyke, fixed the cottage roof, bought some cows and sheep and even acquired a cat to chase away the mice that lived beneath the floorboards of their little house.

'I hate this place,' protested Mother, over and over again, 'I need to go home.'

'This is home, my dear, now please try and be happy,' begged her husband.

'Why can't she try harder?' he thought, as he went outside to see what his seven-years-old daughter was doing.

Rosy didn't mind the new life, in fact she was settling in fine. When she saw her father she ran to him breathless and grabbed his hand, saying, 'Look, Daddy, over there by the hole in the hedge—a huge rabbit, see it?'

'That's not a rabbit, my dear, that's called a hare, and I must say I'm surprised it has come near, usually they stay upon the hillside. They're afraid of humans, you see.'

Wondering what was taking her family's attention the mother went over. The moment she saw the hare a piercing scream came from her, 'That's a hare! Don't look into its eyes or it will entice you away, Rosy.' Saying that, she grabbed the little girl's arm and marched her into the house. Her husband followed, shaking his head in disbelief at the senseless reaction from his wife to a harmless animal. 'What is wrong with you, woman? Do you have to be so awful just because of our predicament? You know if I could afford to we'd be living in the city. Oh, I'm off to fix the far side fence, don't make my tea until I come back.'

Rosy didn't hear her parents arguing, because lately that was all they did. No, she was staring out the window watching the big brown hare. As young as she was, she recognised there was something wrong with the animal. 'Mum, I think the bunny is hurt, look.' But she didn't look: instead she pulled her child away from the window and closed the curtains. Then, with Rosy sulking in her room and her husband gone out, she recalled her old Granny's stories of witches, crows, fairies and magic brown hares. 'They possess a mystical power, and if parents are not careful they will lose their babies to the magical hare who will take them away for the Devil.' Yes, it may have been a long time ago, but she never forgot the terrifying tales. So often as a child she would wake in sodden bedclothes, because of those fearsome visions stirring in her little head.

However, while deep in her own troubled thoughts, she failed to notice that her daughter had sneaked from the house. Imagine the panic spreading in her when she discovered she was gone. 'Rosy, Rosy, come here this minute!' she called, running from the house. She ran from one end of the garden to the other, but not a single sign of her precious child could she see. She called out to her husband, but he too was nowhere to be seen. Tears filled her eyes, as the heart in her chest beat faster than it had ever done. 'My baby has been stolen by the dark forces. I knew it was a mistake to come here, I hate this place.'

Drying her eyes, she noticed a tiny hole in the hedge. 'My baby, I must find my baby!' She swiftly dropped onto her knees and pushed her body through the tiny opening. She searched everywhere—behind trees, in bushes, under boulders; she even, in desperation, rammed her arms inside rabbit-burrows. Poor soul, the more she called and searched, the louder her heart beat, bringing all her Granny said about the dark world closer. Then, as she glanced far off toward the horizon a tiny spark of hope appeared: Rosy's navy blue dress, she saw it disappear under a gorse bush. Quickly she got to the place and was on her knees staring into the thick undergrowth. There was her little girl, and at her side, breathing heavily, was the hare! 'Rosy, my love, I've been looking everywhere for you.'

'Mummy, please help my friend. She is bleeding, I think she might die.'

The young mother froze. Her Granny told her that hares sometimes pretended to be hurt just to gain the trust of their prey. 'Don't go near that creature, come home this instant!'

She pulled at Rosy's sleeve, but her child refused to abandon the injured animal and broke free, diving further into the bushes. Then the child saw why the hare needed her help. 'Look, Mummy, come in here and see.'

She leaned down and there, tangled up in ferocious barbed wire, lay the whimpering body of a baby hare!

'Stay with it, dear, I'll go home and get Daddy's cutters.' She felt an absolute fool for putting herself into a state of blind panic over a childhood story. When she returned she hardly noticed the mother hare had gone. Soon the tiny bundle was suckling hungrily on spoonfuls of warmed milk and within two weeks it was back outside munching on moist grass.

After that the couple put all worries behind them and felt as if they had always lived in the countryside. Little Rosy was born for the wild open spaces and grew strong and healthy. And according to my Daddy she spent many happy days playing up on the high hills surrounded by big brown hares with cleft top lips and long pointed ears.

*I left my baby lying there, a-lying there, a-lying there,*
*I left my baby lying there, and someone stole my baby-o.*

Talking about babies made me think on my father's words back at the berries, when he disclosed I would never have any, and although I'd put this out of my mind at the time I won't say it didn't come into my head now and again. Especially when those blasted hormones took the contents of my brain and scrambled them up like fluffy eggs. I just had to speak to Mammy and see if they were both in agreement about the road my future was to travel. Later that night, as we took our last private stroll of the day, I asked her. This was our conversation.

'Mammy dear, Daddy told me never to go with men.'

'Why, in heaven's name, should he say such a thing?'

'He said I'm the one to look out for the baith of ye when you're too old to see to yourselves.'

'I'm sure we can do that ourselves, pet.'

'But what if the brain goes or the legs, or, oh, I don't know, Mammy, but he said that it was final. Although I cannae see a problem, because it would make life easier for me. I couldn't be bothered by arguing with men and cooking for a dozen weans and a' that kind o' stuff, but I would like the choice.'

'You don't know what the good Lord has planned for you, Jessie.'

'But Daddy said, and I have to obey him.'

'Listen to me, pet, and keep stushie on this, because it's between me and you, right?'

'O.K., Mammy.'

'Now, how do you think Daddy's lungs are coping with all the spray-painting, given as the bugger never wears a mask? You know as well as anybody how the coughing fits come on him during the winter, and the doctor sees mair of him than us. Daddy will not last, Jessie, he knows that. It's me he's thinking of.'

'Why, mother, you're fitter than a young wife wi' a back loaded wi' the siller herrin'.'

'He doesn't want to leave me on my own, Jessie. When he told you that about being the "carer", he really meant being my companion after he's gone, now that's the truth.'

'Oh God, Mammy, surely there's a lot o' spunk in the old divil yet!'

'Maybe aye, and maybe no, but one thing I'm certain of, my bonny wee lassie, is, if a laddie takes yer fancy and he's made o' the right stuff, then go for him. I'll see to myself.'

'Listen to me, now, Mother dear, because I make this solemn promise; whether I marry or not, even if I have a dozen weans, I'll be there with your last breath.'

It was as if a mountain had been lifted off my young shoulders. Honest, reader, if you're young like I was and have problems, and if you have a mother, then share them with her. What a great tonic.

## 28

### A WARM NIGHT

That day while we slowly ventured along the narrow coastal roads of Sutherland I remembered a time far back in my past when we lived in our bus. None of the older girls had married, so we were a happy crowd of travellers without a care. Or so I thought. I know some people believe that each of us has a guardian angel, while others believe we are contacted in other ways. I am certain my guardian came to me one night while I slept and gave me a dream. See what you think.

Being Scottish travellers in the fifties could be hard going. For a start, unless you were wanted by local farmers to spend back-breaking days in their fields working the land, there weren't many places to pull on to. Landowners got a mite stroppy as well, and on many a night we were forced from our beds to pack up and move on. But that was before the Bus. Once Daddy purchased our state-of-the-art mobile home we were on the luxury level, as travellers go that is. He'd been gifted with two good hands, had our Dad, and could master everything from electrics to joinery, although his expertise fell short of plumbing. Well, there was not much room for a lavatory, especially one to accommodate eight females, four older than I and three younger.

Toilet was a walk of privacy to where no eyes could pry. We dug the ground and then covered it over, so nothing was left above to soil or spoil Mother Nature's painting.

So there we were, then, on the road, in our completely renovated bus with beds, carpet, cupboards and the heart of every home—Wee Reekie, the stove. A rounded three-legged glowing fire, for cooking in summer and heating in winter. Reekie was bolted to the floor, positioned behind the driving seat and partitioned off by sheets of asbestos. Of course no one knew the dangers to one's health from this material at the time, and it is thanks be to God we were none the worse. Mammy cooked everything on that wee stove, which resembled Queen Victoria when she was old and fat.

The day was into its gloaming when Daddy called back to us that a wood-end was nearby. 'We'll stop here,' he said, as the end of the giant fir forest came in sight. Branches of thick spruce grabbed the last of the sun's rays, scattering them in every direction. The last sliver of sunshine fell upon the moss-carpeted forest floor while we rushed about gathering as many thick sticks as our arms could encircle before the dreaded midges began to bite. Soon our fire had a heart of spewing blue smoke and orange flames. Mammy took no time in finding a burn and filled the kettle from its wimpling stream of peat-water. Within a short while we were eating ham pieces washed down with milky tea, finished with a chunk of her 'clootie dumpling'. The older girls went off to do what one does in the privacy of trees. Meanwhile my young sisters and I hastily washed off the day's grime in the meandering burn. Mammy tucked us into bed, said a short prayer and warned us that there was no wind, so we should keep the windows shut or else midges would render sleep impossible. That night, though, it wasn't the dreaded midge which surrounded our vulnerable abode but something far more sinister. Something so frightening, that even to this very day hair I never knew I had rises on the nape of my neck.

My older sisters went to bed sickened by the constant nipping of Scotland's cursed mosquito and Mammy followed. Then, after making the fire safe, Daddy pulled the bus door shut and he too called it a day.

The night was clammy. Our bodies became sticky as if we were coated in glue. Uncomfortable and unable to sleep, I pushed back the quilt, making sure not to wake my little siblings, and tiptoed down to the front of the bus, staring out at a pitch dark wall of trees.

As I stared into the forest my eyes soon became accustomed to the depth of night, and bit by bit things began emerging from its midst.

Moonbeams pushed through the high trees. A small roe deer sniffed the air, then dashed off, followed by its sleek shadow. On a hanging branch a hoolit (owl) stretched her wings, then glided up into the sky, only to dive at some poor unsuspecting crawly and end its tiny life. Like the ever-turning light of a solitary lighthouse my head went from window to window, taking in all that the night had to offer. It was through the little window above my parents' bed that something caught my eye. A movement at the dying embers of our fire had me hold my breath. I very gently stretched my body over to peer out. Whatever was out there wasn't going away. I stared and could just make out the outline of a man who was stirring up the ashes with a stick. He piled fresh wood into the flames, allowing me to see his thickset body and unwashed bearded face.

Now, it wasn't unusual to see the odd tramp wander round our fire in the night and take comfort from what was left of its welcome heat, so I didn't wake anyone. Instead I curled my knees up under my chin and watched him from my perch. No doubt, I thought, after warming himself he would blend into the night and be gone, but soon it became clear he had other things in mind. From a bag he pulled out a length of rope, rose to his feet and made over towards the bus. Very swiftly he slipped the rope between the split door of the bus and tied it into knots. Instantly he went back to the fire and lifted a flaming stick, then before I could open my mouth to warn my parents, he shrieked, 'burn, bastard gypsies, fry in your filth!' Suddenly flames darted up the side of the bus, and with demonic ferocity engulfed a curtain tail that had found its way from a small cracked window. I screamed at the top of my voice, 'Mammy, Daddy, girls, wake up! We're on fire!' while pulling at the tied door with all my might. 'Help, help me, there's a shan gadgie trying tae pagger us, he's fired us, wake up, come on!'

The fire was terrible and spreading with a madness I'd never witnessed in all my nine years. But more awful than the unfolding evil was that no one was stirring, it was like they were all dead. I pulled and punched at all of them, yet still they slept. I leapt upon my parent's bed and threw punch after punch onto their heads, but there was no response.

With relentless fury the flames, now totally engulfing the bus, hissed and spat sparks onto the curtains, then ran along the roof, down and under the exposed flesh of my sisters. I watched them fry. Then the flames, as if with a mind of their own, gathered in a giant ball and rolled over me. I screamed and writhed on the floor. And it was within this nightmare that my mother shook me awake. 'You've been dreaming, pet, the thump your body made as you fell out of bed wakened me, are you alright?'

'Oh, thank God for that, Mammy, the bus was on fire, it was a living terror. Yes, I'm fine, I think.' I held her close and sobbed, feeling my skin to see there were no burns.

'There now, go back to sleep, lassie. It's as quiet as the grave this night, nothing but a moth stirs in the place.'

What a relief I felt, but oh, how lifelike it was, that bearded face and fiery red eyes.

Next day we'd packed early, and before eight were once again trundling along another winding country road. Just before midday, as yet another bend approached, Daddy slowed down to overtake an old man standing on the byway. I glanced down at him as we passed by. I was about to give a friendly wave as I always did when passing a road tramp when my hand fell like a dyke stone. Staring up into my eyes was the arsonist of the Devil, who had crept within the deep recesses of my mind the previous night and torched my whole family! The dirty, bearded face and fire-red eyes seemed to recognise me. I changed places with one of my sisters to look out another window.

I shook uncontrollably, calling on Daddy to find an open campsite, anywhere but a wood-end. Thankfully we met up with other travellers and were able to stay several days on a deserted beach, back-dropped by the mighty Ben Hope in the county of Sutherland.

On the last day as we packed to move on, a Highland policeman came cycling along. He stopped and propped his bike against a tree, removed his hat and sat down on a boulder. My mother noticed his face was pale and he'd the look of sickness. 'Would you like us to make a cup of tea for you, lad?' she asked him.

He shook his head, rose and came over to where Daddy was watering the bus engine.

'Do you know of a family of travellers who were hereabouts, a week or two ago?' he enquired.

Daddy asked what their names were. The policeman mentioned a name we did not recognise. My father talked a while with the man before he set off again on his rickety bike. I forgot about him until

I heard my father tell Mammy that a family of travellers who had camped back in the forest had been burned to death in their tent!

'Poor souls,' she said. My mother's next words froze my spine. 'Some folks can be right reckless with fires.'

The unexplainable, perhaps, reader?

## 29

## SUPERNATURAL APPARITIONS

While we're recalling the days on the bus I remember another night visitor, whom I called the 'Tall Man'. I saw him one night—well, not all of him, only the back of his head. It had been one of those darker than normal nights when it takes a wee while for eyes to adjust to the pitch black. I awakened, sat up and saw it, the head, propped on the seat at the front of the bus. 'Is that you Daddy?' I enquired, thinking he'd risen, unable to sleep.

'No,' said the head, 'it's me, now go back to sleep, Jessie.'

I froze solid with fear as I sat there in almost total darkness, before finding enough courage to cry for my parents. Mammy rose and went down to the front seat, only to find no one there. Our door and windows were locked tight. Next day, news came that Granny Riley had passed away. This brought with it all the pain and grief of losing a loved one, and I put the night visitor out of my mind, thinking him a dream anyway. However, months later, he appeared again. Same scenario as before, but this time I noticed his shoulders. My family, plus Tiny, were jolted from their beds at my screaming, and as before he just vanished.

Mammy was sure I'd been eating cheese too near bedtime, and hoping she was right I left that food in the cupboard the next night. However, when the news came that a close relative had passed on, the apparition left a cold shiver lingering in my mind.

Months went by before I awakened in the dead of night again, and there he was, as before sitting eerily silent and still. I forced out the words, 'who are you?', then waited. But nothing came from my visitor. Without a word I slid under my blanket and curled into a ball between Mary and Renie. I lay there, not moving, until I heard a cock crow.

Yes, as before, another of our kin soon went into the soil.

I have no explanation why this visitor thought our bus a place to be days before a relative died, and to this day nobody has given me one. Was he a long-gone relation, or just the product of a child's imagination?

I know for certain, however, I did not imagine his last visit. He'd left my nights alone for almost three years and I'd forgotten him. Then, on the eve of my Granny Power's leaving us, he came back. This time he rose from the seat, stood up and walked up the aisle and out through the rear end of our bus. A figure so tall his head almost touched the roof. In the dark I could not see his face, but something told me he meant no harm. From that night to this I have never seen him again.

I want to share some of our superstitions with you now, friend, for we are steeped in them, we travelling folk.

> We have a massive fear of certain objects that bring bad luck and search constantly for signs of good luck. Take, for instance, when men are getting prepared for a day's work. Now, if they happen to see a crow on the ground to their left, then no work is done that day. It's considered bad luck. If, on the other hand, the bird pecks to the right, then the men will go to work, but not until after midday.

> A bird entering a tent or caravan can signal death. The most feared bird in the traveller world must be the peacock. I remember hearing of a travelling girl who was due to be married to a rich man. As a wedding present he surprised her with a beautiful, custom-built Lonsdale caravan. Trimmed with chrome and lined inside with Scandinavian pine, it was a beaut. However, when his bride-to-be saw the plush curtains the wedding was off. Why? The material was patterned with peacocks.

Never mention the word snake. Call it a wriggly or a curler, and never refer to it on a Sunday.

Don't wash the sugar basin or clean the teapot, this can mean friends will not visit.

Never prepare for a forthcoming baby, this can hinder its life force with the earth. Some travellers swear a stillborn baby was the result of its parents buying clothes before the birth. When a baby is out of the womb and taking its own place in life, then and only then do friends and relatives provide the baby with necessaries.

As new life is surrounded by customs and superstitions, then so is death. This practice is less likely to take place today, but several years ago when a traveller died it was the normal custom to burn their belongings. Whether it be a cart or a caravan, car or lorry, every item belonging to the deceased was burned. Not even a tiny keepsake would be left, all went to the flames.

Monkeys can be considered unlucky along with rats.

My brother-in-law will not put a foot outside the door if he hears folks either singing or whistling the Londonderry Air, or Danny Boy as it is also called.

Among certain travellers the loss of a loved one is mourned for a full four seasons. No celebrations take place, no Christmas, Easter etc. This is to signify that each season has its own memories, and not until the end of the cycle of seasons does life go back to normal. During this time the womenfolk wear black.

Dropping cutlery on the floor can have a varying degree of bad luck: for instance a dropped knife means an argument. A spoon means a long journey. A fork means losing money.

A dog with two different eye colours (ringle een) is to be avoided like the plague. I've seen dozens of poor wee pups checked for this, and into a bucket of water they go if the defect is found. (We'll share a story shortly about such a dog.) Horses also can be considered untouchable if they sport two different eye colours.

Cats! Well, if ever an animal has suffered with superstitions then it is the pussy. Witches, devils, ghosts and demons are all believed to have pet black cats. Personally I think you can't beat them for keeping a cold lap warm in winter.

Never burn green sticks on a fire after midnight, 'ye'll bring an evil imp amongst ye,' was the call from many an older person. Another thing one should not do at midnight is brush hair while looking in a mirror. Many a young lass went pure white-headed when the Devil looked over her shoulder into her reflection.

If a poaching man found himself rising early morning before his dog he point blank refused to go an inch from his tent. There's a belief dogs have a second sight, and if they slept longer than their master it meant something bad was waiting for them both.

Of course, folks, I could go on and on, but that tale about the dog with the 'ringle ee' I promised to tell you, well I think I'll do it now.

# 30

## RINGLE EE

Tam felt the need of a cup and some dinner. All the long day he'd rounded and whistled and trekked the hillsides gathering his sheep. But never again would the old man rise before the cock crowed or the hen laid; there were to be no more snow-storms and wild gales. Never again was he to see the skin ripped from his arms as he scrambled down rocky outcrops to rescue fallen lambs. Nor would he again feel the anger when finding a throat-torn ewe that'd lost her way and lay sickly at the mercy of foxes and ravens. No, Tam was finished as a shepherd, he'd done enough, already he'd worked well over retirement age, and he sorely needed a rest.

When he arrived home, Nell, his dear wife, kissed him and said, 'Ma lad, I've done ye a grand pot of soup, and steaming it is, filled tae the brim wi' carrots and neep.' He gazed around the cosy cottage and thanked God he'd saved his old bones to tend his garden and cuddle Nell, because when folks think on hard-working shepherds they seldom give thought to their wives. She too had suffered many a night when he failed to come home as a blizzard raged. She also had the job of helping through nights at lambing time, and now she too was deserving of the rest. 'Will ye miss the sheep Tam?' Nell enquired after dinner was over and the dishes stacked.

'Well, I'll be honest wi' ye wife, it's nae the sheep but the dogs that'll be missed.'

True were those words indeed, because he always had his faithful dogs.

However sheepdogs only know work, so when the new lad took over, the dogs would go too.

Nell went outside, then came back with something in a box. 'Happy retirement, Tam,' she said and sat the box at his feet on the floor.

'What's this ye've been daein noo, lassie?' He leaned down and opened the box, to see, staring up at him, a scruffy grey puppy. 'I'm no needing a dog Nell, just because the collies will be missed frae the hoose disnae mean I need another one.'

'Now you pay heed tae me, Tam, the worst thing a body can dae when they retire is sit aboot the hoose a' day, ye'll need tae keep your legs supple, so a dog has tae be walked and so dae ye!' She continued, 'Mary Doig in the village was getting rid of her bitch's pups, and I took him, now isn't he bonny?'

Tam had no intentions of arguing with his well-meaning wife so he picked up the pup. Suddenly a cold shiver ran through him. 'Did you notice this, wife—see, look, the dog has a "ringle ee". A dog with a grey circle on its eye is considered amongst some folks as a devil dog, and I happen tae be one o' them—take it back.'

Now Nell didn't believe in superstitions, and laughed at her husband's unfounded fear.

'Here, have a scone with your cuppy and say no more about such nonsense, devil dog indeed! Look, he's a lovely wee thing, and see, he's taken tae ye already.'

The pup was licking and snuggling against Tam's hand, but he pushed it away and said, 'I'll no refuse a well-intended gift, but if ye think I'm petting wi' it ye can think again.' At that Tam turned his back on the young dog and finished his tea.

All night long he lay in bed and felt a strange presence had entered his wee cottage, was it the dog? He couried into Nell's back, glad she'd allowed him to kennel the pup outside in the barn.

What a fright he got to find, when opening sleepy eyes, the dog sitting staring at the foot of their bed. 'How in the name did you get in here?' he said as he marched the dog out of the room.

Nell sat up and smiled, saying, 'the poor animal isnae long off the suckle, he was missing his mother.' Tam came in after tying it up outside, reminding her the house was locked, so how did a puppy get into a secure home? Neither knew, but as they lived in the country it was almost certain Tam had forgotten to lock the door as he'd done many times.

Tam refused even to give the dog a name, so Nell called it Ringy, which further pushed an invisible wedge between the man and his pet.

Two years passed, with Tam keeping his distance; he hardly gave the dog a pat or a kind word, something about it frightened him, and he never allowed it into the house at night. Nell, on the other hand, adored the dog, bonding with it; much to her husband's annoyance, she petted and pampered it.

Soon Tam's fears haunted his very dreams. He became insanely jealous of the dog and thought of nothing more than of how to get rid of what he thought was a hound from hell.

One night when Nell was asleep, he sneaked from the house, tied a rope around the dog's neck and walked it far out into darkened fields. He'd brought a spade, and finding a secluded ditch dug furiously until he'd a hole big enough to bury the dog. Then he set about tying it up, first its mouth, then its legs, until it could neither struggle nor bark. The strange thing was, it didn't put up a fight, nor did it bark. Soon Tam had the dog buried deep in the hole. 'You'll not get out of there,' he cried at the earth before heading home. Nell was still sleeping when he arrived back, and as he slid between the warm sheets, a feeling of freedom spread through him.

'Hello, Ringy, some cookit rabbit for your breakfast, ma handsome lad.'

Tam sat bolt upright in his bed on hearing his wife's voice. 'Please make it be a dream!' But no, there was the dog, eating heartily on a fine breakfast. And as the old man approached, it stared at him through those cold, grey-circled eyes.

A pain shot through Tam's chest and spread bolts of lightning down his arms. What kind of creature was this dog? Did it bite through its bonds from the previous night's burial? Could he be imagining the whole thing? He did not know, but one thing he did know, was that the dog had to go.

Nell came in from gathering eggs, noticed how pale her husband had gone and immediately gave him some water. 'What ever is the matter wi' ye ma man?' she asked. 'I think ye should see the doctor.' She covered his knees with a shawl and fussed over him, while Ringy lay, staring all the time into the frightened old man's eyes.

Tam didn't answer Nell, all he could think was 'that dog must go.' He put the attack of pain down to muscular strain, and within three days was thinking on yet another way to destroy the dog. It came on the Saturday whilst Nell was in the village shopping. He knew, while there, she'd visit friends, taking up most of the day in the process. He folded a sack, leashed Ringy, then set off. Several miles away there was a steep track that he'd followed many times in search of lost sheep. At its source a burn spurts from the ground to twist and turn, cascading from high rocks to form a powerful waterfall. So many times he'd watch helpless as sheep would slip and fall to meet their death in the deep pool below. 'Nothing survives. The perfect place to get rid of a demon dog,' he thought.

It took several hours, but soon he was standing perched at the top. 'Now, hound, this time you'll not get back to eat rabbit or anything else from my home again.' As before, Ringy did not struggle and allowed Tam to tie his legs. When he was tied and stuffed in the sack, the old man lifted his live bundle and with all his strength hurled the dog into the turbulent water. He watched as it bounced and battered from off the rocks, then disappeared into the gurgling pool far below. Tam scanned the swirling water until completely satisfied that Ringy was drowned.

He felt free and happy as he wandered home. Nell was there, smiling, a smell of cooking wafted from the kitchen. 'Been awa for a walk, ma love? That's good. Now come ye in here and git yer tea. I've done a braw stew, the way you like it.'

Tam sat comfortably down at the table, thinking he'd better wait until tea was finished before telling her a lie that Ringy had fallen into the falls whilst out walking.

He went over to wash his hands at a basin on the sideboard, and kissed Nell's cheek. 'Yes, free at last,' he thought, then asked, 'well, lass, how was your day?'

'My day was just grand. I bought some material to make new bedroom curtains and met Mrs Doig, who told me her bitch had died.'

Tam thought for a moment and said, 'what bitch?'

'Ringy's mother, of course.'

'Oh, I've something to tell you, lass, aboot the dog. I had him awa up at the Brae waterfall, and while I turned ma back poor Ringy fell ower.'

'Whatever are ye saying, man? Ringy's oot there eating a plate o' stew.'

Like a demon possessed he ran from the house, and there it was, the devil dog, eating healthily on a plateful of stew, pausing to stare up through a grey-circled eye as Tam keeled over and hit the cold ground.

Tam, the old shepherd, was buried a week later. A small gathering of locals attended his quiet funeral. After they left, Ringy, the grey scruffy mongrel with the 'ringle ee', stood at the graveside for a few minutes, then slipped away into the fields and was never seen again.

I have conversed with many travelling folks who can tell similar tales of the 'ringle ee', and one told me it's not an evil thing but a messenger who comes from the other side to help some over.

A certain English gypsy further informed me that his good brother bought a ringle-eyed horse at Appleby Fair one year. He hobbled it with other ponies, and during the night all the horses began screaming and pulling at their hobbles. It took all the next day to find them, and next night the same thing happened. It was decided to separate the ringle eye from the others after that.

He was tied to the wagon and during the night it went on fire. The occupants escaped with a few burns and cuts, but lost all their worldly goods. The horse freed itself, and neither hide nor hair was seen of it again.

My father remembered seeing a ringle-eyed dog once. He was only ten years old at the time and saw it standing by a swing gate next to a river. When he approached to pet it, it ran off. Next day, while he was passing, the dog was on the other side of the gate beside the water. This time Daddy ignored the dog and went home. That night a terrible howling wakened his family. Next morning my father took Grandad to where he'd seen the dog, but it could not be found. Next night, once again, a terrifying howling was heard for miles around. It was so bad Granny insisted they up stock and move. They did so, and that night the whole campsite where my father's family had stayed was completely flooded by a deluge of torrential rain. If they hadn't moved when they did, then for certain they would have been drowned.

So there you have varying stories, folks, of ringle-eyed animals, beasts that make the traveller think twice.

# 31

## BLAIRGOWRIE

$A$s I write this, reader, I feel the excitement mounting as I'm thinking about Blairgowrie. It was berry time once again. Would Cousin Anna and Berta be there? Would Lena, Mammy's sister, and Uncle Tommy, with all the Reekie bunch, be there? I so longed to see them and get the crack. Things had been quiet since we left England, and I'd spent empty days without company. My three sisters were turning their backs on the wildness of their travelling lives, and spent more time indoors playing cards or reading. And with me being the forever traveller, this meant they were turning their backs on me too. They had also taken a scunner to Mammy's hawking basket, whereas I, well, I couldn't get enough. Mammy had taught me the ways of hawking and I had many a grand time round the doors on my own.

Someone else came into my mind as we headed for Blair— Geordie with the wandering hands. When I thought about how hard I'd kicked the poor soul between the legs upon yon braeside behind the berryfields, amongst cows and corn lice, all manner of things flooded my mind. Had he become a priest because I'd ruined his ableness? Perhaps he'd gone in another direction, taking a liking to his Mammy's clothes and speaking with a squeaky voice? These thoughts made me feel quite guilty, but hey, who was I kidding? When we met I could hardly believe it, the bold laddie had a young wife, and with the size of her belly I'm quite certain he had suffered no lasting damage. From then on I secretly named him 'Stone Nuts'.

Farmer Marshall's field was full to bursting with travellers, just the way I liked it. However, not one single relative of ours was there, I hoped they would arrive soon. More important than that was making lots of money. I was a big girl now who needed plenty underwear and the likes, so putting my loneliness on a back burner I set to work pulling pound after juicy red pound from heavy, fruit-laden bushes, keeping half of my earnings to myself, giving the rest to Mammy for my keep.

Daddy was spray-painting from dawn till dusk, and Mammy constantly worried about his lungs. One day my old friend Grumbling Appendix had me staying in bed hugging a hot-water bottle. It was while there I heard my father coughing, and by God I'd never heard him that bad before. When I told Mammy she made murder with him either to give up the painting or the fags. He did neither, until a visit to a doctor put the frighteners on him.

'You stop smoking, Mr Riley, and you've a good chance of seeing your old age. Continue, and you won't see past the next ten years!' For the rest of that summer he stopped smoking and wore a mask while working. It certainly helped; his mood changed too, he'd a brighter smile and only coughed if the cold virus was spreading throughout the family.

It was over a month since the first day we'd arrived, and Daddy said that in one more week we'd head for Crieff to settle for the winter. Crieff would fill our pockets with tattie money and the younger girls could attend school. The harvesting of the tatties meant I'd a good chance of meeting up with travellers, so this cheered me up a wee bit.

But not half as much as our Sunday visitor: it was dear old Portsoy Peter, who'd arrived from somewhere only God and some toff knew. He came laden with presents and promised they were not 'shan chories'. Mammy's jaw dropped when he presented her with a beautiful Crown Derby fruit bowl. She thanked him, but she was well aware it must have cost somebody an arm and a leg, so she put it away and refused to display it as other travelling women would have been proud to do.

After a bite to eat he stayed for a blether, then went away. I never saw Portsoy again.

That day's end joined a dreamy dusk which settled upon the quiet site. I wandered down to where we'd camped the year before. The place where our caravan had sat was jammed with balers and discarded ploughs. It had taken a flood during the winter, leaving the farmer no option but to section it off from travellers. I climbed upon the old baler, looked on the ground and saw the circle our fire had left. I remembered Mac of the 'tent tales' and the last tale he shared with me. I hope you like it. Got that tea poured?

## 32

### DEAD MAN'S FINGERS

Purney felt a warm spring breeze whistling through the broom and thanked God another winter was at the tail-end. He could throw up the flap door of his wee canvas tent and let the air in. 'At long last,' he thought, 'I'll get ma fire lit without it blowing out and hear the leric singing his love song to his mate.'

Apart from her with the pointed nose passing every so often, he'd seen neither hide nor hair of a living soul come past his wee tent on the field at the opening of the forest, and that was exactly how he liked it. He'd long since decided the strange old herb-gatherer was a witch, and wouldn't even spend a minute in conversation with her.

It was many years gone that he had come upon this heaven of a place to work for the farmer who owned the very land he dwelt on. And from that day to this he'd worked the soil, never feeling the need to travel on as his ancestors did before him. A quiet man, was Purney, who enjoyed his own company along with the birds and creatures that lived within the neighbouring forest. Nothing meant more to him than his perfect peace and quiet, just to watch a red squirrel nibbling at some crumbs he'd scattered on the ground was enough contentment for this worker of the soil.

One day, not long after he'd seen out the summer, her with the pointed nose came by, as she was prone to do, and gave a wee nod before scuffling away on two big cloth-covered feet. Suddenly she slowed her pace, stopped, turned and came back. 'You've company,' she said, then dashed off and was soon concealed by fir and beech tree.

'Company? What the hell is yon auld witch muttering about now?' Purney laid aside a knife he was sharpening with a ruggle stane and walked to where he'd a view of the winding farm road. Sure enough, heading in his direction was a big muckle lorry. Dark green it was, and covered by a khaki-coloured tarpaulin. He watched it change direction and trundle towards the farm, where it came to a crunching stop. A big, gruff-looking, bearded man with a belly that hung like a jelly pendulum over a leather belt, stepped down. Purney watched as the wild man conversed with the farmer, then they both turned and stared up towards him. He wondered why the farmer should be pointing in his direction, but oh, dearie me, he didn't have long to wait for an answer. The fat man went behind his lorry wheel, reversed and headed for Purney's wee haven. All manner of reasons for his actions jetted back and forth in Purney's mind while he waited and watched the lorry turn the last bend and soon grind to a halt feet from him.

'What brings ye, my man, have ye news for me?' Purney asked in hesitant tones.

The green lorry man ignored him as he stumbled down and went round to the back of his vehicle and lifted the back flap. Next instant poor old Purney near had the breath leave his body, as bairn after bairn jumped like freed zoo monkeys from the lorry. There, in front of his very eyes, he watched the gruff man erect a massive tent. A woman pushed a rosy red face into his and said, 'where's the water?'

Purney took it she was looking for the burn, and pointed over to the fountain he'd dammed with stones. Without a word of thanks she thrust a battered pail into the pool and filled it to the brim. In no time his small campsite was overflowing with unruly children and flea-ridden, mangy hounds. Soon they had a roaring fire going, with sparks shooting everywhere; some landed on his wee tent and sent shivers of fear through his old bones. Why were these unruly folks thrust upon him? The only thing for it was to see the farmer, who told him, 'you have been getting a wee bit bent-backit, Purney, and wi' me purchasing three more fields I need extra hands. I thought you'd be pleased, seeing as they're tinker folk like yerself.'

'How long have ye fee'd them for, farmer?' he enquired.

'Och, I though they'd be fine company for ye, Purney lad, so I said as long as they were content they could stay.'

Purney, rather than say a word against his own kind, pulled his bunnet back over his head and headed home. When he got there, two big lads had removed his guy rope, resulting in his tent leaning dangerously in the direction of his fire. 'Ye stupid buggers, my tent has been in this spot for thirty years, now why did ye dae that?'

He watched them laughing and mocking him, and that was after he'd had words with the parents. Purney went into his tent, and for the first time in his life allowed the day to waste away without a cup of tea. All night long he lay listening to the noise and unruly behaviour of his new neighbours from hell. The biggest lads fought over a knife, while the mother and father cursed and swore at each other over him taking more of the bedcovers than her. And just to cap it all, the hounds had caught a rabbit and were tearing each other to pieces for a feed at it.

Purney had to find a way to get rid of this wild bunch, and before morning a plan began to form in his head. However he had to gain their trust, especially the two teenage sons; this is the age when people are most susceptible to suggestion.

The sun was pushing itself into the sky like a giant yellow fan, birds began to tweet and sing from the crow to the wren, and Purney breathed the air—his air, not theirs but his. He looked over at the dirty brown dome tent and wondered about the awful smell and mess of filthy bodies about to gatecrash his heavenly space. Well, he'd be waiting for them. They could take any bit of God's earth they wanted, but not his!

The mother rose first, crawling like a snake from beneath the flap. 'Someone get this fire on for me, or ye'll eat raw sausages.' Purney watched a stirring from within the canvas, as the gruff with the jelly belly followed his woman from the hole. He then picked up a stick and hit the tent side, shouting, 'come on, big yin, an' gather sticks for the fire.' The oldest boy crawled out, rose and threw Purney a look, marched across and blatantly helped himself to a pile of tidy piled sticks he'd stored against the dyke. Grabbing a handful he shoved a fist into his face and said, 'ye dinna mind me helping maself, dae ye?'

'Be my guest, laddie. By the way, are you thinking on going into the wood today?'

The lad threw Purney's sticks over for his father to start a fire, and asked why he should bother where he was going, that day or any other day.

'Well, seeing as you folk are new to these parts, I'd best warn you about the dead man lying half buried in the forest.'

'Who killed him?' was the only response the boy gave, before adding, 'ye'd think him no very good at murder if he wisnae able tae bury a decent grave.' With that he kicked a toeful of dust into Purney's face then strutted off.

He'd not get much from him, but he was, after all, the oldest, it was the younger two who'd be more likely to listen. Purney watched them eat, and thought the dogs had better manners. Soon the boys, with catty firmly clasped in unwashed hands, set off into the forest to seek out birds and squirrels, to see how many they could shoot down. Purney followed them. When he thought them far enough out of earshot of the rest he called out, 'you lads, I hope you remember not to go near the undergrowth.'

Curiosity roused, they asked why. 'He disnae like being disturbed from his sleep, some folks claim they've been chased by him.' Purney deliberately sat down and the boys came over. 'Thank God,' he thought, 'maybe now I'll get some fear intae them.'

Watching their eyes grow wider with every word he went on and on about the 'dead man'. 'In the darkest night some say his black hands lift up the corner of tinkers' tents at the spot where young lads like you sleep. Once a family of travelling people came and camped just down the road a bit. I heard screaming in the night and went to see the folks next morning, and all that was left was a dead dog and a flattened tent. Oh, a bad do, right enough!'

The boys were by now showing signs of genuine fear, so he laid it on like syrup. 'They say he can conjure up thunderstorms and forked lightning, and an old man was struck once leaving a smoking pile of ashes on the scorched ground. A bad do, right enough, you wouldn't catch me creeping under the brush bushes.'

The older of the two had heard more than he'd wanted, so grabbing his brother by the collar, he shouted that he was going to get his father and big brother to skelp Purney for frightening them.

No sooner had they ran off screaming, when jelly-belly Daddy, red-faced Mammy and bully brother came storming into the forest.

'Come here, you,' shouted the belly, 'I'll tank the face aff ye for shanning ma laddies.'

Poor Purney, it looked as if his plan had backfired, as a kick from one landed on his leg and a slap from another came hard upon his neck. Just as he thought they were about to skin him alive, a voice from behind a tree had them fall silent.

'Have any of you people been into this undergrowth here?' It was her with the pointed nose. She cautiously approached with those big cloth-covered feet and added, 'it's the dead man's fingers, they've been moved. Have you got them?'

Red-faced Mammy let out a scream and said, 'we're biding aside a deevil and a witch, come on, let's pack and get tae hell oot o' here!'

Jelly-belly, bully-brother and the rest from hell took off in the direction of the mother.

Purney could hardly believe his luck. By the time he'd arrived home the invaders were trundling down the windy road and were never to bother his tranquillity again. They'd left a mess, but in no time he'd got it tidied and soon all trace was gone. That afternoon, as he sat warming himself at a bright fire, the pointed-nose one came by and for the first time he spoke to her. 'Excuse me, dear lady, but how come you heard me tell those lads about a dead man in the undergrowth?'

'I dinna ken onything about a deed man.'

'But I heard you ask thon rough folk if they'd moved the dead man's fingers.'

'Aye, they're ma favourite mushrooms, they grow at the foot o' the beech tree and yon certain patch is always covered by brushwood. Now, if ye'll excuse me, sir, I've a bunch o' herbs tae gather before I go home.'

Purney pushed his wool cap to the back of his head, scratched his temple and said, 'Bloody mushrooms! Well, bless my soul. Cheerio, wife, maybe if tomorrow you pass, stop and share a bite tae eat with me.'

'Well, seein' as you've lost your neighbours I might just dae that.' She smiled, and Purney was certain he saw a wee wink at the corner of her eye as she shuffled off back into the peaceful forest.

Far be it from me, folks, to speak ill of my own kind, but in all society there is good and bad, and that's life!

*Note*: Dead Man's Fingers, *Xylaria polymorpha*. With its blackish, club-shaped fruit-bodies, which often arise in clusters, this fungus deserves its morbid name. It is strange, though, that the experts declare it is inedible, yet pointed-nose said it was her favourite mushroom. It is also known as a delicacy to believers in Black Magic, when eaten with roasted raven!

# 33

## FORGET US NOT

My last year at the 'berry picking' went out like a damp squib. Not a single friend or foe came to share our fireside. I stood on the same braeside where 'Stone Nuts' took my forceful kick the previous year, and scanned every inch of my beloved memory-laden berryfields. I doubted if we'd come back, and with that knowledge, knew life would never be the same again. Another brick in the traveller's house of freedom crumbled. Tears rolled over my cheeks, leaving a salt trail of misery, and I couldn't have cared who witnessed it.

Deep inside the pain was almost unbelievable. It was like Death himself visited my heart like a phantom surgeon to wrench out my roots. I could hear the Ancient Ones, those hardy craturs, my ancestors, calling me. I closed out the river of tears and heard them in my mind. 'You had better believe the inevitable, lassie, Scotland doesn't look kindly on the travellers. Only way to get on is to be ashamed of us.'

'Never, as long as I live, will I deny my roots,' I called back to them through the window of my mind. 'I'll never be a zombie!'

Every day I say a silent prayer for my people. This is for them.

§

A circle of tents snuggled into a secluded forest, it was a freezing January.

There was a woman with a newborn baby. The tiny bundle came into the world after two days of pain-wracked labour. The young mother was screaming at her husband. He took her baby, their first child, a beautiful boy. The poor little mite was blue dead. She bit into her horsehair mattress and heard the starving dogs eat her child. They hadn't eaten for days, but now they were fed would be able to hunt for food to feed the members of that lonely circle of nomads forced to live on the edge of society.

The tinker children buried their innocent little faces into mother's skirt. 'Don't look, my lambs,' she warned them, 'else this memory will stay with you all the days of your lives!' Doing as she asked they closed their eyes, and didn't see the men from the nearby village batter their father to death with hammers and axes.

'Run, ma bairn, or the bad men will get you too.' She ran as fast as she could, not faltering or turning to look back once. The bad men took turns doing things to mother, things that innocent young mind did not understand. Then they left her stone-dead on the bleeding grass. The child waited hours in the thick rye grass before going back. She sat all through the night holding mother's cold hand, then at daybreak took a stone and hacked off a piece of mother's flaxen hair to remember her by.

The old man came back from gathering sticks. An eery silence had spread itself over the moor and not even the dogs barked. With shaking legs he crept slowly towards his campsite. The sight that met his eyes had him fall upon the ground: they'd come visiting, the body snatchers. What could he have done, if he'd been there? Nothing! He piled his family's bits and pieces and set fire to everything, then sat under a laburnum tree to wait for the scythe of death. It was well known amongst travellers that because of their non-registered existence they were easy prey for dissection-hungry doctors willing to pay whoever brought them good healthy specimens.

'Go and stand in the corner, you're a waste of my good teaching skills.'

'Tinky, tinky, cold bum, yer mammy canna knit, yer faither kicked the polisman an' is lying in the nick.'

'Please, miss, I can't sit here beside her, she's a dirty tinker. I'll catch a disease, my mother said.'

'Wullie, how can we get the tar and feathers frae aff the bairn?'

'Please, Mammy, don't send me back to that horrible school.'

'I've been asked to inform you that the school nurse said she hasn't enough liquid paraffin to treat your children's lice. Please don't send them to school.'

Then, just when I thought my heart would burst with sadness I saw the weddings, the music and the laughter. Storytellers and balladeers entertained with pipers and box players. The hot summers with happy-faced bairns running and playing upon heather-thickened moors. Cutting bracken and maggot-scouring the sheep. Children seeing how long they could string the daisies before one separated the chain.

No, my ancestors, I'll never forget you. This is my pledge to you. You can take this Traveller off the Road, but you'll never take the road off this Traveller.

# Scotland's Outcasts

*Ye canna sleep them awa,*
*They'll aye be here in the morning.*
*Ye canna dream them awa,*
*They'll surely turn up wi' yer dawnin.*

*Ye canna expect them tae go,*
*Or scarper ower the heather,*
*They widnae abandon the show*
*They're joined tae you forever.*

*Ye canna just sweep them aside,*
*They are here like an oncoming tide.*
*Ye canna just wish them away,*
*Ach, ye widnae anyway.*

*Sometimes they're sullen an dour,*
*But they're nae hidden treasure.*
*They've nae misgivings, they're sure,*
*They're travelling folks forever.*

*If a spanner were tossed in yer works,*
*They'll stand firm: 'Esprit de Corps'.*
*They're the essence o' what yer aboot,*
*Ach, they canna just sling their hook.*

*They'll ne'er shake hands wi the deil,*
*For they're yer bells, yer steeple.*
*So never doubt how they feel,*
*They're Scotland's travelling people.*

*They're the grandest show on the road,*
*Forced to carry this cumbersome load,*
*Their facet is your visage too,*
*They're the splendid part o' you.*

*Tae the watery skies abune,*
*Tae oor hallowed glens within,*
*Tae oor ancestors steeped in past,*
*Here's tae Scotland,*
*They're still yer outcasts.*

Charlotte Munro

## 34

### CRIEFF, THE FINAL FRONTIER

When I read about Crieff in bonny Perthshire it is mostly described in terms of tourism. Fair enough—a fine picture is painted, and justly so. But when I think of this little town nestling in the foothills of the Grampian mountains I see the whole face of Scottish history being changed, or how it would have done if the folks who used to live here took a different route. Why? Well if you've a cuppy, then sit yourself down and listen to this.

After the great upheaval of the Reformation, France and the Stuarts had one great plan between them: to seek the throne of England. If it was in their hands then Rome could claw back her Catholic states, which were disappearing daily.

Prince Charles Edward Stuart (who my friend Mac didn't believe was monarch of anywhere) was their last hope. Aided by France, he tried to land an army of French soldiers in England in 1744, but his fleet was lost at sea during a storm.

The next year, 1745, France could no longer render military aid to Charles, so with only seven men he landed on a small island on the west coast of Scotland.

He certainly was an able lad, however, for by August he'd collected a large army of mainly Highland clansmen. He made for Perth, then Edinburgh, and while there, proclaimed himself King at the Market Cross. On 21 September he attacked Sir John Cope at Prestonpans, and quickly cut through his army, leaving them fleeing from the field of battle. Triumphantly he marched on, taking recruits as he went, and soon his army consisted of 6,000 men. After defeating Cope, Charles marched on to England, reaching Derby without opposition. He'd heard many places were still strong in Jacobitism. But to his great disappointment he found that his support was weak, and to proceed any further south would have been folly. Anyway, word reached him that the Government had dispatched two armies, one on either side of the line of his advance, while a third was retained to defend London. There was nothing for it, then, but to retreat to Scotland.

The Jacobites and the Covenanters had been locked in combat for many a year, so the banner of the Stuarts found little support in the lowlands of Scotland. Still, it is a well-documented fact that there were still a great many in the west willing to die for Charles's flag, and by the time he reached Glasgow his army numbered 9,000.

General Hawley with the English army had followed up Charles's retreat until he arrived at Falkirk. Here both armies met on 23 January 1746, where the English suffered defeat.

This is where I bring bold Charlie to Crieff. It was on his arrival here that he quartered his troops upon the hardy folks of the town. He also had the southmost arch of the bridge over the river Earn destroyed, in order to impede the advance of the English army. There is no record as to the length of time he stayed in Crieff, but what is well known is that he was not a welcome visitor. As it happens the Crieffites had long since changed their beliefs to that of the Presbyterian faith. They regarded Jacobitism as a thing to be detested and opposed.

He had loyalty in Strathearn, though, especially among the landed gentry. He sat in the Auld Hoose o' Gask where the old lady cut off a piece of his hair, an incident still sung about in folk circles today.

It is known that Charlie sent most of his men north by way of the Sma' Glen and Highland roads, while he sat at a window in the Drummond Arms Hotel in James Square until he saw the first of the Duke of Cumberland's men descending by the old Muthill road. He then ordered his horse and left to spend the night in Ferntower House. Its ruins still stand today on the edge of Crieff Golf Course.

The Duke did not follow the Pretender's army through the wild treacherous roads they had taken, but preferred to take a safer route by Perth and the East coast to Aberdeen. He then turned towards Inverness, where both armies met on Culloden Moor. There Jacobitism was utterly destroyed.

Lord Perth of Drummond Castle was a true friend who risked and lost everything for Bonnie Prince Charlie. But neither he nor any of the other local landed gentry could now offer much support or assistance to the Pretender. Only two or three recruits went along with Lord Perth to stand by the banner of the Stewarts on Culloden. After the defeat, for his act of high treason, a great price was put on his life.

He tried however to muster as many of his estate workers as he could. One local story tells of twin brothers, aged only thirteen years, who disobeyed their parents and tried to follow Charlie. Fearing their lives would be lost in battle, their father and relatives tied them to a strong oak tree down by the Earn's bank. It is where the river dips before reaching Powmill. Sadly, after a terrific thunderstorm, the river rose and burst its banks, drowning the boys.

The estates of Drummond fell into the hands of the Government, which appointed a local factor by the name of Campbell who owned some land in Argyllshire.

Instead of Lord Perth it was a Captain Drummond who belonged to a collateral branch of the family who was considered worthy of recognition by the Government because of his services to Britain during the American War of Independence, and so to him went the estate of Drummond and the Castle.

Captain Drummond had a male heir, but sadly he died in childhood of the croup. The story goes that the baby's nursemaid, an elderly woman by the name of Mary Moir, who lived in King Street, took the infant up onto Turleum Hill to cure it. It was believed the top of Turleum had healing properties, and she sat all night with the child hoping to save his life.

Captain Drummond had another child, known as Miss Drummond of Perth. This young lady married Lord Willoughby de Eresby. Both lived in London, visiting the Castle once a year. Their name still holds the seat to this present day.

Now do you see what I mean by the course of history being changed?

If the people of Crieff had not embraced Presbyteranism but had clung to the hand of the old faith, then Charlie would have found many more thousands throughout Strathearn to take on the Duke's army at Inverness.

So then reader, what do you think of this?

Crieff rejected a Royal Prince, yet accepted a wee Scottish nomadic lassie—me!

§

Just like the drovers who came to Crieff hundreds of years before, eager to make enough money to see them through the long, bitter Scottish winter ahead, so came the 'tattie howkers'. Clans of Macallisters, Reids, Macphees, Macdonalds, Burns, Johnstones, Rileys, Stewarts, Donaldsons, MacKenzies, Williamsons, MacLarens, Shaws, Douglases, Patersons, Robertsons, Browns, Whytes and many more descended upon Crieff.

In this little town nestling at the mouth of the Highlands, the traditions of an age-old culture flourished. If during the summer one failed to pass roads with relatives then a certainty was that all would meet at the tatties. Field after field, mile after brown mile, farmers grew and grew potatoes until not an inch but had a shaw protruding from the earth. The potato may be a humble part of our diet, but here in Crieff it was the agricultural backbone that brought prosperity to the whole Strathearn valley. And it was to my folks, the lowly travellers, that a great deal of thanks is due, because they converged in their thousands to harvest the tatties and make landowners and farmers rich.

Ask the farmers and see if they agree with me, of course they do. It was many a furrowed brow they had if their usual tribe failed to appear on time.

So here I am then, reader, in Crieff at tattie time. We found a proper site with toilets and washie house, which pleased Mammy no end. Daddy was still painting, but back on the fags. My sister Babsy went to the very same school I went to the last time we lived here. Renie and Mary went to the tatties. Cousin Nicky joined us for the tatties along with Mammy's brother, Mattie's son of the same name.

The site, named Arnbro, was built near the ruins of a prisoner-of-war camp halfway along the Broich road; it is still there today, run by the same family.

My older sister Chrissie, who was married to a Crieff lad, lived on the site, and having them there with their two boys was sheer joy for my parents. Now and again Janey came to visit with her lot, and soon the family were happy and content.

When the tatties finished, Nicky and Mattie drifted off home, and Renie and Mary started working in local shops. I felt the need to head off some place for the winter, so saying my farewells to everybody I set off, with battered brown suitcase in hand.

I spent a week here and there with cousins, aunts and, latterly, sister Shirley, with the wanderlust still strong in my legs.

I hardly gave my folks a thought, when out of the blue came a letter from Chrissie that Mammy had fallen and hurt her back.

Her being ill had me heading back to Crieff. Poor soul, she'd fallen on the concrete step at the washie, and slipped discs in her back so severely she'd been hospitalised.

Before going down the road to Arnbro I had to pop into the Cottage Hospital to see her. When I asked how she was faring, she said, 'stiff as a board—and see that old woman over there, if she doesn't stop shouting at the poor nurses I'll throttle her myself.'

Although her back was a hindrance, there was nothing wrong with her spirits, thank heavens.

Painful days lay ahead, but without doubt she felt much better seeing me, she knew as long as I was there Daddy would get his soup (only I made it like her), and I could keep a check on his smoking.

This after all was my purpose in life, to care for my parents. Funny, though, I didn't think I'd be doing it this early.

Mammy received a bit of bad news from the doctor, who told her she'd be in hospital for six weeks. Being away from us for this length of time fair knocked her into a right mood. I'd intended to tell her that Daddy's cough sounded more like a barking dog, as the fags were chained to his lungs, but thought she had enough to worry about. Instead I took it upon myself to make a doctor's appointment for him. He shouted and protested, but when I said I'd tell Mammy about the coughing, he reluctantly went. This time the doctor let him have it. He left the surgery drained of all colour, came home and threw a twenty packet of fags into the fire.

'Well, Da, what made you do that?' I asked.

'Yon doctor wi' the rid hair, Dr Lindsay, telt me tae stop spraying and smoking—if not, then my lungs will cease to work in the space of a few years!' Poor Daddy, we all knew that farmers had no use for a mole-catcher or rabbit-trapper, and rags fetched a mere pittance. So what would he do, how could he provide for his family?

Everybody believed him to be missing Mammy, and yes he was, but only I knew why he was so down after that.

I tried my best to cheer him up by saying that Renie and Mary could share their wages and I'd get a job. 'That might be all right, lassie,' he told me, 'but a man needs his money. What good is the head of a family without a shilling in his pocket?'

Six weeks went past, and Mammy was home. What a happy caravan we had, filled with her smell, that fresh 'lily-of-the-valley' toilet water she wore seemed to lift our spirits, it even cheered Daddy up. I thought the better of telling her of his doctor's visit. After all, his cough had cleared up considerably, and the fag withdrawal symptoms had subsided.

One Saturday Mammy received a letter to say her sister-in-law was coming to visit. I remember the panic when she realised there wasn't enough tea, sugar or biscuits. I told her not to get so flustered, I'd go and get some at Wooller's shop in King Street. As I left the shop I accidentally put my toe in a box of vegetables and tripped, sending messages flying in all directions. When I leant down to retrieve them, a young lad gave me a hand. I was so embarrassed I hardly noticed what I'd dropped.

'Here,' he said, 'a packet of sweetmeal biscuits for a sweet wee lassie.'

God, did my face burn or not? You bet, what a beamer. 'Thanks,' was all that came from a half-closed mouth, as I turned and ran off feeling like a right eejit.

Approaching Arnbro gates I heard a voice calling behind me and looked back, it was him holding up a bag. 'You forgot the sugar, you must be far too sweet then.'

There was no need of me going red because I still was, my cheeks shining like toffee apples.

'What's yer name?' He was holding out a hand, long fingers with a bluebird tattoo. I touched his hand and drew back, remembering my spinster's role in life and said, 'Jessie, what's yours?'

'I'm David to my mother, Spook to my mates, but you can call me Davey.'

'I can understand the David and Davey, but Spook?'

'Oh, I used to be a milkboy and when I used to get into school from my rounds with a pale face and my hair blown stiff with the wind, a certain teacher began calling me "Spook", as in ghost.'

Then with two hands pushed into jean pockets he turned and sauntered up the road. 'I'll be seeing you,' he shouted back, then added, 'that's a promise.'

That night, as my relatives blethered about everyone and everything, I didn't hear them. My mind was filled with the fair-haired lad who'd followed me home with a bag of sugar in his bluebird-tattooed hand. It would be several weeks before we met again, and not for one minute did he leave my thoughts.

Meanwhile, despite immense protesting, Daddy went back to the painting. He'd made up his mind to give Mammy a nice big residential caravan, one with a washing-machine and sink. I knew this meant our travelling days were well and truly over; somehow I had felt it back in Blairgowrie but prayed I was wrong. I also knew it might be the last job Daddy ever did. I prayed even harder on that one, folks.

Something else I'll share with you now, reader: he decided it was time for a driving licence—mine! 'You think I'm learning to drive in big Fordy, then think again, Daddy.'

I did! It was nightmarish trying to manoeuvre yon great brute of a motor along the narrow bends of Broich Road, Madderty, Auchterarder, Muthill and so on. I remember most of the way I was on the grass verge instead of the road. What a useless article behind a steering wheel, by the time I'd mastered staying on my side of the road I'd sent the frighteners into every tractor man for fifty miles radius. One sighting of the orange van and out of the tractors they jumped. Chrissie's man, plus uncles, cousins and Daddy, took turns at tutoring me, but if ever there was a useless learner driver then I was it. There was nothing else for it but a proper instructor.

So, by my seventeenth birthday I was a learner driver, Mr Bertie Don did the business. What a difference having a qualified gent instruct me on the ways of the road. After twenty lessons I was facing my test. It was a cold wet Thursday morning, the Examiner's name was Mr Lindsay. After what I thought was a perfect half-hour examination he turned to face me and said, 'take this list of failures, and when you can drive come back and re-sit the test.' Honest, reader, to this day I feel anger and shame swelling inside. I was certain my driving skills were red hot. So angry was I that the piece of paper he handed me was thrown into his face; on reflection, if he had wished, the man could have had me arrested for assault.

Daddy hardly said a word, instead he blamed poor Mr Don, stating that anyone worth a grain of salt could teach a body to drive. Then he changed his mind and said I couldn't have been paying attention.

I immediately re-applied for my test, and employed the help of a certain George Gauld. Six lessons later, I was heading home with a pink slip in my hand, giving me permission to take up my place on Her Majesty's Highways.

'Thank God,' said Daddy, 'at last I've got a driver.' The great thing was that Daddy had sold his Jag (I couldn't see me getting to cruise in yon status symbol) and purchased a Ford Zodiac, six cylinder, which went like a rocket! I refused to drive anywhere in big Fordy, so was allowed the privilege of hitting the road in Flashy Fordy. It was a Lovat-green-coloured, sleek, handsome, powerful car, just the tool for a travelling girl.

However, before I was given the freedom of this car I had to prove my road skills. So, if I wasn't going in to Edinburgh for paint, I was taking him and Mammy to Perth where they'd found a form of entertainment they liked—wrestling! They wouldn't miss it. One of the wrestlers was named Mick McManus, and because Mammy's Granny went under the same name she was convinced he was a relative of sorts. Mick was hardly a nice wrestler, in fact it seems he was always the baddy, yet my mother, thinking him a distant kin, would shout for him to win. Daddy said she was the only fan the 'bad man' of the ring had. He, in all seriousness, warned her not to be telling folks she was a relation of yon ape-acting wild man. Why? Because 'he wisnae awfy bonny'!

Driving was a form of freedom for me and sometimes I'd sit behind the wheel, foot to the boards, cruising like Stirling Moss along the old A9. One day Daddy asked me where I'd been. I asked him why he wanted to know. 'Because there is one hundred and fifty miles on the clock!'

What did my father do then, folks? Well, he had the wheels made so that they wobbled—when my speed reached fifty the car shuddered; to stop it happening I was forced to lower my speed. One thing he didn't know, however, was the other way to stop the shudders—that was to hit sixty and keep up the speed! I was just a wee devil, me with a vehicle.

In the meantime I got a job outside Comrie in a mink farm. This was for me a totally new experience, as I hated the idea of caged animals, but the vet who treated them convinced me that, as they were born in captivity, the small furry creatures knew no difference. I never took any part in the kill, but I am ashamed to say I skinned and boarded the pelts. However, now that I'm older and wiser, you'd be hard pressed to see me take any part in animal farming. Then I was just a teenager and knew my wage-packet far outsized anybody else's of my age. My workmates were two Aberdonian lads plus Davie the feedman, from Comrie, and a family of Irish folk called Comer. Mary was my favourite; she was as rough and ready as any man, with a heart as big. To this day she and I share a crack and a laugh. Once, when working overtime at the pelting, I collected the family in the works van, a wee green Mini. There had been an almighty snowstorm, leaving great drifts on either side of the A85.

Between Comrie and St Fillans I came upon a bend in the road, took it far too fast and span round. Well, as it happens my Irish workmates had been celebrating the night before, and just happened to be the worst for it when the door swung open, spewing each of them onto the road. God, what a fright. I thought they were all killed, but thankfully up they jumped, and soon were walking into the farm none the worse.

Next day I almost drove over old Sandy 'the cock o' the north' Stewart. This bold fella was one of Perthshire's road tramps, and although I seldom spoke to him he'll always stay in my memory because he wore two Black Watch coats, a Glengarry tammy and a crooked stick. He was a fine lad who'd never miss the Highland Games, wherever they were held.

Mammy got her state-of-the-art modern residential caravan and was over the moon.

Remember Davey? Well, one night some Muthill girls I'd befriended took me to the dancing in Auchterarder. As we queued to pay at the door I saw someone, a young lad, lying out for the count along a corridor. If it wasn't for the tattoo, there's no way I'd have looked twice at someone the worse for alcohol. When I stooped to see if it really was him, he opened his eyes and said, 'promised I'd see you again.'

'What a waste of space,' I thought, when joining my friends. 'If that drunkard comes within a mile of me he'll feel my hand across his face.' Well, he did, and when I discovered it was his birthday I understood. Stupid me! However, walking home that night I told him my parents didn't want me seeing boys. He asked if we could be friends, and not seeing the harm in that I agreed. So from then on Davey was a permanent feature in my life, although Daddy refused to speak to him. I think Mammy had told him I could easy take care of her, whether married or not. But nothing doing, my father was adamant—no man in my future.

## 35

### FOR THE LOVE OF RACHEL

I've been going on far too long about my life, folks, so how about another tale from the tent?

Here now is a story of love.

§

Three months passed and Rachel was becoming increasingly worried that she had heard not a word from James since Father Dillon had brought the last crumpled letter.

'My lassie, it has rained for weeks,' was the first line the old priest read, before saying, 'Aye, and no' just on the soldiers fighting in France, but here in Glen Coe, we've had oor fair share, is that no' right, Rachel?'

'Aye, aye, Father. Now please read on, maybe ma laddie has been hurt and you sitting there going on aboot the weather.'

Father Dillon sat back into the soft chair Rachel had placed by her campfire to make him as comfortable as her meagre means allowed. He was a very important person, was the old priest, for what would she do without him? Tinkers in those days seldom learned to read and write, and she was no exception. Neither could her good man James: his saviour who put pen to paper on his behalf was an army minister.

The priest continued reading to Rachel who had gathered her wee sons, Jamie and Harry into her bosom, so that they too could listen to their father talk from within the crumpled letter held gently between his sinewy fingers.

'We are fine here in France but my pal Joe who comes from Brora took a bad one and is in the field hospital. Hope he makes it. Are the boys behaving themselves? Tell Jamie to keep chopping wood, and Harry you mind and gather twigs for kindling, I'm on guard duty tonight so best get my bully eaten and take up position. Love you till the heather grows feet and walks off the hills, James'

'Thank you, Father, you've no idea how much better we'll sleep knowing he's still safe.'

Father Dillon said nothing as he handed her the letter. She stared at it for ages, touching it and smelling it as if a piece of James were in her hands, then she gently folded it and slid it into a small box under the tent door.

The memory of that day three months ago was all she had to cling to. 'When will he be in touch again?' she thought, then prayed he remained safe.

As October headed to its end it was becoming colder with each passing day. The women of Ballachulish were knitting and baking, because weather predictors had already foretold a bad winter looming. Rachel became concerned about her two children living in her tiny canvas hovel—oh, how she needed James. Suddenly a voice she knew well boomed from a small, bent man making towards her. It was Father Dillon. He held something in the air and waved it, a letter. 'Oh, praise God, word from my man!' She ran to meet him, with Jamie and Harry at her heels. 'Read it, father, read it. Hurry up, what does it say?'

'Come now, lassie, ye've waited this length of time, a few more minutes won't matter. At least let me settle my bones.' Breathless, he dropped onto the familiar seat, took a grey handkerchief from his pocket and wiped the sweat from his furrowed brow.

Rachel and the boys sat wide-eyed, with the biggest grins on their faces, eagerly waiting to hear what James was saying and doing in the mud-filled trenches of France.

The priest read on, not losing a moment to bring joy to this small family of tinkers.

'Dear Rachel, Jamie and Harry, Daddy here again I hope you are fine, I have managed to stay clear of the bullets. Not much time so this letter has to be short. Rachel I want you to take up roots and head over to Glen Etive. As you know my folks have a wee cotter hoose there. I had a feeling last night you are going to see a lot of snow this winter. I'd feel a lot better knowing you and the boys were with the auld yins. By the time Father Dillon finishes this note I want you packed.

Look for me among the heather, love always, James.'

'Well, I'd have thought he could have put a wee bit more into the letter, Father. Surely he's not that busy, fighting the Germans?'

'Lassie, I'm sure he'll write a longer letter next time. You never know, but maybe there's one waiting for you when you arrive at Glen Etive—you know how long it takes for mail to arrive, goodness, this letter must have taken weeks to get here.'

'Aye, Father, I'm sure you're right as always.' She began gathering her belongings into a tablecloth that she tied in two large knots. Jamie and Harry skilfully did the same with their own things. Jamie, who had just turned seven, already owned a knife and wood-axe, while five-years-old Harry pocketed a catapult and a handful of marbles he'd won from a local laddie.

'Father,' asked Rachel, untying and piling her skeleton ribcage of hazel sticks on which stretched the tent canvas, 'would you be so kind as to store our tent in the shed by the manse? I'll collect it when James and I come back here again.'

'Why, of course ye can, pet. Now, away with ye and take the path through the Buchailles. No short cuts, mind.'

She'd shared many a story with the kindly old man, about James and her running over Beag and Mhor as children knowing every inch of the traverse.

'Not with the boys, Father,' she promised. 'Anyway, this nippit wind and heavy sky tells me my soldier laddie's feelings are coming with a herald o' truth in them.'

Father Dillon raised his head upwards and agreed with her. Already Aonach Eagach saw a top tapping of white, even further down the Paps were dusted like fairy cakes.

They parted, and the priest watched her turn the bend in the road with a pack bigger than herself, wee boys following on; she was like a ewe with her precious twin lambs. He waited until Rachel and her bairns disappeared from view before he set off back to his duties, because even in that small, sparsely-populated area, there was already news to break. A mother would find no sleep that night, nor ever see her son again.

Reaching the spot that cuts a fine path through the mountain feet of Buachaille Etive Beag and Buachaille Etive Mhor, Rachel ushered her boys onwards. About a mile in, she stopped to sniff the air. 'My God, if that's not an ice-filled wind I don't know what is. I pray we make it before the storm. I haven't set eyes on a deer or a grouse, and they are scarcely seen when foul weather is coming.'

Young Jamie looked at the concern wrinkling his mother's brow and asked why she was so afraid of the snow.

Rachel ran a hand over her son's head and said, 'bairn, when it snows here, it's like a tunnel that fills, burying everything in its path, and we're in its path.'

No sooner had she uttered those fearsome words when the snow fell, gently at first, with half-crown-sized snowflakes covering the ground and also their life-line to Etive: the winding narrow path. Rachel gathered her sons to walk behind her; she'd shelter them from the fierce wind, now building up in force with every minute. On and on the small band trekked, until it was almost impossible to go any further; snow filled their way, progress was at a standstill. She had only one chance to save her children, to reach higher ground, but that in itself held great danger, with hidden crevices and jagged rocks. However, no way could she fight the constant build-up of white piling in front, so taking the boys firmly by the hands she began to climb. Finding what she thought was a level track, she began to go forward again round the hillside. Up there she was safe from a snow burial, but her path had many dangers: the precipitous crags meant one wrong footing and she and her boys were dead. Her knowledge of the area meant nothing in a storm with power-ful winds forcing her eyes shut. Panic was quickly taking hold, she threw off her bundle and pulled the boys tighter for warmth. 'What am I going to do?' she thought, 'I know I'm lost, there's no way I can go on in this nightmare. God help us this day.'

Jamie pulled on his mother's sleeve and called up at her, 'Mammy, look, along the track. I can see a man, see, there is a man.' Rachel screwed her eyes and stared into the blizzard, and yes, praise be, she could just make out a form ahead. 'Come on, lads, I think we might be found.' With a stronger hold she took her boys' hands and headed toward the man, who was waving his arms above his head. As they drew closer to the man she heard a voice, a familiar voice, it grew louder. 'Rachel, go left, my love, left, save yourselves, go left.' It was James. He was calling to them. Then, as he began to fade back into the storm, Rachel screamed, 'James, James!' but as quickly as he came he was gone. Thank God, before she was able to run to find him, Jamie pulled hard on her arm. 'Mammy, Daddy said go left.' With that he pulled her and Harry down into an opening on their left, where they sheltered from the horrendous storm. All night they sat huddled together in their godsent tiny cave, praying James had found his own shelter.

Dawn came with a clear crisp, blue sky before they peeped their tired heads from the opening. The sight that was spread out before them made Rachel's heart leap to her throat, because an inch from the cave was a sheer hundred-feet drop. If James hadn't shouted 'go left', then they would without a doubt have been dashed to pieces far below!

Now, with a clear view and clear sky, she knew exactly where they were and was soon headed down toward Glen Etive and her in-laws' home; but where was her man? Surely he was coming to meet them, to see if they were safe?

Tired, cold and hungry, Rachel and her laddies arrived at Granny and Grandad's door, who were overjoyed to see them.

'Guid Mother, James, where is he?' Rachel told them about the previous night.

'Rachel,' her good father laid a hand upon her shoulder and said, 'lassie, James was killed at the Somme this month past, has no news reached you yet? Whoever you saw on the mountain last night it could not have been him.'

Rachel fell upon a chair and looked at her sons in utter bewilderment. 'Jamie, Harry, tell Grandad who called out to us in the blizzard last night.'

Jamie, unable to speak, was resting his head in his hands, while little Harry stood up, went over to his Granny and said, 'Granny, we saw Daddy last night, he had on a green hat and coat. But you've not to worry, because he's in among the walking heather.'

Rachel put gentle hands on her small son's shoulders and said, 'No, pet, the snow was far too thick and fearsome for you to see what he was wearing. It couldn't have been Daddy, it must have been a shepherd or somebody else.'

Little Harry kissed his Mother's tear-streaked face and said, 'Mammy, last night while you and Jamie fell asleep, Daddy came. He sat down beside me and held me tight. He kept me warm because I was shivering. His clothes were army green and I gave him one of my marbles because he asked for one. When the snow stopped and you were stirring, he took my catty, then said he'd walk with the heather.'

Rachel, overcome by her child's words, ran outside into the crisp snow and stood proud, facing a fresh wind, 'I'll look for you, my love, in the heather, I promise.' As she turned to walk back something came whizzing past her nose and landed by her feet. She leant down and picked up a small glass marble. Unable to explain or understand the supernatural event she wiped her tears, and popped the glass ball in her pocket.

The hills were resplendent in their white coats, they'd stay that way until the long winter was over. She had sons to raise and elderly people depending on her. She'd keep her tears until the purple came back upon the mountains, then cry for her lost love.

You have been told a true story. My people have taken time on many occasions to tell me stories of loved ones coming back, so to speak, and helping in time of need.

Here is a similar tale.

## 36

### THE OLD TREE BY THE BURN

Anne had to face life without her husband, as just another young woman widowed by the war. She was left with only memories for company, those and her teenage daughter. But she was strong, she had to be; and not just for Penny, but also for her mother-in-law.

On that particular day it was the interfering old lady that Anne could well have done without, she'd a washing needing doing and Penny's cardigan was looking for two new elbow patches. But when mother called she had to drop everything and run. All the emotions would be showing, yet again, about her dear son, and why did he have to die, and on and on she'd go, completely ignoring the fact that it was also Annie's husband and Penny's father who had lost his life. Why did she always have to be such a pain? A sudden flash of lightning streaked across the sky and earthed somewhere in the wood, followed by an almighty crack of thunder. It caused her quickly to close all the windows, momentarily pushing annoying thoughts of mother-in-law to the back of her mind. 'Penny, bring your wellies out of the cupboard and try to find my brown umbrella.'

Her daughter called out, while rummaging for her rainwear, that Granny was terrified of thunder, and that they'd better hurry or else she'd have a fit. Anne smiled rather wryly and thought, 'it would solve all my problems, that,' and then scolded herself for being so nasty.

Outside Penny linked arms with her mother and went on about Granny being so afraid, hurrying Anne on. 'Mummy, shall we go the quick way by the burn and the old tree?'

'Oh, I suppose we had better, or else she'll be scolding us until the cows come home.'

As they splashed on through sodden grass and fern, Anne remembered how often she and Bob used to run as teenagers up by the burn and lie beneath the old tree. The many kisses and stolen embraces they shared came back to her. The more she thought, the heavier grew the pain hidden just below the surface of her hardened resolve. It was only for Penny she pretended to be strong, but so often when no one was there she'd sit holding Bob's photo and sob into her handkerchief. Another clap of thunder jolted her back to matters in hand. The burn was rising with every step they took. This worried her because they might not get across, leaving Granny to face the storm alone. As much as she disliked the old woman, she would never wish her harm, after all, she was her husband's mother.

'Come on, Penny, best run or the burn will burst its bank and we'll not get over to Granny.' Anne held her teenage daughter's hand and ran as fast as she could. Just as they reached the old tree another almighty crack split the heavens and momentarily lit up the sky. Over by the old tree Anne saw an old woman with a shawl covering her head; she was pointing towards the wood and calling out, 'run away, don't cross the burn, run towards the wood!' Anne wiped the rain from her eyes, and saw it was Granny, of all people, out in the storm.

'Look, Penny, the stupid old woman has gone mad—she's over by the tree, can you see her?'

Penny, who was struggling with an inside-out umbrella, glanced over but could see no one.

Anne looked again, and yes, it was Granny pointing toward the wood. A shiver ran up her spine, and grabbing her daughter by the arm she ran away from the burn and its old tree. Penny protested, but another crack of lightning and roar of thunder had her following Anne, discarding the brolly. They hid under a bush of gorse, watching a storm so fierce they'd never seen its likes. Suddenly another terrifying crack lit up the whole place and wrenched apart the old tree. With a shattering crash its main branch thudded down, shaking the ground beneath them. Anne was certain that Granny was over there; she crawled out and said, 'Penny, let's get to Granny's house, I feel something is wrong.' Soon, soaked to the skin and breathless, they were standing outside Granny's house. They knocked, then without waiting for an answer went inside. It was very quiet, and the fact that there was still no sign or sound of the old woman sent a shiver through Anne. She stepped into the bedroom, and lying in bed, peaceful and very still, was her mother-in-law. She had passed away in the night, said the doctor who was there with her.

Did Anne really see her mother-in-law telling them to go away from what was obviously a death trap, or was it something caused by the effect of a thunderous sky?

However, from then on, along with her late husband's memory, Granny's memory was the most precious thing for Anne. She owed the old woman her life, but more importantly, she owed her that of her daughter too.

There are strange things that happen on this earth of ours, reader, but it is not for us to explain them.

I hope you liked that wee story.

## 37

### THE END OF TRAVELLING DAYS

Lets us go back to Crieff now and see how my family and I wind up our travelling days.

Daddy spent another bronchitis-struck winter, seeing more of his pillow than a mirror. Thankfully, though, there must have been a breakthrough in medicines for chest troubles at that time. His pockets bulged with inhalers and pills that helped him no end. Mammy had discovered Bingo. Chrissie and her family moved up to a house on a country lane and loved it.

Mary, who'd been going out with a lad, fell pregnant, and much to my parents' sadness, refused to marry him.

Aunts and uncles grew old and died, and now and again I took myself off to some quiet, secluded place down beside the River Earn to remember them. And it was while I was there day-dreaming upon a sandbank that Davey found me.

We chatted about the river and the sand-martins who burrowed like rabbits, and all the travelling folks who came and went in and around Crieff. Then, much to my utter shock and horror, he just stood up and asked me to be his bride! His face beamed bright red, and all I could do was laugh. This was definitely the wrong response, because without a word he scrambled up the embankment to get away from me, but his feet began to slide which sent him tumbling back toward me. However, as he rolled he gathered up speed and couldn't stop, catching me on the downhill. Can you imagine then, reader, a more unusual proposal? Just before we hit the water I called out—'YES!'

I hadn't realised it, but my friend and I had fallen in love. It sort of grew on me like ivy round an old fence post. Still, it had to be kept a secret until I found the right time to tell Daddy. He certainly would not want me coming home with news like that.

Mary meanwhile gave birth to the most beautiful baby girl we'd ever seen, with lots of fluffy hair and the biggest round blue eyes, she was gorgeous and quite a novelty in our home. Perhaps it was her newness—you know that special smell babies have that made me yearn for one of my own.

Davey was desperate that we marry, and so wanted to ask Daddy for my hand, to do it right and all that. I told Mammy to have a word with him, she did and we set a date. Mammy baked nice cakes, while I cleaned and spruced the caravan. The rest of the family went out to give us privacy. Although I had a feeling that another reason was that they didn't want to be there when Daddy hit the roof. Davey arrived about seven as planned, hair brushed back with a ton of hair cream through it, clean white shirt with tie, shoes polished spit-sparky clean. But no Daddy. Hour followed hour, until eleven o'clock struck loudly from Crieff's tower clock, and then he came in from God knows where, ignored Davey and sat down. Still, I have to take off my hat to the lad, because he went right over to Daddy and said, 'I want to marry Jessie.'

'Oh, now, is that a fact, and what do you do?'

He knew very well what he did, I'd told him a thousand times.

'I'm an apprentice joiner, Mr Riley,' he answered proudly.

'Well,' said my thrawn father, 'when you're a time-served one, come back and I'll think about it.'

The lad had been far too well brought up to answer my Father back, although by the look on his face I'm damn sure he'd have liked to. The poor man ran from the caravan, with me apologising for my father's behaviour. I followed him, but Daddy called me back, 'just a minute, lassie, I want a word with you.'

I was furious with my father, and for the first time in my entire life let him know. 'Where have you been all night? Don't you think it the height of ignorance to leave my boyfriend sitting here? You knew how nervous he must have been.'

'Jessie, I said you were never to marry, remember? Anyway, lassie, you're too young to be marrying. Now this conversation is over.'

Mammy smiled and said, 'why don't we all go to bed, things will be clearer tomorrow when we can hae a crack about this.'

Next day I ignored my father, we discussed nothing, while he thought it best to take the car keys just in case I eloped with it. Later I met Davey in our usual spot up town. 'Let's get the bus into Perth,' he said. We did and headed for the first jewellers on our road. It was mid-June and we chose my engagement ring, a twin diamond twist set in a thick gold band. It cost twenty five pounds—every penny of Davey's saving since he left school. He wanted a quick wedding, a summer one, but I needed my father's blessing and persuaded him to wait.

I never got Daddy's blessing, and I think I'd still be waiting on it. Meanwhile, a home of our own became paramount. A house either to buy or rent was out of the question, so we went over to Arbroath Caravan Park and paid a small deposit on a sixteen foot, four-berth caravan. I was still employed at the mink farm, so we managed to afford the payments. Chrissie let us stance it in her back yard. Mammy helped me to sew curtains and Davey's mother bought some cushions and carpets to match. There was a cosy wee coal fire, so our first home at least would be warm.

So on the last day of the year 1966 I became Mrs David Smith, and what a Hogmanay that was. If you like, I'll tell you about it. You would? Oh, I'm so glad.

Mary was my bridesmaid, while Davey's pal Alan Brock was his best man. Our banns had been posted with Perth Registry Office in Tay Street, for the ceremony to take place at twelve noon. Mary and I, for the first time in our lives, had a hairdresser pamper and style our heads. Having long hair, Mary opted for a hairdo that resembled a wind tunnel. Thankfully, mine was short and easy to style.

I asked Daddy for the car three times that morning, before he set the keys on the table and said, 'help yourself!' Mammy had been an absolute angel; she'd ordered a one-tier wedding cake from Campbell's the Bakers and sent invitations to relatives far and near. She'd also decorated the caravan with balloons and paper flowers, it was so lovely. By the time we set off it was doubtful if we'd be there on time, I began to panic. Any other day of the working week would have been OK, but on Hogmanay in Scotland—what

Registry Officer would keep an office open when he'd his Ne'er day bottle to purchase?

At last the four of us were heading out of Crieff. Butterflies were thronging inside my belly and, like most brides, I was wondering if I was doing the right thing.

'Hang on, you three,' I warned, 'because it's twenty minutes to twelve, I'm going to put the foot down all the way, so hold onto your seats!' Now, three miles outside Crieff, at Gilmerton, there's a bend in the road, which if you're not careful throws you over the road. No, I wasn't careful and over I went. Flash Fordy spun round several times, before crashing through a wooden gate and bogging down in a field. Thanks be, the night before there had been a hard frost that hardened the ground to the extent that Mary, Davey and Alan were able to get behind the car and push. It took ten precious minutes to get us back on the road again. The lads' nice blue-grey suits were splashed by the gutters that hadn't frosted and Mary's wind-tunnel resembled the leaning Tower of Pisa. We arrived in Tay Street at twelve thirty—half an hour late. Would the Registrar be there? Someone who was, however, was a nasty, limping parking attendant, who with several waves of his arms instructed me to get my stationary car out of the way. Drastic measures were called for, so grabbing my hat, bag and flowers I got out of the car and handed the wee attendant the keys. 'Come on you lot,' I shouted at my husband-to-be, his pal and sister Mary, 'if Limpy here can't find a spot then I sure as hell won't.' The poor man looked at the car keys, then at me, and didn't have a word to say, which was probably the first time this had happened since he got the job. Now, folks, I swear to you but that Registrar was still there waiting on us. Oh aye, he had the face of anger on him right enough, but there he was, God love him, standing on the steps watching for us, his bunch of office keys jangling from his fingers.

'David, do you take Jessie to be your wife?'

'Yup.'

'Jessie, do you take David to be your husband?'

'I do.'

'I now pronounce you man and wife,' said the old Registrar with a smile, and added, 'you can now congratulate each other.' I kissed Davey, he shook my hand, big nervous oaf!

Well, there I was, reader, a married woman. My in-laws had paid for our wedding dinner, which we had in the York Hotel in Perth, and it cost a full ten pounds. We then set off for a walk round the town, where I bought a chicken for our New Year's Day dinner and my new man purchased his bottle of whisky.

Back in Tay Street we went looking for my father's pride and joy with a wee bit apprehension. Did the flustered attendant have it pounded or tipped into the silvery Tay? No worries, because wee Limpy had positioned Flash Fordy in a safe spot opposite the Police Station. A note under the wiper read, 'Congratulations, but next time don't be so cheeky!' (Next time, aye, that'll be right.)

A super surprise was waiting back at Arnbro for us; many friends and relatives had arrived in answer to their invitations, which made me feel just that wee bit special. So, after a hearty feed, a lump of wedding cake and a dram we sang, danced and cracked. It mattered not a jot that Jack Frost was attacking every finger and nose, the party went on all night. Davey and I left our guests around three in the morning and headed the two miles home to our wee trailer. He held me tight, because not only was I freezing to death, but I was nearly four months pregnant. Thought I'd keep that little detail out of my wedding day photographs, folks.

From all of my memories of that day this was to me the most special—when we arrived at our tiny caravan, much to our surprise, someone had been in and lit the fire and pulled down our bed. It was such a warm and cosy welcome, to this day I can still feel it.

When I popped into bed there was a present propped beside my pillow, whoever had lit our fire left it. It was a radio loosely wrapped with brown paper and twine. I read the small card—'From Daddy'. I cried myself to sleep, because at long last he'd accepted my decision to marry.

Because the family I grew up in consists of eight girls I thought I'd pop this next wee story in for you.

# 38

## BRIDGET AND THE SEVEN FAIRIES

Here is an oldie now for you. One that I always remember because I have seven sisters. I recently read a version of it in a book by my old friend Bob Dawson. He heard it from a travelling man, while they sat sharing a cup of tea round a campfire in Arran in the sixties.

Once there lived an old tinker man who had six beautiful daughters and one not so pretty. They lived in a tent and were always poor and hungry. 'I am sick of this poverty,' said the eldest lassie, 'I think it time for me to go and seek my fortune.'

Saying her farewells to the family she set off, however she had not been long on the road when she came upon a fairy caught in a gin trap. 'My, fairy, you're the most horrible creature I've ever seen,' she told it.

'Dear tinker girl, let me out I beg you,' pleaded the fairy.

She looked at the fairy and said, 'Ugh, you are too ugly to be rescued,' so she picked up a stone and threw it at the trapped fairy.

'For that evil act you shall lose your beauty and become ugly, I'll send you home with a donkey's tail.' No sooner said than done, she grew an ass's tail. Terrified to be seen, she turned and ran home. When her father asked how such a thing had happened she told him about the ugly fairy.

Soon the second daughter went out to seek a new life, and she too came upon the ugly fairy trapped in the gin trap. The same thing happened—when the poor creature asked for help it was refused, and this sister ran home to hide with a pair of large donkey ears sticking prominently from her head.

The third sister went, and so did the fourth, the fifth and the sixth. All refused to help the fairy and came home with ass's hoofs and hindquarters and hair all over the body. Into the tent they went and hid beside the others.

Now it was the turn of Bridget, the seventh daughter, who wasn't pretty, in fact she was a dowdy girl.

When her father asked her why she had to go, she said, 'to find the fairy and plead with her to forgive my sisters.'

Her father told her not to go near the ugly fairy, because it would put an even worse curse on her, but she went anyway.

She searched for days before she found the ugly little fairy that gave her sisters the body parts of a donkey. When she saw just how awful the fairy was to the eye she could see why her sisters threw rocks at it. 'Please help me, tinker girl,' it said, 'I've been stuck here for years.'

'I certainly don't want to become a donkey,' she thought, so leaned down and set the fairy free, then pleaded that she break the spell on her sisters. 'Your sisters were devilish to me, but you were kind. For this act I will present you with a gift. Your sisters were beautiful, but you will be the most lovely of them all, so be on your way.' As soon as this was said, Bridget's dark hair turned golden yellow and shone like the brightest sun.

Next day she came across another ugly fairy in a gin trap. She released this one also, which in turn gifted her with skin as white as milk.

Next day the same happened, with this fairy gifting Bridget with beautiful, slender, flawless legs. The next gave her perfect breasts, and the next sea-blue eyes.

So in all she'd saved the lives of five fairies who were forever grateful.

Next day, as she skipped happily along, she came upon a sixth fairy. This one however had horns and red jaggy teeth. Its face glowed fiery red, and Bridget was very afraid. She thought, 'she is far too ugly to let out, I'll hurry past and ignore her.'

The fairy was hopping mad within the gin trap; so hard did she jump her leg became very sore, and she screamed at Bridget, 'for not releasing me you will surely die!'

Bridget ran off, frightened and in tears. She didn't see another tiny fairy in a gin trap until she'd tripped over her. 'Oh, forgive me, little fairy, I was running away from a nasty fairy who cursed me with death.'

'That's my sister, and she has a powerful magic, but although I can't lift her spell I'll change death to sleep. You'll sleep for a hundred years. Go home, and there it shall come to pass.' So Bridget went home, went into her tent and fell fast asleep. At the same time her father and donkey sisters froze solid in ice, and they all stayed that way for a hundred years.

One day, after the time had elapsed, an ugly, long-legged, three-nosed, four-eyed man came down the road and saw the small tent all rotted and rain-leaking. When he looked inside he saw Bridget, and thinking her dead he leaned down and kissed her. Immediately she opened her eyes, and he covered his ugly face in case she was afraid to look upon him. 'Oh thank you,' she said. 'You have released me from a terrible spell.'

He turned and left the tent, only to meet the nice seventh little fairy, who thereupon changed him into a handsome tinker lad with a sharpening stone and bag of good tools. Bridget and he married, while the rest of the good fairies changed the scraggy tent into a grand house. As for the donkey sisters, well, it was thought they'd learned their lesson and they were made proper again, not into beautiful girls but into strong-backed donkeys. Bridget gave them away one by one to weary travellers who came by in need of an animal to carry their bundles.

I remember when at school, a teacher told the story of 'Sleeping Beauty.'

I defiantly told my teacher it wasn't called that, but rather, 'Bridget and the Seven Fairies'.

## 39

### THE PROMISE KEPT

Two months passed and we moved down to join my parents in Arnbro. Davey continued to work out his apprenticeship with a local firm called Dodd's. However his skin began to react to sawdust, leaving him with a severe skin condition. On his doctor's advice he was forced to give up his job. This was quite a blow, because he'd only a year left to serve before qualifying as a joiner. I too had to stop work, on account of my pregnancy, and money was scarce. So scarce that our instalments on the caravan couldn't be met.

Now, far be it from me to encourage gambling, but one night Mammy asked me to go bingo-ing. I only had a ten bob note to my name. With it I bought one book.

One hundred and seventy pounds had been accumulating over several weeks, 'a jackpot' folks called it. I smiled, watching all the wives biting their nails as the caller called out number upon number. Suddenly I was waiting on a seven, my tiny baby was turning somersaults in my abdomen as I sweated, then it happened—'beautiful seven'. It meant the end of the caravan payments—I had won the jackpot on my first time there! Those ladies with five and six books were not amused, I can tell you, but when they saw my pregnant state and knew how young and hard up I was, they smiled and wished me well with applause. So I went off to Arbroath with one hundred and ten pounds, and the caravan was ours. I had enough money left to buy a pram for the wee junior he or she, and a second-hand car. One of Davey's pals sold us a 1954 green Standard Eight car, which had a 1964 souped up Triumph Herald engine, for twenty pounds. It went like a rocket, however with me having such a monstrous lump Davey drove, even though I was the one with the driving licence.

One morning in April I rose feeling awfy sorry for myself. Davey said, 'what you need is a wee drive around Loch Earn, that'll pick ye up, ma lassie.'

When I had finally eased myself into the small passenger seat we headed up to take in the touristy delights of our countryside. I even packed a picnic basket. And I must say, by the time we were on our way home my earlier feelings of despondency had drifted off, but as we approached the north side of the loch we met an almighty 'gowk storm.' Now for those of you who have never felt the fury of mother nature's spring blizzards then you'll not be aware of their ferocity, but for those who have, then imagine what I now share with you, reader. Our window wipers refused to budge! Torrents of thick heavy snow blasted our view, it was horrendous. 'What will we do?' I asked.

Davey, being in charge of the vehicle, said, 'If you run alongside the car, I'll drive real slow while you wipe the snow off the window so I can see where I'm going.'

I bet you're thinking, 'what a thoughtless young man, and his poor wife pregnant too.'

Yes, no doubting that, but hey, do you know what I did?

I got out and ran alongside the car, wiping the snow off so he could see.

We arrived home and I slept for two solid days.

At long last, on 25 May 1967, I was rushed into Perth Maternity, where doctors discovered my pelvic area was unable to allow a natural birth (I don't know the medical terminology). By early evening our tiny infant was being strangled by its own cord, so the only thing to do was a Caesarian section. So there I was—Jess, who had planned to flood the world with enough bairns to side a football team—being told that all my births, if I had any more, would have to be sections. Poor Davey, was my last thought as I drifted under the anaesthetic, he so wanted a big family.

Poor Davey indeed, there was I giving him a seven-pound, seven-ounce son, and he was across the road in a pub listening to Celtic win the European Cup.

I slept for the next three days, hardly aware of the stream of grandparents and relatives who came and went. It was after day three I was able to fully take in my beautiful son. We decided on calling him Johnnie, after my father's friend who saved his life during the war. Mammy always said if she had a boy that would be his name. I had the boy and gave him the name.

Davey, unlike me, had no sisters but he did have two brothers. His youngest brother was called Alex, who had the brain of a genius, always studying. Sadly, though, his older brother whom he idolised was killed in Germany while serving with the Remies. He and several lads who were heading back to barracks took a short-cut over a railway line. No one knows the details, but their army vehicle got stuck and was hit by an express train. I always felt heart-sorry for his parents, because they never got over losing their eldest son. Still, to have our grandson put some happiness back into their hearts made me feel good in a small way.

Daddy was chuffed to have another boy in the family (Chrissie had two, Shirley one and Mona also had one). When he peeped into the tiny mite's cot, he smiled and assured me 'he's the look of a soldier about him.' The strange thing was that Johnnie, by the age of sixteen, was a member of Her Majesty's Armed Forces.

Before I leave the maternity ward, let me share this last bit with you, reader. It was on my fourth day when the metal clips and stitches were tightening their grip on my abdomen and I felt like screaming with pain. A nurse brought me mail, a wee letter from Mammy to cheer me up, lovely. However, when the smiling nurse pointed out the address I nearly fell from the bed. Instead of writing PERTH ROYAL INFIRMARY, my sweet, innocent mother wrote 'Jess Smith, R. I. P.' (Royal Infirmary Perth). It caused hilarious laughter through the Matty that day, I can tell you, folks. I saved that envelope as a keepsake.

A terrible thing happened after that. It was July, and Janey and her family came to Arnbro for a few weeks holiday. She had three lovely wee girls and was six months pregnant. Across from where our caravan was stanced, her man parked theirs. Between us was the access road. Wee Irene was their youngest, just starting to walk. She was with me when her mother called her over. None of us saw the car. Baby Irene was killed outright.

That was when as a family we cracked. My parents and two remaining sisters went far away up to Macduff on the Banffshire coast to retire, living in a house for the first time in many a year. Mary married and moved to England. Janey had another girl whom she called Angela, she said she'd lost an angel and now had another one.

Within no time my youngest sisters met and married fine northern lads, leaving Mammy and Daddy, oh, and wee Tiny, all alone.

For a time Davey wandered about the country with me being a true traveller. I was fine, but unknown to me my man hadn't the stomach for a lifestyle alien to him. And to rub salt on his wounds, the skin condition which robbed him of the chance of being a joiner dug deep. Poor lad, although I tried to treat his weeping sores, it became apparent he needed to see a skin specialist. I remember the doctor saying only daily emulsifying baths would help. There was nothing else for it but to find a house.

He also began drinking heavily, so we headed back to Crieff. I thought if he were on home ground then he'd pull up his socks and we'd make a go of it. We moved into a flat in Gallowhill. In times gone by this was where sheep stealers and murderers hung for days. Our wee ground floor flat looked out onto the very place.

Soon Davey found work in a pallet factory along the Broich. I was pregnant again and not very well. For a start all my relatives had moved away, I had no one to turn to, while Davey drank more of his wages than paid bills.

It was between Christmas and New Year. You know, the time when a lot of Scots lads don't need an excuse to down the 'cratur.' My husband included.

If our marriage had chances, then they were thinning rapidly. I decided to have one last go at healing the cracks. This is what I did.

A thick frost was covering everything; even my washing hung stiff on the line. I stared out through the kitchen window and felt the tiny feet inside my belly kick hard against my ribs. 'I think you're another wee laddie,' I told the unborn child, running my hand gently across my swollen belly.

Johnnie was only eighteen months and looking up at me with sleepy eyes for his 'sooky', a piece of flannel he took to bed to suck on. I pulled it down off the pulley where it hung still damp, and gave it to him. I'd done all my housework and it had gone two p.m., so I thought I'd take a nap with my toddling boy. Davey had gone 'for a pint' earlier, and I didn't expect to see him until five, teatime. When Johnnie and I cuddled in, time seemed to slip by, and soon he was prodding me to get his tea. I got up, heated him soup, and by eight o' clock he was bathed and ready for bed once more. The house was very quiet, and as I had bought some cocoa powder I made a chocolate sponge.

I was used to Davey not arriving home for tea, so thought I'd wait until he arrived before cooking. I put on a nice big coal-stapped fire and settled down with a book. Hour followed hour, and minutes after midnight had struck loudly from the town clock Davey wobbled through the door. 'Not much use in putting soup into that beer-filled gut,' I thought, so smiled and asked him if he wanted a nice slice of chocolate sponge before going to bed?

'If that is what you call feeding a grown man—chocolate bloody cake—well, think again!' He then threw my offering against the fireplace and collapsed on the settee. As I watched the cake blob and splat onto the floor I made my fateful decision—tomorrow morning, when the day dawned, he would be dead!

From the washing line I removed a pair of solid, frozen pyjamas. I then opened the back door; very calmly I pulled the alcohol-unconscious man I'd foolishly married from off the settee until he lay upon the floor. I then removed every stitch of clothing and replaced it with those still frozen pyjamas. The next part (which was hardest with me being so heavily pregnant) was to pull him outside. He'd be found in the morning, and even the most suspicious law-enforcer would never imagine that poor wee pregnant me could have any hand in his demise. He'd be dead and my bairn and me would be free.

I calmly locked every door and window and happily couried under my bed covers with the knowledge Davey was no more. I was now wee Jess—mankiller!

Johnnie wakened me needing his breakfast. I, remembering, rose from bed with a thumping headache, streaming nostrils and a terrible cold, while my victim lay cuddled into my back, sound asleep, wearing those same pyjamas and none the worse after my attempted murder!

I promise you this, reader, to this day I have no idea how he got into the house, it remains a mystery. But the strange thing was, Davey, from that day to this, has behaved in every way as the good and wise husband and father.

The unexplained, wouldn't you say, folks?

I was right about the child being a boy, and we named him Stephen. Then, despite my doctor protesting 'no more', I went ahead and tried for a girl. She came along three years later and we named her Barbara.

Not many years later Shirley separated from her husband, leaving her devastated with two children to bring up on her own. My parents worried about her, so they upped sticks and settled in Glenrothes. It was here at the ripe old age of twenty-one that Tiny, our wee fox terrier cross, died. God bless that wee dog, there never was a more loyal jugal than him.

A little while later, while visiting Janey at Brechin, Daddy suffered a collapsed lung and was rushed into Strathcathro Hospital, where his youngest brother happened to be a charge nurse. 'How long have I got, Joe?' he asked him. Joe said he wasn't allowed to disclose such information. But Daddy reminded him that travelling brothers don't keep secrets like that from each other.

'Then, see'n as ye pit it like that, cove,' answered Joe, 'six months! Better get things in order, Charlie.'

That was in June. He hired a small car, and after spending two weeks with every one of us he and Mammy went back to Glenrothes to spend what little time they had left together. By mid-December his six months were up. It was then that he took the decision to finish his life. 'I will not drink water, Jeannie, or food, so don't give me any, lassie.'

Mammy began to panic: this wasn't how she'd imagined his end to be, not as drastic as this. But she knew her man. Black and white was Daddy, she knew he'd never put her through years of nursing a vegetable, and that was exactly what he'd be if air didn't reach his lungs to feed his brain, he'd told her many times. She was frightened, so we all rallied round, taking turns to stay with her and keep the pecker up. Daddy relented and drank a little water, but took no food. When Mammy could no longer watch the man with whom she'd shared almost fifty years withering in front of her eyes, she begged the doctor to put him into the Victoria Hospital in Kirkcaldy. At the end of January, Daddy took a massive stroke. We were all there around his bed. Each one of us kissed him and said our goodbyes. When it was my turn he opened his eyes and whispered in my ear, 'Remember your promise to take care of Mammy.'

I stood there staring down at his pale, lifeless body. My precious father, the travelling man who never once denied his roots, joined the Ancient Ones still holding up his head, proud and steadfast in the old ways. My mentor was dead, aged sixty-nine years.

He was buried in Crieff, where he wanted to rest. So his funeral tea was held in our wee house in Monteath Street. May I say this in all honesty, that when a traveller dies it is out of respect that travelling folk come, some hundreds of miles, and they certainly came that day. It was a freezing cold February. My house was bursting. The womenfolk stayed inside while the men lined up outside in our garden and even spilled onto the street with cups of tea and scones in shivering hands. I still wonder what my 'scaldy' neighbours were thinking.

Mammy went back to Glenrothes to mourn. I told Davey that Daddy had chosen me to be her keeper if she ever needed one. She certainly was as healthy a specimen as ever she was, but we said any time she wanted to come to Crieff then she only had to ask. After three months we received a phone-call, it was Mammy, she was ready to move in with us. For two years she shared her life with us, Davey, me and our three teenage kids.

However I began to see signs of strain on her face, and although she'd never say so, I knew a sink of her own was what was needed and a little peace and quiet.

My sister Renie's man, who adored Mammy, bought her a pictur-esque cottage in Crieff. She was in seventh heaven, it was beautiful. With a little secluded garden, that one-bedroom home was all she desired. After it was decorated and furnished, she held my hands and said, 'Jessie, this'll dae me till I die.' And it did.

Eleven years Mammy stayed in her wee cottage. Every single day I popped in to keep an eye on her. Mary had brought her a wee dog called Laddie, and if ever a jugal was ruined then he was, he even slept at the feet of her bed. Sometimes we'd walk and talk about when the end came, this was quite natural for her although I would quickly change the subject. 'Lassie, I'm seventy-odds, don't ye think me and yer faither have been apart far too long?' (On reflection I remembered the faraway look she'd sometimes have and I could see she was drifting back to the old days with him at her side.)

I'd laugh, but inside my heart was breaking so I'd pick up a stick and throw it to Laddie just to avoid the conversation. However her eyesight was failing, and once or twice she'd had a heart scare. So one night while she suffered a wee turn we lay in bed and she told me what her wishes were. 'All the gifts your sisters have given me through the years, I want them to have them back. There will just be enough money in my piggy bank to pay for the funeral. I want it paid in cash, mind, nane o' yon cheques, OK. And most important, make sure my knickers aren't showing if I crumple down. God, it's a red face I have when thinking of my clothes up over my knees.'

I cuddled into her and said, 'Mammy, dear, you'll be here a while yet.'

It was mid-June when Renie phoned to see if Mammy was all right, she'd spoken with her and thought her voice sounded weak. I said she and I had shared a baked tattie with chicken mayonnaise for lunch and she seemed fine, although she had complained of a sore stomach in the night.

That evening as usual I called her on the phone to see if her blanket was on and if the dog was in, but there was no answer. I froze and Davey had to prise the phone from my fingers.

We rushed down the few hundred yards from our house to hers.

My Mammy lay dead on the paisley-carpeted floor. Only a tiny inch of petticoat peeped out from beneath her Black Watch tartan skirt. Arms were crossed over her chest. Everything was just as she wished but I had taken no part in this. No one can convince me that the Ancient Ones hadn't prepared her for my eyes, my last sight before she was laid.

I called the doctor who pronounced her dead, and before putting her into bed to await the undertaker I held her eight times, a cuddle from us all, her precious daughters.

My promise kept.

So now, my dear friends, we come to the end. My travelling days never found the way back onto the road, because I travelled a different one. One with a husband and children. However, as I said before, 'you can take the traveller out of the road but never take the road out of the traveller.' I believe my road is still there, finding new bends and new campsites. Yes, of course they are all in my mind, but that's okay. As a storyteller and singer I share them with everyone. When people ask me as they always do, 'where do you belong?' I still say 'wherever the feather falls.'

Where do you belong?

*I belong*
*Wherever the wind blows.*
*I am the feather*
*That soars above the billow's crest,*
*That wheels above the moorland crags,*
*That lines the nest in far places.*
*I am the seed*
*That is borne aloft on the breeze,*
*That lights down on distant pastures,*
*That is the life of my people.*
*I have the strength of the tempest,*
*The gentleness of the zephyr.*
*I'm the spirit of the whole land.*
*I am within the unbroken circle*
*That has no beginning and no ending.*
*Around I go like the story of life.*

Michael G. Kidd

Reader, you have been fine company as we travelled together through these memory-filled pages. Thank you.

# Glossary of Unfamiliar Words

*Abune*—above
*ahent*—behind
*barry*—fine, smart
*bent-backit*—bent-backed
*bidey-in*—live-in
*bint*—woman
*bitty*—a little bit
*boking*—retching, vomiting
*braw*—good
*cant*—traveller dialect
*catty*—catapult
*chats*—earrings
*chavie*—young man
*chittie*—iron tripod positioned over an open fire
*chuckit*—useless
*clootie dumpling*— rich pudding, steamed in a cloth
*cobble*—short, flat-bottomed rowing boat
*courie doon*—snuggle down
*couried*—hidden, snuggled
*crabbit*—peevish, irritable
*deek*—see, look
*een*—eyes
*gadgie*—man, fellow
*gan-about*—traveller, gypsy
*gouries*—young girls

*graip*—pitchfork
*guffy*—pig
*guid*—good
*hantel*—group or crowd of people; *country hantel*, non-travellers
*haun*—hand
*heechy*—mad moment
*hoolit*—owl
*hornies*—police
*jugal*—dog
*kushtie*—great
*leric*—blackbird
*Lorne sausage*—square sliced sausage
*louped*—leaped
*lowie*—money, wealth
*luggie*—container with one or two handles (used for collecting berries)
*lunzie*—tramp's bag or pouch
*lurcher*—a dog crossed between a collie or sheepdog and a greyhound, often used by poachers
*menses*—food
*merl*—blackbird
*muckle*—a lot, big

*pagger*—a beating
*puckle*—a few, small
*purn*—bobbin
*quine*—girl, young person
*roused*—angry
*ruggle stane*—natural river stone used to sharpen knives
*scadded*—rubbed, chafed
*scaldy*—settled, i.e. non-traveller
*schnell*—sharp, biting
*scunner*—nuisance, annoyance
*shan*—frighten; *shan chories*, stolen goods; *shan gadgie*, an untrustworthy man
*shanning*—scaring, frightening
*shaw*—stalk
*siller*—silver, money
*skelp*—hit, beat
*smir*—fine drizzle
*sookit*—sucked
*stapped full*—jammed full
*stardy*—jail, police station
*stushie*—fight, commotion
*tank*—to skin
*thrawn*—stubborn, contrary
*tottie*—small
*washie*—washhouse
*wayn*—large amount, cartload
*wean*—child
*weel kent*—well known
*yin*—one